CONFEDERATE CHARLESTON

CONFEDERATE CHARLESTON: AN ILLUSTRATED HISTORY OF THE CITY AND THE PEOPLE DURING THE CIVIL WAR

ROBERT N. ROSEN

University of South Carolina Press

Published in Columbia, South Carolina, by the
University of South Carolina Press

Printed in Canada

Library of Congress Cataloging-in-Publication Data

Rosen, Robert N., 1947–
    Confederate Charleston: an illustrated history of the city and the
people during the Civil War / Robert N. Rosen
            p.   cm.
    Includes bibliographical references and index.
    ISBN 0–87249–991–X (acid free)
    1. Charleston (S.C.)—History—Civil War, 1861–1865.
2. Charleston (S.C.)—History—Civil War, 1861–1865—Pictorial
works.   I.   Title
F279.C457R66 1994   94-13751
975.7'91503—dc20

To my father, Morris D. Rosen, for a lifetime of encouragement; to my mother-in-law, Joyce Ann Corner, for her generous support; to the memory of Nelson Mitchell, Esquire, the most admirable of the Confederate-era Charleston lawyers; and to my wife, Susan, without whose help you would not be about to read this work.

In proud and grateful remembrance of their devotion
Constancy, and valor, who, against overwhelming odds
    By Sea and by Land,
Kept Charleston virgin and invincible
    To the last.

—From the inscription on the Confederate monument,
Magnolia Cemetery, Charleston, 1882

Exactly four years after the surrender—that is, on April 14, 1865 —Robert Anderson
returned to raise his old flag over Fort Sumter. By then, the sounds of battle had
given way to the stillness at Appomattox and the issues that inflamed the antebellum
years had been settled. Slavery was dead; secession was dead; and six hundred
thousand men were dead. That was the basic balance sheet of the sectional conflict.

—David M. Potter, *The Impending Crisis* (1976)

CONTENTS

PREFACE

As a child growing up in Charleston, I did not like the Civil War, or as we called it then, the War Between the States. I was torn between a fierce pride in the city of my birth and the idea of a war brought about by slavery. As a student at the University of Virginia in the 1960s, I learned from Paul Gaston, Willie Lee Rose, and the writings of C. Vann Woodward that one could be a Southerner, take pride in the South, and not feel compelled to defend the indefensible.

The Civil War is endlessly fascinating because, like a Lowcountry hurricane, it uprooted settled ways, covered everything, went everywhere, and involved everyone. It brought out the best and the worst in people. For generations afterward, indeed to the present day, Charlestonians—both black and white—have vigorously defended their ancestors' roles in the war. The conflict has been called by many names: the War of Secession, the Confederate War, the "late unpleasantness," and the "War of Northern Aggression."

I have tried to tell the story of Charleston and Charlestonians during the conflict as well as the story of Charleston's many unwelcomed visitors. This book is a popular history for the general reader, and I have left the footnotes and scholarly details to other authors. I have tried to describe the war from many perspectives: the Southern as well as the Northern version; the stories of the secessionists and Confederates, of African Americans, women, and ethnic groups, of the generals and the privates. This is not a traditional version of the war, although I have relied on many traditional interpretations. It is, I hope, an accurate and inclusive version. I hope, in fact, that it will be an eye-opening experience for the reader to learn—as I did during my research—that the war included a wide variety of people, most under a great deal of stress. The story of the Civil War is not just the simple story of the one-dimensional characters of Hollywood movies.

I want to thank my research assistants Pat Hash, Chris Harte, Sandra Foster, and especially Jennifer Cohen for their help. I am grateful also to my partners at Rosen, Rosen & Hagood, P.A., for their generous support, and especially to my brother, Richard S. Rosen. Thanks also to my sister, Debra Rosen, for her encouragement; to Jane and William Pease; Henry Fair; William Cathcart; P. C. Coker; Joseph H. McGee; Jim Moody; Sister M. Anne Francis Campbell, O.L.M.; Stephen Hoffius and the staff of the South Carolina Historical Society; the National Park Service (Fort Moultrie and Fort Sumter) and Anthony Brown in particular; Eleanor Richardson and the staff of the South Caroliniana Library; Dr. Charles V. Peery; and especially Solomon Breibart. I wish to thank my legal staff: Cheryl Jansen and my secretaries, Sherry Kubach, Gerry Brown, Lissa Pellum, Renee Ellison, and Beverly Blanchard. Claudia Kelley, my administrative assistant, somehow miraculously brought the manuscript to a conclusion and wrestled all of the illustrations from a multitude of museums, societies, and galleries. These amazing feats deserve much praise and thanks. I also want to thank Emily Adkins and Sue and Buzz Corner for the best of all gifts, Civil War books, and my children, Annie I. Rosen, Alexandra L. Rosen, and E. William Rosen, for keeping me company while I was writing and for listening to all of my stories about history.

CONFEDERATE CHARLESTON

PROLOGUE

Ironically, the tune of "John Brown's Body" was taken, according to the historian Henry Steele Commager, from an African-American melody "popular in the Carolina Lowcountry, where it was sung to the refrain

Say, brothers, will you meet us?

On Canaan's happy shore?"

Other historians believe that a free black Charlestonian, William Steffe, wrote the song and that a Vermonter, Tom Bishop, picked up the tune while traveling in South Carolina. Bishop used it in writing "John Brown's Body." Bishop later joined a Massachusetts infantry battalion, and Julia Ward Howe heard the melody as his battalion marched through Washington. She used the melody for "Battle Hymn of the Republic," the Union's most stirring marching song. Thus, as the film-maker John Mitchum explained to a reporter for the *News & Courier* in 1991, "the song is black music, with white words, and welded the whole union back together."

On May 23, 1988, the Fife and Drum Corps of the United States Army Band, resplendent in colonial uniforms, paraded down Broad Street from St. Michael's Church to the Old Exchange Building on East Bay Street. There the South Carolina General Assembly was to meet in joint session to celebrate the two hundredth anniversary of the ratification of the United States Constitution by the state of South Carolina. As the band came to the Old Exchange, it played "Battle Hymn of the Republic," that stirring, patriotic song derived from "John Brown's Body," the old abolitionist marching song. No one noticed. Charleston had come a very long way from 1861.

In May, 1788, Charleston proudly hosted the convention of the people of South Carolina to consider "ratifying or rejecting the Constitution framed for the United States by a Convention of Delegates assembled at Philadelphia in May last." Meeting at the Old Exchange Building, the delegates voted overwhelmingly, as the Founding Fathers were sure they would, to ratify the Constitution. The vote was 149 to 73, and Charlestonians had led the way. After all, four Charlestonians had attended the Constitutional Convention in Philadelphia, and all four had signed the Constitution.

Before the ink was dry on the Constitution, Americans began debating the nature of their "more perfect union." The idea of secession was as old as the Constitution, but it was articulated best by John C. Calhoun, the brilliant U.S. senator and vice-president who married his cousin, a Charleston heiress, and now lies buried in St. Philip's churchyard. The nullification controversy of the 1830s, which centered in Charleston, led inexorably in the 1850s to the "fire eaters," the radicals best exemplified by another Charlestonian, Robert Barnwell Rhett, who is sometimes called the Father of Secession.

Senator Robert W. Barnwell wrote in 1845, sixteen years before the war, "Our institutions are doomed and the Southern civilization must go out in blood."

For reasons almost impossible to understand today, the Democratic party held its national convention of 1860 in Charleston, allowing Southerners and Charlestonians to disrupt the proceedings, defeat Stephen Douglas, and ensure the election of Abraham Lincoln.

On December 20, 1860, seventy-two years after the United States Constitution had been ratified by the people of South Carolina, a new convention met in Charleston to repeal that vote. "We the People of the State of South Carolina," the Ordinance of Secession read, declare that the "Ordinance adopted by us in Convention, on the twenty-third day of May . . . whereby the Constitution of the United States of America was ratified . . . [is] hereby repealed; and that the union now subsisting between South Carolina and other states, under the name of The United States of America, is hereby dissolved."

The eminent Charleston lawyer James L. Petigru, hearing the church bells ring on that December day in 1860, asked where the fire was. He was told there was no fire, that South Carolina had just seceded from the Union. Petigru retorted, "I tell you there is a fire; they have this day set a blazing torch to the temple of constitutional liberty and, please God, we shall have no more peace forever." He wrote to his daughter Susan in 1860, "The Constitution is only two months older than I. My life will probably be prolonged till I am older than it is."

The Old Exchange Building, built from 1767 to 1771 as the colonial Exchange and Custom House, was the site of the ratification of the United States Constitution by the state of South Carolina in 1788. Three years later President George Washington greeted the citizens of Charleston from the balcony of the Old Exchange.

A. Toomer Porter was an Episcopal priest in Charleston before, during, and after the Civil War. He founded Porter Academy (originally The Holy Communion Church Institute) on the site of the old Federal arsenal on Ashley Avenue, now the Medical University of South Carolina.

But the Constitution did survive.

The great American Civil War was about to begin within sight of the Old Exchange Building, the very place where the United States Constitution had been ratified by a previous generation of South Carolinians. It was to begin at a fort named in honor of a national hero of the American Revolution, Thomas Sumter, the fiesty and daring guerrilla general known as "the Gamecock."

Charleston was viewed by Americans of the 1860s and is viewed by historians today as the cradle of secession, the birthplace of the Confederacy. There is a serious question as to whether the first shot would have ever been fired if the Charlestonians had not done it. The officers of the Union army certainly thought Charleston was culpable. "Should you capture Charleston," General Halleck wrote to General Sherman in 1865, "I hope that by some accident the place may be destroyed." The whole army burned "with insatiable desire to wreak vengeance upon South Carolina. I almost tremble at her fate," Sherman replied. Indeed, Charleston was destroyed by the Civil War.

In 1905, when the famed novelist Henry James visited the city, he found that he "might have looked straight and far back into the past. The past, that of the vanished order, was hanging on there." He found "the Battery of the long, curved sea-front, of the waterside public garden furnished with sad old historic guns." He saw a defeated city in a "*bled* condition . . . and I asked myself, on the Battery, what more one's sternest justice could have desired."

The "late unpleasantness," as Charlestonians used to refer to the war, is still remembered in Charleston. It is etched in the landscape of the city. Virtually all of the major monuments in modern-day Charleston commemorate the conflict. The city is best known as the place where the Civil War began.

This then is the story of Charleston and the Civil War in words and pictures. It is not a pretty sight. But as General William Tecumseh Sherman wrote, "Any one who is not satisfied with war should go and see Charleston, and he will pray louder and deeper than ever that the country may in the long future be spared any more war."

As Boston was regarded as the cradle of American liberty, where the infancy of the Union was nurtured, so Charleston, in later days, came to be considered the nursery of disunion. Therefore, during our Civil War, no city in the South was so obnoxious to Union men as Charleston. Richmond was the objective point of our armies, as its capture was expected to end the war, but it excited little sentiment and little antipathy. It was to South Carolina, and especially to Charleston, that the strong feeling of dislike was directed, and the desire was general to punish that city by all the rigors of war.

—C. R. P. Rodgers, Rear Admiral U.S.N. and Chief of Staff during the siege of Charleston, writing years after the war in *Battles and Leaders of the Civil War* (1887)

*The interior of South Carolina Institute Hall at
134 Meeting Street during the National Democratic
Party Convention as shown in* Harper's Weekly.
*Here also the Ordinance of Secession was signed in
December, 1860.*

CHAPTER 1

THE LONG ROAD TO SECESSION

When Captain George S. James gave the order to fire the first shot of the Civil War, the conflagration that resulted was the culmination of nearly forty years of political feuding and bloodletting; social and religious agitation; and economic, industrial, and commercial revolution. The United States had grown from the agricultural nation that it was at the beginning of the century to a product of the industrial revolution. The Southern states generally and South Carolina and Charleston in particular had not shared in that development but had come instead to rely on a one-crop economy supported by slavery.

Charleston had always been at the center of the debate over slavery and its relationship to the Federal government. The Charlestonians at the Constitutional Convention in Philadelphia in 1787 had insisted on strong Constitutional protection for slavery. And the labors of Charles Cotesworth Pinckney, Charles Pinckney, and Pierce Butler had paid off in sections of the Constitution concerning the regulation of the importation of slaves, the counting of slaves as three-fifths of a person for voting puposes (which increased the political power of white Southerners), and a provision concerning the escape of persons "held to service or labour" to other states. The words *slave* and *slavery* do not appear in the Constitution.

The agitation against slavery had begun in the early 1800s. Charleston was a focal point throughout the century for the defense of slavery because the city was, after all, virtually the capital of Southern slavery. A great percentage of all Africans brought to the United States came through the port of Charleston. They were quarantined on Sullivan's Island, which Peter Wood has described as "the Ellis Island of black America." In 1820 and 1840 three-fourths of all "heads of families" in Charleston owned at least one slave. In other Southern cities the percentage of whites owning slaves was substantially lower.

In 1822 South Carolina had enacted the Negro Seaman's Act, which forbade free black seamen to come ashore in Charleston. In fact, a group of them had been arrested and held in jail in defiance of Federal authority. In the same year, Charlestonians uncovered a massive plot by Denmark Vesey, a free black, and others to free the slaves and kill white slave owners. The reaction was harsh: 35 blacks were executed, 31 were deported, and 131 were the subject of an intensive investigation organized apart from the ordinary legal process.

It was no wonder then that by the 1830s, when the abolitionists began printing pamphlets and newspapers, petitioning Congress, preaching, and politicking, Charlestonians began to react. The events of the 1830s and 1840s created ever-increasing political tension between North and South. The nullification crisis of the 1830s, in which South Carolina contended that it could refuse to obey Federal laws with which it disagreed, centered in Charleston. Andrew Jackson moved the customs house to Fort Moultrie, considered a military operation against Charleston, and communicated with local

Slave auction in Charleston just to the north of the Old Exchange Building on East Bay Street. This drawing was made in 1853 and was published in the Illustrated London News, *November 29, 1856.*

unionists about the potential "delicate use of force." Major General Winfield Scott, who would later serve Abraham Lincoln, was ordered to Charleston with artillery units. Jackson threatened to hang all traitors, and the crisis passed.

In 1831 the antislavery advocate William Lloyd Garrison began publishing the *Liberator* in Boston and denounced the Constitution as "a covenant with death and an agreement with hell." The slave revolt led by Nat Turner in Virginia in 1831, the war with Mexico, the activities of the abolitionists, and the virtual war over the new territories such as Kansas and Nebraska led to a sense in Charleston particularly and South Carolina generally that their society could not survive as a part of the United States.

By the mid-1850s this concern had led to a growing consensus in Charleston that the South could not remain in the Union. Charleston had become the political and intellectual cradle of secession. In 1850 it was the South's second-largest city; only New Orleans had a greater population. A local press had published the definitive defense of slavery, *The Pro-Slavery Argument*, in 1852. William J. Grayson wrote *The Hireling and the Slave*, a long poem in defense of the institution. The leaders of the secession movement, the so-called fire eaters, were Charlestonians. The Charleston *Mercury* was edited by a fanatic secessionist, Robert Barnwell Rhett, Jr., who provided the rhetoric that fueled the movement across the South. The *Mercury* went so far as to threaten to publish and thereby blacklist those Charleston merchants who did business with Northern firms whose members belonged to the church of the abolitionist minister Henry Ward Beecher.

It is easy to understand why Charleston would lead the way to secession and civil war. As the capital of Southern slavery, Charleston, more than any other city, was irrevocably

View of Charleston in 1851, drawn by John William Hill and published by Smith Brothers. In 1850 Charleston was the South's second-largest city with a population of 42,985 (20,012 whites, 3,441 free blacks, and 19,532 slaves). New Orleans had a population of 116,375, of whom 89,459 were white. Richmond had a population of 27,570.

THE PRO-SLAVERY ARGUMENT

There was almost unanimity among the white people of Charleston that slavery was, in Calhoun's words, "a good—a positive good." There were even free African-American Charlestonians who thought slavery was a perfectly legitimate institution: they owned slaves themselves. Such a family was the Ellison family of Charleston and Stateburg, which owned more than sixty slaves. And prior to 1861 the country at large was not antislavery. Indeed, prior to the Civil War, an overwhelming majority of Americans, North as well as South, felt slavery should not be disturbed where it existed. Rabbi Morris J. Raphall of New York said in a sermon,

> On the most solemn occasion recorded when God gave the Ten Commandments on Mount Sinai . . . slaveholding is not only recognized and sanctified as an integral part of the social structure, when it is commanded that the Sabbath of the Lord is to bring rest to "thy male slave and thy female slave," but the property in slaves is placed under the same protection as any other species of lawful property when it is said " Thou shalt not covet thy neighbor's house, or his field, or his male slave, or his female slave."

Books, articles, and pamphlets were published in Charleston defending the South's "peculiar institution." A writer in the *Southern Quarterly Review* described slavery as "the same form of government to which the abolitionists subject their wives and children," namely a "patriarchal government." One of the best-known works defending slavery was *The Pro-Slavery Argument as Maintained by the Most Distinguished Writers of the Southern States,* published by the Walker company in 1852, containing essays by a number of prominent Charlestonians including the lawyer, planter, and writer William Gilmore Simms.

Simms was born in Charleston in 1806. He became a lawyer in 1827, but his talents as a writer overtook his legal career. He was a prolific author who produced numerous novels or romances, as he called them, ranging from stories of the American Revolution, such as *Katherine Walton,* to colonial Indian wars (*The Yemassee*) to stories about the "border country" of Alabama and Mississippi (*Border Beagles*). A patriotic South Carolinian, he wrote a history of the state and a biography of Francis Marion. Simms was very well known to the writers and intellectuals of his day. His stories and articles were published in national publications, and he was well thought of in the publishing world. He was a part of the literary world dominated by Sir Walter Scott and his American counterpart, James Fenimore Cooper. "The modern Romance," Simms wrote, "is the substitute which the people of the present day offer for the ancient epic." He wrote to vindicate his native soil and described himself as "a genuine Southron, well hated by New England, hostile to the Tariff, abolition, etc. not to speak of a hundred other Yankee abominations."

Simms was intensely political. He served as a magistrate for a number of years and was elected to the South Carolina House of Representatives. He was pro-Union in the nullification controversy, but, like many moderates, he was eventually won over to the cause of secession. He ultimately became a vociferous supporter of disunion.

As one biographer put it, "Simms experienced to the full the cataclysm of the war." His town house in Charleston was destroyed; his home in Barnwell was burned by accident in 1862; Sherman's troops destroyed the only portion of the home that was rebuilt; his wife died in 1863. Simms had gone to Columbia as a refugee when Sherman invaded South Carolina and burned that city. He survived and wrote again after the war, but his life was marked, as were the lives of many Southerners of the time, by grief and poverty.

Simms's fellow Charlestonians erected a monument to him in White Point Gardens in 1879. It is the only monument to a literary man at the Battery and one of the few monuments to an author in the state. But, like the bust of Henry Timrod in Washington Park, it is also a monument to a spokesman for the Southern way of life, and thus it is a Civil War monument also. The monument originally bore only the name Simms, but as time went by no one knew who Simms was. The city fathers eventually had carved on the pedestal "William Gilmore Simms, 1806–1870, Author, Journalist, Historian." They probably should have added "Defender of the Faith."

William Gilmore Simms, Charleston author.

To show that there is an individual monster in the slave States, argues nothing against their morals. It must be shown that his case is not the exception, but the ordinary history. There is a work of fiction, recently published by Mrs. Stowe, which is just now the rage with the abolitionists; the great error of which, throughout, consists in the accumulation of all the instances that can be found of cruelty or crime among the slaveholders. Admit all her statements to be true, and they prove nothing. Her facts may be susceptible of proof, while her inferences are wholly false. Take an example from this very work of fiction (*Uncle Tom's Cabin*), which illustrates this error of reasoning among our enemies. She shows us a planter of Louisiana, as one of the most heartless, bloody, brutal, gross, loathsome and ignorant wretches under the sun. She gives us the most shocking details of his inhumanities; but, in doing so, *she herself isolates him.* She shows that he *resides in a remote, and scarcely accessible swamp region, where his conduct comes under no human cognizance.* How is society answerable for his offenses? How does he represent the condition and character of the slaveholder? The very isolation of his position and of the case, is conclusive against its application. When to this we add, that the equal necessities of truth and fiction seem to have compelled her, though a Yankee, to admit that this brutal specimen is a Yankee also, we may reasonably, without shaking our skirts, refer his responsibilities back to his native parish.

—William Gilmore Simms, "The Morals of Slavery," in *The Pro-Slavery Argument* (1852)

committed to defending the institution and the way of life it supported. Charleston had more to lose than other cities. The relationship between secession and slavery is nowhere better articulated than in the words of the secessionists themselves. The South Carolina Declaration of Causes of Secession (December 24, 1860) denounced the actions of "the nonslaveholding states" in denying the slaveholders' property rights: "They have denounced as sinful the institution of slavery.... They have encouraged ... our slaves to leave their homes.... A geographical line has been drawn across the Union." Lincoln's election could not be accepted because "he has declared that 'Government cannot endure permanently half slave, half free.' " Because Lincoln's party will wage war "against slavery until it shall cease throughout the United States," the people of South Carolina must secede.

The Confederate Constitution specifically recognized in Article I, section 9, "the right of property in negro slaves," a right that could not constitutionally be denied or impaired. Near the end of the war, Senator Robert M. T. Hunter of Virginia exploded in a debate in the Confederate Congress, "If we didn't go to war to save our slaves, what did we go to war for?" Alexander H. Stephens, the vice-president of the Confederacy, wrote in March, 1861, that the cornerstone of the Confederate States "rests upon the great truth that the negro is not equal to the white man." Indeed, Charlestonians were to refer to Union troops as abolitionists throughout the war. Colonel Alfred Rhett referred to the Union navy as "The Abolition iron-clad fleet" in an official report.

The intellectual foundation for the protection of the South's "peculiar institution" had been laid by its most brilliant political thinker, John C. Calhoun, in the 1820s. Calhoun had refined the doctrine of nullification, a state's right to nullify and refuse to enforce those federal laws it found contrary to its sovereignty. Calhoun was the greatest apologist for slavery and the strongest proponent of states' rights in American history. Where George Washington and Thomas Jefferson had seen slavery as a necessary evil, Calhoun defended it as "a good—a positive good." Calhoun died in 1850, but he had become an icon to Charlestonians by 1860. At the Democratic National Convention, held in Charleston in April, 1860, Caleb Cushing of Massachusetts, the chairman, referred to the statue of "the great statesman of South Carolina" to loud cheers from the audience.

On the other hand, Charleston was in some ways a tolerant society. There were three thousand free blacks in Charleston in 1860, a third of the state's free black population. Many of them owned slaves themselves. Since free blacks rarely owned plantations and their wealth consisted of urban real estate, most of the slaves they owned were employed as house servants or in trades. The elite of Charleston's free African Americans were brown-skinned people. As Michael P. Johnson and James L. Roark have written in *No Chariot Let Down*, "while color and freedom distinguished Charleston's brown aristocrats from slaves, their property elevated them above most free Negroes."

The vote taken on secession in the Southern states in 1861 shows unmistakably that the counties that contained larger percentages of slaves voted much more heavily for secession than those with smaller percentages. Indeed, the state of West Virginia was created in 1861 when the western portion of Virginia (containing few slaves and many independent mountaineers) "seceded" from Virginia to "rejoin" the Union.

The long history of conflict over slavery (The Missouri Debates, the Wilmot Proviso,

The Great Nullifier, John C. Calhoun, was also the foremost defender of slavery in the antebellum South. Although he fought throughout his career to preserve the Union, he laid the intellectual foundation for secession. He served as vice-president under Andrew Jackson in the 1820s, preached nullification in the 1830s, and became the virtual political dictator of the state during the 1840s. He was United States senator from South Carolina from 1832 to 1843 when he served as secretary of state. He served in the senate again from 1845 until his death in 1850. He was an intellectual and political thinker and, according to Richard Hofstadter, "probably the last American statesman to do any primary political thinking." He is buried in St. Philip's Churchyard. Calhoun Street is named in his honor.

Angelina Emily Grimké was born and raised the affluent daughter of an aristocratic Charleston slave-owning family. She left Charleston, joined the Quakers, and became one of the most militant opponents of slavery and an early feminist.

THE ANTI-SLAVERY ARGUMENT

Following the Denmark Vesey uprising there were few Charlestonians who favored the abolition of slavery. The two most eloquent antislavery advocates Charleston produced were sisters, Sarah Moore Grimké (1792–1873) and Angelina Emily Grimké (1805–1879). Their parents, Judge John Faucheraud Grimké and Mary Smith Grimké, were aristocratic Charleston Huguenots who owned slaves and were proud of their heritage. Early on, Sarah questioned the morality of slavery and sought answers to her questions within Charleston society. On a trip to Philadelphia, she met a group of Quakers and had a religious experience that impelled her to move there and oppose slavery. Both Sarah and Angelina left Charleston in the 1820s and became Friends, although both of them quarreled for years with the Quaker sect.

In the 1830s Angelina became a leading spokeswoman for the abolitionist movement; she was able to write and speak against slavery very effectively and credibly because she knew slavery, as most abolitionists did not, from long personal experience. Indeed, her parents and family continued to reside in Charleston and keep slaves. In 1836 Angelina wrote a pamphlet entitled an *Appeal to the Christian Women of the South,* in which she called on Southern women to rebel against the institution of slavery. "The women of the South," she wrote, "can overthrow this horrible system of oppression and cruelty, licentiousness and wrong." The pamphlet was burned by the postmaster in Charleston, and Angelina Grimké was warned by her family never to return to her home.

Angelina Grimké's speaking out in public against slavery was shocking in the 1830s. Women then rarely spoke in public, and certainly, most people believed, a lady would not even consider doing so. Angelina was condemned by her fellow abolitionists, many of whom did not believe in the equality of the sexes. Ironically, the Grimké sisters thus became leading feminists as a result of their fight to be allowed to speak their minds on the issue of slavery. In her *Letters on the Equality of the Sexes and the Condition of Woman* (1838), Sarah Grimké maintained that "the page of history teems with woman's wrongs" and that "it is wet with woman's tears."

According to the *Dictionary of American Biography,* "Angelina, in her *Appeal to the Women of the Nominally Free States* (1837), strongly insisted on women's equal responsibilities for the nation's guilt and shame and on their interest in the public weal. Gradually many of the opponents of slavery were won over to the cause of woman's rights, and the introduction of the question into the antislavery agitation by the Grimkés was an important factor in the development of both causes." The Grimké sisters were a national phenomenon. The poet John Greenleaf Whittier called them "Carolina's high-souled daughters."

Angelina became so bold and so well known that in 1838 she was invited to address a committee of the Massachusetts legislature, thereby becoming the first woman in American history to address a legislative body. She spoke passionately about the land of her birth:

> I stand before you as a southerner, exiled from the land of my birth by the sound of the lash and the piteous cry of the slave. I stand before you as a repentant slaveholder. I stand before you as a moral being and as a moral being I feel that I owe it to the suffering slave and to the deluded master, to my country and to the world to do all that I can to overturn a system of complicated crimes, built upon the broken hearts and prostrate bodies of my countrymen in chains and cemented by the blood, sweat and tears of my sisters in bonds.

In 1863, when Angelina learned of the battle of Battery Wagner in Charleston harbor, she wrote to a friend, "Do you not rejoice & exult in all that praise that is lavished upon our brave colored troops even by Pro-slavery papers? I have no tears to shed over their graves, because I see that their heroism is working a great change in public opinion, forcing all men to see the sin & shame of enslaving such men."

Angelina married Theodore D. Weld, one of the nation's leading abolitionists. She and her sister convinced their mother in South Carolina to deed slaves to them as their share of the family estate, and they immediately freed them. Because of her health, Angelina retired from public life and helped her husband administer a liberal school in Belleville, New Jersey. In later years the family moved to Hyde Park, Massachusetts, where both sisters eventually died.

the Compromise of 1850, the issue of slavery in the expansion to the West); confrontation with British and European opinion, which had turned against slavery; confrontation with the ever-growing antislavery movement; the growing tensions in Charleston—all of these factors brought on the movement for secession. By the late 1850s the majority of white Charlestonians, like many white Southerners, viewed themselves as prisoners in their own country, condemned by what they saw as a hysterical abolition movement and cut off from world opinion. Emma Holmes wrote in her diary of the "malignity and fanaticism" of the Republicans.

In October, 1859, when John Brown raided Harpers Ferry in Virginia and attempted to incite a slave rebellion, it was the beginning of the end. South Carolinians, especially Charlestonians, took the lead in the fight for secession. Maybe Charlestonians really believed, as George C. Rogers, Jr., argues, that "they had the perfect society. . . . Charleston thus became the center of an idea, a southern way of life. And from this center these ideas began to penetrate throughout the nation."

Yet perhaps it was something else. That ancient Charleston hedonism, the love of posturing, the unrestrained Lowcountry aristocracy whose power knew no bounds, and the lack of any real challenge to the elite's views also played a part. When an individual planter had the power of life and death over his slaves, when the state government did as the planters willed, when no other class or faction could fight back, it is easy to understand why the radical secessionists of Charleston could believe no one in the nation would dare oppose them. After all, no one *had* ever opposed them. Their forefathers had challenged the British Empire and triumphed: the American Revolution, to a great extent, had been won on the battlefields of Upcountry South Carolina. Charlestonians believed there would be no war, that gentlemen of noble birth could stare down the nation.

By the 1860s the South, particularly Charleston, was at a crossroads. Thomas Jefferson once described the slave owner as having "the wolf by the ears, and we can neither hold him nor safely let him go." The South did not dare let go of slavery. It is all well and good to look back 125 years or more and judge a people who inherited slavery, a way of life, and a problem of potential or perceived racial conflict and find them guilty by modern standards. But after the fanatic John Brown's raid at Harpers Ferry to liberate the slaves of Virginia, did white Southerners have a choice?

The North, in large part, thought John Brown was a hero and honored him as a martyr to freedom. Yet he came to kill white Virginians. "These are indications," the Charleston lawyer Christopher Memminger told the Virginia General Assembly in January, 1860, "you cannot disregard. They tell of a state of public opinion which cannot fail to produce further evil. Every village bell, which tolled its solemn note at the execution of Brown, proclaims to the South the approbation of that village of insurrection and servile war." Memminger argued persuasively that the Northern public's approval of a war on slavery and the outcome of elections in the North since "the Harpers Ferry invasion" showed that abolitionist strength was growing. Northern members of Congress, Memminger said, had become more active and more adamant against slavery. The Republicans, a sectional party whose very existence was based on opposition to slavery, had taken power; the dominant party would have at its disposal "immense patronage"; the South was losing ground in the House and Senate and ultimately would be an ineffectual minority unable to defend slavery. Northern public opinion against slavery had become more pronounced and

Charleston was then a proud, aristocratic city, and assumed a leadership in the public opinion of the South far out of proportion to her population, wealth, or commerce. On more than one occasion previously, the inhabitants had almost inaugurated civil war, by their assertion and professed belief that each State had, in the original compact of government, reserved to itself the right to withdraw from the Union at its own option, whenever the people supposed they had sufficient cause. We used to discuss these things at our own messtables, vehemently and sometimes quite angrily; but I am sure that I never feared it would go further than it had already gone in the winter of 1832–'33, when the attempt at "nullification" was promptly suppressed by President Jackson's famous declaration, "The Union must and shall be preserved!" and by the judicious management of General Scott.

—William Tecumseh Sherman, recalling Charleston in the 1840s in his *Memoirs* (1875)

But I will now say a few words on the subject of Abolitionism. Doubtless you have all heard Anti-Slavery Societies denounced as insurrectionary and mischievous, fanatical and dangerous. It has been said they publish the most abominable untruths, and that they are endeavoring to excite rebellions at the South. Have you believed these reports, my friends? Have *you* also been deceived by these false assertions? Listen to me, then, whilst I endeavor to wipe from the fair character of Abolitionism such unfounded accusations. You know that *I* am a Southerner; you know that my dearest relatives are now in a slave State. Can you for a moment believe I would prove so recreant to the feelings of a daughter and a sister, as to join a society which was seeking to overthrow slavery by falsehood, bloodshed, and murder? I appeal to you who have known and loved me in days that are passed, can you believe it?

Act on this subject. Some of you *own* slaves yourselves. If you believe slavery is *sinful,* set them at liberty, "undo the heavy burdens and let the oppressed go free." If they wish to remain with you, pay them wages, if not let them leave you. Should they remain teach them, and have them taught the common branches of an English education; they have minds and those minds, *ought to be improved.* So precious a talent as intellect, never was given to be wrapt in a napkin and buried in the earth. It is the *duty* of all, as far as they can, to improve their own mental faculties, because we are commanded to love God *with all our minds,* as well as with all our hearts, and we commit a great sin, if we *forbid* or *prevent* that cultivation of the mind in others, which would enable them to perform this duty. Teach your servants then to read &, encourage them to believe it is their *duty* to learn, if it were only that they might read the Bible.

But some of you will say, we can neither free our slaves nor teach them to read, for the laws of our state forbid it. Be not surprised when I say such wicked laws *ought to be no barrier* in the way of your duty, and appeal to the Bible to prove this position. What was the conduct of Shiphrah and Puah, when the king of Egypt issued his cruel mandate, with regard to the Hebrew children? "*They* feared *God,* and did *not* as the King of Egypt commanded them, but saved the men children alive." Did these *women* do right in disobeying that monarch? . . .

But why, my dear friends, have I thus been endeavoring to lead you through the history of more than three thousand years, and to point you to that great cloud of witnesses who have gone before, "from works to rewards?" Have I been seeking to magnify the sufferings, and exalt the character of woman, that she "might have praise of men?" No! no! my object has been to arouse *you,* as the wives and mothers, the daughters and sisters, of the South, to a sense of your duty as *women,* and as Christian women, on that great subject, which has already shaken our country.

—Angelina Grimké, *An Appeal to the Christian Women of the South* (1836)

I wonder if it be a sin to think slavery a curse to any land. Sumner said not one word of this hated institution which is not true. Men & women are punished when their masters & mistresses are brutes & not when they do wrong—& then we live surrounded by prostitutes. An abandoned woman is sent out of any decent house elsewhere. Who thinks any worse of a Negro or Mulatto woman for being a thing we can't name. God forgive *us,* but ours is a *monstrous* system & wrong & iniquity. Perhaps the rest of the world is as bad. This *only* I see: like the patriarchs of old our men live all in one house with their wives & their concubines, & the Mulattoes one sees in every family exactly resemble the white children—& every lady tells you who is the father of all the Mulatto children in every body's household, but those in her own, she seems to think drop from the clouds or pretends so to think—Good women we have, *but* they talk of all *nastiness*—tho they never do wrong, they talk day & night. . . . My disgust sometimes is boiling over—but they are, I believe, in conduct the purest women God ever made. Thank God for my country women—alas for the men! No worse than men every where, but the lower their mistresses, the more degraded they must be.

—Mary Boykin Chesnut, March 18, 1861, to her diary

Charleston in 1860

fanatical. "And what is the prospect before us?" Memminger asked the General Assembly of Virginia. "Is it likely that the torrent which is in motion will be stayed in its course?" His answer is worth pondering:

> The generation which now has possession of the political power of the North has been regularly trained from childhood to the course which they are now pursuing. At their mother's knee they were taught that slavery was a sin. . . .

> To these teachings the pulpit adds its religious sanction. . . . Slavery is denounced as a sin, and the conscience is misled to assume jurisdiction over Southern conduct. The press then advances, with its thousand tongues. . . . And here the party leader, with his political craft and skill, intervenes. . . . Thus we have every element of opinion and every power which operates on mind brought into requisition to effect one result. . . .

> We are brought then to this conclusion: The South stands in the Union without any protection from the Constitution, subject to the government of a sectional party, who regards our institutions as sinful, and whose leaders already declare that the destruction of these institutions is only a question of time.

And Memminger's thoughts were those of one of Charleston's moderates. Judah P. Benjamin said that "it was not so much what the Republicans had done or might do as the things they said." It was the assumptions made by what Benjamin called "the pestiferous breed—the fools and knaves of New England—that the Earth belongs to the Saints and they are the Saints of the Lord," that caused Southerners to react. One Southerner, Edward B. Bryan, could ignore the threats, but what made his blood boil was "the untiring efforts which are constantly made by the people of the North to degrade the South in the eyes of all who come within their reach." Robert E. Lee, who opposed secession, wrote after the war, "I have fought against the people of the North because I believed they were seeking to wrest from the South its dearest rights."

"If, in our present position of power and unitedness, we have the raid of John Brown, . . ." the *Charleston Mercury* asked in October of 1860, "what will be the measures of insurrection and incendiarism, which must follow our notorious and abject prostration to Abolition rule at Washington, with all the patronage of the Federal Government, and a Union organization in the South to support it."

Whatever the reason, events moved rapidly, though not rapidly enough for the radical secessionists. The Charleston Vigilance Association was formed in December, 1859, to protect the peace and suppress the slaves. Secessionist activists Robert Barnwell Rhett, Sr., and Robert Barnwell Rhett, Jr., William Porcher Miles, William Henry Gist, and Isaac W. Hayne redoubled their efforts. Moderates like Christopher Memminger reluctantly concluded that slavery would be safe only outside the Union. "We quit the Union," they said, "not the Constitution." They believed they were setting in motion a conservative counterrevolution to preserve the old Union and the Constitution of long ago. "We have rescued the Constitution," Alexander Stephens said, "from utter annihilation."

Soon only a small handful of unionists remained. One was the witty lawyer James L. Petigru, who, when asked his opinion of secession, replied, "South Carolina is too small for a republic and too large for an insane asylum."

S hall I tell you what this collision means? They who think that it is accidental, unnecessary, the work of interested or fanatical agitators, and therefore ephemeral, mistake the case altogether. It is an irrepressible conflict between opposing and enduring forces, and it means that the United States must and will, sooner or later, become either entirely a slaveholding nation, or entirely a free-labor nation. Either the cotton and rice-fields of South Carolina and the sugar plantations of Louisiana will ultimately be tilled by free labor, and Charleston and New Orleans become marts for legitimate merchandise alone, or else the rye-fields and wheat-fields of Massachusetts and New York must again be surrendered by their farmers to slave culture and to the production of slaves, and Boston and New York become once more markets for trade in the bodies and souls of men.

—William H. Seward, United States Senator from New York, in a speech given in Rochester on October 25, 1858

William H. Seward believed he, not Abraham Lincoln, should have been elected president in 1860. Seward was one of the foremost leaders of the newly emerging Republican party. He coined the phrase irrepressible conflict, *which enjoyed much political currency in the 1860s and has gone down in history as one of the shorthand explanations for the Civil War. But he believed that he could personally effect a political deal in which the South would stay in the Union.*

CHAPTER 2

CHARLESTON HOSTS THE DEMOCRATIC PARTY NATIONAL CONVENTION OF 1860

There are radical and inextinguishable feuds in the Democratic party, and they must come out here and now.
—Murat Halstead, reporting from the Democratic National Convention at Charleston, April 24, 1860.

The last party, pretending to be a national party, is broken up and the antagonism of the two sections of the Union has nothing to arrest its fierce collisions.
—*Charleston Mercury*, May 3, 1860

War, von Clausewitz wrote, is "the continuation of politics by other means." The first shot of the Civil War was certainly fired in Charleston, but in a political sense it was fired a year before the bombardment of Fort Sumter. The Civil War began at the Democratic National Convention held in April, 1860. There the political cloth which held the nation together began to tear in earnest. "No American political convention has ever held so much meaning for party and nation," wrote Robert W. Johannsen in *Politics and the Crisis of 1860*, "as that conclave of determined Democrats which gathered in Charleston, South Carolina . . . to nominate a candidate for the presidential office. Upon the decision at Charleston rested not only the future of the Democratic Party but also the continued existence of the Union." Like the valve of some giant, overheated steam engine, the Charleston convention became the focal point of all the sectional animosity and tension which had been building for decades.

The choice of Charleston as the site for the convention of the only truly national political party bordered on the bizarre. Charleston was not a large city. It had never hosted a national party convention before, was not centrally located, and physically could not comfortably handle such a large gathering. It was far from an ideal place for a political party to meet and reach an agreement on a nominee for president. Indeed, Charleston was, as David M. Potter has written, "the city least likely to support the cause of bisectional harmony." In fact, the choice of Charleston was a consolation prize given to the South by Northern Democrats after the Southern bloc's defeat at the 1856 convention, where James Buchanan had been nominated. The selection committee, chaired by a New Yorker, believed holding the convention on a Southern site would bring harmony to the party!

By 1860 it was clear to all except some Southerners that Charleston had been, in the words of Allan Nevins, "heedlessly selected" and "ill-chosen." Hotel accommodations were limited, and hotel owners had agreed to fix higher room prices arbitrarily. Transportation problems were monumental. A passenger had to change trains six times between

This photograph, taken before 1861, shows the Circular Congregational Church and South Carolina Institute Hall (also known as Agricultural Hall), where the Democratic Party National Convention met in April, 1860. When the delegates from the Deep South walked out of that building, it signaled the collapse of the nation's two-party system and the real beginning of the breakup of the Union. Both buildings perished in the Great Fire of December, 1861.

Charleston and Washington, and, of course, delegates came from as far away as Oregon and California. F. O. Prince, a Massachusetts delegate, wrote Adele Cutts Douglas from Charleston,

> I have never been taught to believe in eternal punishment, but the journey here has led me to recognize the contrary "platform," to use the term now current, since it has appeared to me, that those who were instrumental in locating the convention here can only be adequately punished therefor by *Brimstone* and *Caloric ad infinitum*. Not that I complain of Charleston, for it is a most charming city, and the Charlestonese incarnate every quality that graces humanity—most especially, beauty, wit & hospitality . . . but my objection in coming here, is on account of the fatigues & miseries of the journey. Such slow coaches—facetiously termed steam cars! Such abominable hotels! . . . If Mr. Douglas is not nominated pretty soon, I shall become a *pauper*.

The Northwestern Democrats and Douglas supporters had tried unsuccessfully to persuade the national committee to change the site of the convention. "For Douglas and the Democratic Party no choice of convention site could have been more unfortunate," Johannsen stated. "The choice of Charleston placed the advantage squarely with the Southern leaders."

On the national level things had gone from bad to worse. When Congress assembled in December, 1859, it was paralyzed. There was certainly no leadership from Buchanan's White House. The House of Representatives could not even elect a Speaker because of the close division between Republicans and Democrats and the factions within each party. Stephen A. Douglas, the front-runner for the Democratic nomination, was attacked on all sides by President Buchanan and his political allies for personal and political reasons having nothing to do with slavery. His opponents were determined he would not be president. The mood was bitter. Tempers flared. Fistfights almost broke out in Congress. Leadership on the national level was sorely divided.

The Democrats too were badly divided. To a significant degree, the 1860 Democratic party national convention was sabotaged by radicals who wanted Lincoln to be elected. The secessionists and the moderates both disliked Douglas. He was viewed as untrustworthy by Southerners because he championed popular sovereignty in the Western territories (letting the settlers themselves allow or disallow slavery as opposed to acknowledging the slave owner's absolute right to take his property where he willed). After the United States Supreme Court handed down the Dred Scott decision, which affirmed the slaveholder's right to take his slave anywhere in the country, Southerners, led by Senator Jefferson Davis of Mississippi, determined to enter into no more political compromises on the question of extending slavery into the territories. After all, the Supreme Court had held in effect that a black man had no rights which a white man was bound to respect. The country in general and Northern Democrats in particular would have to accept the absolute constitutional right of slave owners to take slavery into the territories. They demanded, in fact, a federal slave code in the territories. No more popular sovereignty. No more ambiguous deals. No more compromises. It was now all or nothing.

It was apparent that no "true" Southerner could be elected, and in the view of the secessionists, Douglas and those who wished to find the so-called middle ground would only postpone the fight. Charlestonians were not necessarily of one mind, however, on tactics. Some thought a compromise candidate could be nominated in Charleston, and war could be averted. When the convention opened, no one knew what to expect.

Charleston hosted the most divisive national party convention in American history. Lincoln called it "the Charleston fandango." It was the longest in history except for the 1924 convention, and none was more bitter and complicated. It was the only convention in American history which failed to nominate a candidate for president. Delegates began arriving as early as Wednesday, April 18, for a convention which was to begin on Monday, April 23. The site of the convention was Institute Hall at 134 Meeting Street, known to contemporary Charlestonians as Agricultural Hall. The Mills House hotel was on the next block south of Institute Hall and was therefore the most convenient place for the delegates to stay. Fifteen-hundred Douglas delegates from various states took it over, and it was, according to one observer, "as lively as a molasses barrel with flies." Douglas delegates also rented Hibernian Hall next door to the Mills House. There they could sleep in a dormitory-like space on the second floor of the building at a great savings over the cost of hotel rooms. The Charleston Hotel, a little farther away, north of the convention site on Meeting Street, housed the radical secessionist delegates. The so-called administration senators, supporters of Buchanan and therefore enemies of Douglas, were headquartered in luxury in a hotel on King Street, "a large old-fashioned building" overlooking an "ice-cream garden."

The New York, Pennsylvania, and Massachusetts delegates came to Charleston by steamboat. This solved both their transportation and lodging problems, the latter because they could sleep on their boats in Charleston harbor. The *Nashville*, home of the New York delegation, arrived with a complete store of liquor and "amiable females." The Pennsylvanians brought five hundred barrels of liquor and three hundred kegs of lager beer on the *Keystone State*. The Bostonians arrrived on the *S. R. Spaulding*, lacking, it appears, both liquor and females.

When the convention began, Institute Hall was crowded with more than 3,000 people, including 606 delegates who could cast 303 votes, the national committee, guests, reporters, and 2,000 spectators, some of whom were ladies in a gallery set aside just for them. People jammed the city and the convention hall, which, while large by Charleston standards, was pitifully inadequate for a national convention. Few could actually hear the proceedings. The acoustics were poor, the doors were open, and Meeting Street was "paved with bowlders . . . and the incessant clatter of the wheels [was] deafening," wrote Murat Halstead, a reporter from Cincinnati. It was so hot in the hall that men took off their jackets.

On the first day, the convention elected an anti-Douglas chairman, Caleb Cushing of Massachusetts, and debated the unit rule, which held that a state had to vote as a bloc. The rule was upheld. The next day, the Douglas delegates agreed to a vote on the platform before the nomination of candidates. Historian Roy F. Nichols observed in *The Disruption of American Democracy* that this was "a fateful decision which may have spelled [Douglas's] doom." Once the decision was made, the convention began to bog down in the political quagmire of slavery. It was the best way for Douglas's opponents to beat him. Murat Halstead reported that there "is an impression prevalent this morning that the Convention is destined to explode in a grand row. . . . There is tumult and war in prospect." While convention participants may have spent some evenings in the city's many bars and taverns

It was April, and Charleston in any April can evoke a poet's ecstasy. Its air was warm and soft, its foliage luxuriant, its architecture elegant, its manners polished and languid. It was the great cultural center of southernism; a spiritual capital, it might be called. Here were the most fervid traditions of southern loyalty, the most elegant pattern of southern civilization. It was a Mecca which many southerners, whether they realized it or not, approached in a frame of mind resembling reverence. Also it was the only one of the ten large cities in the nation which was not forging ahead with rapid strides. Time had a tendency to stand still there. Thither the Democracy was thronging.

Never before had an American political convention been held in such an exotic environment. Charleston was unique, a place by itself; and it was fateful chance which had chosen it. The imps of Satan must have chuckled with devilish glee to learn that the Democratic party was to meet that year in the South, and in Charleston of all places. A bitter struggle for control was imminent, and the life of the party hung in the balance. Men of desperate political fortunes were to meet other men exalted by fanatic zeal to defend all they held dear. In numbers they were almost evenly matched. The environment was one of the most powerful influences which were to turn the balance.

—Roy Franklin Nichols,
The Disruption of American Democracy (1948)

Institute Hall burned in the great fire of 1861. There is now an office building on the site, designed with an architectural nod to the original structure. In her diary, Emma Holmes described Institute Hall as "one of the largest [halls] in the South [and] the scene for many years of almost every public event. There were held all our fairs, concerts, presentation of flags, The Democratic or National Convention of 1860, and, above all, there was signed our Ordinance of Secession, the instrument which broke the fetters with which the North is seeking to bind us down to everlasting slavery and disgrace. That loss can never be replaced, those hallowed associations will linger around the ruined walls."

William L. Yancey, the prince of the "fire-eating" secessionists, was born in Georgia, lived for a time in South Carolina, and then moved to Alabama. Along with Robert Barnwell Rhett, he agitated for Southern independence for many years.

or in delightful walks to the Battery, where a band from Boston serenaded delegates and locals alike, the days were given over to fierce debate. "Charleston," wrote Nichols, "had never had a show like this." The debate raged all week. The Northern and Western Democrats simply would not agree to force slavery on the territories.

Halstead wrote on April 30, "I have several times this morning heard the remark, 'The President will be nominated at Chicago' [the site of the Republican convention]." The Northern and Western Democrats were as frustrated as the Southerners. The South was insistent that the platform be unambiguous, so worded that it could be interpreted only as pure Southern doctrine, by which they meant the protection of slave property in the territories and the unequivocal repudiation of the Douglas doctrine of popular sovereignty. The Northern delegates, however, were extremely concerned about the political consequence of yielding completely to the slaveholders. "Their political existence" Halstead wrote, "depends absolutely upon their ability to construe the platform adopted here to mean 'popular sovereignty,' in other words, upon such a form of words in the platform as will allow them to declare, in the North, that the officially expressed Democratic doctrine is that the people of the Territories may, while in their territorial condition, abolish or exclude slavery. They cannot, dare not, yield the opportunity for pressing this pretext. The South will not allow it. Here, then, is the 'irrepressible conflict'—a conflict between enduring forces."

W. L. Yancey, the fire-eating secessionist from Alabama, made an impassioned speech for Southern rights and for the party to embrace slavery outright. He was not a legislator or even an organizer, but he was an orator par excellence. He was certainly one of the greatest demagogues in American history. In his speech, which was the highlight of the convention, Yancey said in part,

> Ours is the property invaded; ours are the institutions which are at stake; ours is the peace that is to be destroyed; ours is the honor at stake—the honor of children, the honor of families, the lives, perhaps, of all—all of which rests upon what your course may ultimately make a great heaving volcano of passion and crime, if you are enabled to consummate your designs. Bear with us, then, if we stand sternly upon what is yet that dormant volcano, and say we yield no position here until we are convinced we are wrong.

The crowd went wild. Rarely in American history has one speech affected the course of events more dramatically.

Later that evening George Pugh of Ohio addressed the convention, now at the height of the debate over slavery. He told the Southerners that the rest of the country would never agree to the unconditional extension of slavery proposed by Yancey. "Gentlemen of the South," he implored, "you mistake us—you mistake us—we will not do it." Halstead reported the situation thus:

> This thing is in a hopeless jumble. The South has driven the Northern Democracy to the wall, and now insists upon protection of slavery in the Territories. In other words, insists upon the political execution of every Northern Democrat, and the total destruction of the Democratic party. The Northern Democracy [however] . . . are unwilling to submit themselves to assassination or to commit suicide. And the South will not yield a jot of its position as master of the party.

South Carolina's delegation was composed of unionists, as its secessionists had

The interior of Hibernian Hall in 1860. The pro-Douglas Northwestern delegation slept here during the Democratic Party National Convention. Hibernian Hall is just down Meeting Street from Institute Hall, where the convention met. Built by the Hibernian Society, it was a monument to the success and affluence of Irish Charlestonians.

boycotted the state party proceedings. The other Southern states, however, sent delegations firmly committed to secession, and after the platform vote was finally taken on April 30, most of the Southern delegates, led by Alabama, walked out, urged on by the radicals in Charleston. The South Carolina delegation withdrew against their wishes. "If they had not retired," Rhett wrote, "they would have been mobbed." Speeches justifying the walkout were made by a member of each delegation. "The speech of Mr. Yancey had been the speech of the Convention," Halstead reported. "Some time before it was concluded the day had expired, and the gas had been lit about the hall. The scene was very brilliant and impressive. The crowded hall, the flashing lights, the deep solicitude felt in every word, the importance of the issues pending, all combined to make up a spectacle of extraordinary interest, and something of splendor."

Many of the Northern spectators and some of the delegates began to leave the convention for home. As fewer delegates attended, more Charleston ladies crowded into Institute Hall. "South Caroleena beauty is well represented," Halstead wrote. "Many of the ladies have fine features but most of them, bad complexions. They are splendid in eyes and hair, with fine profiles and bright countenances, but not excellent forms. The ladies are a great feature of the Convention. The delegates are desperately gallant."

It became increasingly clear that the convention was a debacle, that Southern and Northern Democrats could not agree on the slavery question and the nomination of the Democratic party would be worthless. As it dragged on, the galleries were filled with Charlestonians determined, as Nichols wrote, "to see the first act of the great tragedy which was to have so many of its scenes set in their city."

The Charleston newspapers, the *Mercury* and the *Evening News*, bombarded the delegates, urging them to make no compromise. Intemperate speeches were the order of the day. The streets of Charleston and the galleries of Institute Hall were filled with secessionists. The tension in the city itself prolonged the convention and helped to deadlock it. As a result, Stephen Douglas could not garner enough votes to be nominated. According to the historian Emerson D. Fite, the nation was "awestruck." When the convention adjourned on the seventh day, everyone knew that it had failed and that "the party of Andrew Jackson had been reduced to a shambles and the fate of the nation had been sealed." The party reconvened the convention in Baltimore, where Douglas was duly given the useless nomination. "Something more than the convention had come to an end when the delegates of the cotton kingdom walked out of the hall," Allan Nevins concluded in *The War for the Union;* "the Democratic Party had been riven asunder, and the stage set for secession and disunion. The melancholy words which a veteran leader of the South, ex-Senator Foote, wrote decades later, were all too true; the Southern extremists who had declared that they would never tolerate a Republican President had taken the very steps to make Republican victory certain, and thus deliberately sealed the destruction of the national fabric."

It was readily apparent that Charleston and Charlestonians had helped to disrupt the convention of the Democratic party, which had been until then the governing party of

The steamship S. R. Spaulding *transported New England delegates to Charleston for the Democratic Party National Convention. Once in Charleston, the delegation stayed on board the ship rather than move to one of the overpriced local hotels. Caleb Cushing, the Convention chairman, stayed on board.* Harper's Weekly *reported that the delegates "can thus live more cheaply, and probably more comfortably, and certainly more healthily, than in the overcrowded hotels of Charleston."*

St. Andrews Hall on Broad Street, next door to John Rutledge's home, played a prominent role in the events of 1860. When the Southern delegates withdrew from the Democratic convention, they met at St. Andrews Hall. The Secession Convention of December, 1860, also met in the hall, and it was here that the vote on secession was taken. The Ordinance of Secession itself was actually signed at Institute Hall. St. Andrews Hall was destroyed in the Great Fire of December, 1861.

American politics. It was the party of Jefferson and Jackson. It was the party of the incumbent president. There had never been a Republican president. The night after the walkout by Southern delegates, Halstead described the city as follows:

> There was a Fourth of July feeling in Charleston last night— a jubilee. There was no mistaking the public sentiment of the city. It was overwhelmingly and enthusiastically in favor of the seceders. In all her history Charleston had never enjoyed herself so hugely.

What John Brown's raid started in 1859 was finished by the Republican party's nomination of Abraham Lincoln in 1860. A popular joke of the time ran, "Stephen A. Douglas was a greater man than Abraham Lincoln, for while Lincoln split rails, Douglas split the Democratic party." Lincoln was viewed as a radical opponent of slavery, though he had consistently said he would never interfere with slavery where it existed. He did, however, argue against the *spread* of slavery, and this position appealed to the working people of America, who wanted the West to remain free so that the white laborer could prosper.

When Lincoln defeated Douglas, the Democratic nominee, and John Bell and John C. Breckinridge, nominees of third parties, no one in South Carolina was surprised. That was what the majority wanted—a reason to secede. "Lincoln's election," wrote Steven A. Channing in *Crisis of Fear*, "*meant* the ascendancy of abolitionists to national power— *meant* convulsive slave insurrection—*meant* emancipation of the Negro hordes" to Charlestonians—unlesss they acted immediately to protect themselves. Secession now became inevitable. And war? To most Charlestonians it still appeared distant and unlikely.

The bright smiles and handclappings which Charleston ladies bestowed upon the receding delegates were applause for an irrevocable step toward war; the bouquets which they brought next day to fill the empty seats of the seceders were symbolic of the flowers soon to be cast upon multitudinous Southern graves.
—Allan Nevins, *The Emergence of Lincoln* (1950)

Charleston was the past incarnate, the city that had forced time to stand still, carefully preserving a cherished way of life which had a fragile and immutable pattern, and it would listen to no demand for change. And although Charleston stood apart, it did not stand alone.
—Bruce Catton, *The Coming Fury* (1961)

Stephen A. Douglas would have been president in 1861 instead of Abraham Lincoln if the Democratic Convention in Charleston had not been disrupted by Southern secessionists and their Charleston allies.

CHAPTER 3

THE CRADLE OF SECESSION

Abraham Lincoln as a candidate for president of the United States in 1860.

As late as September, 1860, secession and Civil War did not appear inevitable. James L. Petigru thought "no possible issue could be more untenable than to make [Lincoln's] bare election a casus belli, without any overt act against the Constitution. . . . If our planter were in debt, or cotton was at 5 cents, . . . [secession] might be likely; but our magnanimous countrymen are too comfortable for such exercise." Most Charlestonians and many Southerners, however, believed the North would never go to war and that Great Britain would intercede to protect its supply of cotton. After all, Cotton was King, and Great Britain had imported 78 percent of the South's cotton crop in 1859. "I firmly believe that the slave-holding South is now the controlling power of the world—that no other power would face us in hostility," Senator James Henry ("Harry") Hammond of South Carolina wrote. "Cotton, rice, tobacco, and naval stores command the world; and we have sense to know it, and are sufficiently Teutonic to carry it out successfully. The North without us would be a motherless calf, bleating about, and die of mange and starvation."

South Carolina had been so radical for so long that it became necessary for other Southern states to act first. Leaders of the secession movement in South Carolina helped to orchestrate the needed action in Georgia, Alabama, and Mississippi. The conservative leadership in Charleston also recognized in the fall of 1860 that they had better take over the secession movement or the radicals like Rhett would displace them. Men like William Denison Porter, the president of the state senate; James Simons, the speaker of the state house of representatives; and Andrew G. Magrath, the local federal judge, all became strongly committed to immediate secession that fall.

On November 7, 1860, when it was clear that Lincoln had been elected, high local federal officials quit their offices. Both the United States district judge, Andrew G. Magrath, and the United States attorney, James Connor, resigned. Indeed, the political machinery of secession actually began as the votes for the presidential electors—chosen in 1860 by the General Assembly, not by popular vote—were counted. The General Assembly met on November 5, 1860, and after appointing electors, stayed in session to call for a state convention for the purpose of dissolving the Union. "The way to create a revolution," W. W. Boyce told the General Assembly, "is to start it. To submit to Lincoln's election is to consent to death!"

The depth of hatred for Lincoln personally in South Carolina has no equal in American political history. Charleston book shops closed their accounts with *Harper's Weekly* and *Harper's Magazine* because these periodicals had published a portrait and biography of Lincoln. The *Mercury* called Lincoln "the beau ideal of a relentless, dogged, free-soil Border Ruffian, a vulgar mobocrat and a Southern hater."

Andrew Gordon Magrath was born in Charleston in 1813 and died in 1893. In November, 1860, after Lincoln's election, he resigned his position as a Federal judge and announced that as far as he was concerned, "the Temple of Justice, raised under the Constitution of the United States, is now closed." He became an instant local hero. He served as secretary of state of the short-lived Republic of South Carolina and as a Confederate judge. Four years later he was elected governor of South Carolina. He fled his office in February, 1865, when General Sherman arrived in Columbia. He later became the first president of the South Carolina Bar Association.

A crowd gathers at City Hall in Charleston in November, 1860, when the news of Abraham Lincoln's election to the presidency is announced. Lincoln's election was viewed by most Charlestonians as a virtual declaration of war because of his opposition to slavery.

On November 9, a large public meeting was held at Institute Hall in Charleston. "It was plain, from a brief glance," wrote J. W. Claxton, "that the respectable citizens of Charleston were there. The speakers were persons of note. They, one after another, in burning phrase, counselled immediate secession.... As they uttered their fierce words, the multitudes rose from their seats, waved their hats in the air, and thundered forth resounding cheers." The president of the South Carolina Senate, William O. Porter of Charleston, observed, "The city which is most exposed and must bear the brunt in great part, is clamorous for secession." Even the mercantile community was caught up in the frenzy. They too believed Lincoln's election meant the end of slavery, and even the most conservative businessman could not abide abolition. "So unanimous is public sentiment," stated William Grimball, "that in the city of Charleston, formerly from its commercial interests the most union-loving and conservative portion of the State, no other candidates will present themselves to the people." Senator James H. Hammond wrote on November 12, 1860, "People are wild. The scenes of the French Revolution are being enacted already." The women of Charleston were as fervent as the men. Indeed, Emma Holmes noted in her diary that "secession was born in the hearts of Carolina women."

As Frederick Jackson Turner pointed out, "Charleston was peculiarly suited to lead in a movement of revolt. It was the one important center of real city life." It was a focal point, a gathering place for the planters. "Thus South Carolina, affording a combination of plantation life with the social intercourse of the city, gave peculiar opportunities for exchanging ideas and consolidating the sentiment of her leaders." Charleston was the political center of the state and the only real city, but it was the planters' city. When asked to invest in an industrial corporation in Charleston, Nathaniel Heyward, who owned seventeen rice plantations, is said to have remarked that "such industrial enterprises would ruin Charleston for what it was intended to be, a summer home for rice planters." Charleston was located in the center of the lowcountry black belt, surrounded by a huge black population. The city was, as James M. Banner, Jr., said, "at one with the surrounding land." The planter influx made her both cosmopolitan and provincial, urban and rural.

The fear of revolts, arson, and poisoning by slaves, so much a part of Charleston's history, now pervaded the entire white community, although there was no actual revolt. "The negroes are all of opinion that Lincoln is to come here to free them," Petigru's niece wrote to her husband, but she added that "they are perfectly quiet and *nothing* is apprehended from them." The city was tense with rumors of slave revolt. But no one really expected war. The *Mercury* argued that "it is utterly impracticable for Mr. Lincoln and his rump government to make effective war upon us." An invasion would only consolidate Southern nationalism. "What is indisputable," Channing declared, "is that the overwhelming majority of South Carolinians believed in the imminence of a peaceable acquiescence by the North to the secession of the state." Confederate Major General Samuel Jones, an apologist for the war, argued afterward in *The Siege of Charleston*,

> If evidence were needed to show that the States which first withdrew from the Union did not contemplate a war of coercion as one of the first consequences of secession, none more conclusive could be presented than the defenseless condition of those States when the war commenced. For it is inconceivable that intelligent men charged with the conduct of public affairs would have plunged their States, so unprepared, into so unequal a war.

ROBERT BARNWELL RHETT

Robert Barnwell Rhett, "the father of secession," was born in 1800 in Beaufort, South Carolina. Elected to the General Assembly in 1826, he eventually became a radical proponent of states' rights, believing that John C. Calhoun was too moderate on the subject. As state attorney general and as a congressman, he championed the most radical position—immediate secession—the earliest. He wrote the address to the Nashville convention in 1850. He succeeded to Calhoun's senate seat in 1850 and called on South Carolina to secede alone and at once. When this call was rejected, he resigned from the Senate.

During the 1850s he and his son Robert Barnwell Rhett, Jr., the editor of the *Charleston Mercury,* worked untiringly for secession. The *Mercury* was the leading secessionist newspaper of the time. Its influence outside Charleston was probably greater than within. In 1858 Rhett met with William L. Yancey and other radicals in Montgomery, Alabama. Their new plan was to ensure a Republican victory in 1860 and push for secession immediately after the election of Lincoln, while tempers flared and emotions ran high.

When South Carolina seceded, Rhett was widely perceived as the chief tactician and ideological spokesman for the move. He wrote the Address to the Slaveholding States, which called for the creation of a Southern confederacy. When Major Anderson moved to Fort Sumter, Rhett became very excited. According to Abner Doubleday, a union officer stationed at Fort Sumter, Rhett rushed over to inform Governor Pickens that "'the people demanded that Fort Sumter should be taken without any further procrastination or delay.' The governor made a very shrewd reply. He said, 'Certainly, Mr. Rhett; I have no objection! I will furnish you with some men, and you can storm the work yourself.' Rhett drew back and replied, 'But, sir, I am not a military man!' 'Nor I either,' said the governor, 'and therefore I take the advice of those that are!' After this, there was no further talk of an immediate assault. The action of the governor in this case almost gained him the reputation of a wit among the officers of his command."

Rhett's career went downhill after secession. He was never seriously considered for the presidency of the Confederacy by anyone other than himself and his family but was apparently disappointed when he was not elected. He received no appointment from Jefferson Davis, and his political proposals were rejected by the Confederate government. An agitator, not a statesman, Rhett did not have the confidence of the moderate leadership. "Rhett," T. R. R. Cobb wrote his wife, "is a generous hearted and honest man with a vast quantity of cranks and a small proportion of common sense."

In 1863 Rhett was defeated in a bid for election to the Confederate Congress. He died in Louisiana in 1876, believing to the end in the rightness of his cause, a separate Southern nation.

There were no Charlestonians in the very front ranks of the Confederacy. Perhaps if Calhoun's successor, the venerable senator Robert Woodward Barnwell, had accepted Jefferson Davis's offer of the office of secretary of state, Charleston would have had a higher profile in the Confederate government. As it was, Charleston's place in the Confederate cabinet went to Christopher G. Memminger, a quiet, unexciting, and—as it turned out—ineffectual secretary of the treasury.

Robert Barnwell Rhett, the Father of Secession. He thought John C. Calhoun was too moderate. On Calhoun's death in 1850, Rhett was elected to succeed him in the United States Senate. His son Robert Barnwell Rhett, Jr., was the editor of the fiery Mercury.

When a bill was enacted by the General Assembly on November 10 calling for a secession convention, the city celebrated. Elections for delegates to the convention were to be held on December 6. "Charleston proceeded to hold high carnival," as David M. Potter described it, "with wine flowing, palmetto flags flying, and hot-heads reveling in martial display." Robert Barnwell Rhett exulted, "The tea has been thrown overboard— the revolution of 1860 has been initiated." Rev. Toomer Porter wrote later of a "laughable story" about Petigru. Petigru was walking up Main Street in Columbia, Porter related, and was met by some countryman who asked whether Petigru could tell him where the lunatic asylum was. "Yes, my man," Petigru said, "It is off down that street, they call that the asylum, but it is a mistake. Yonder," pointing to the State House, where the General Assembly was in session, "is the asylum, and it is full of lunatics." William Seward reported to Thurlow Weed that "the Republican Party today is as uncompromising as the Secessionists in South Carolina. A month hence each may come to think that moderation is wiser." A prominent free black Charlestonian, James M. Johnson, wrote his brother-in-law on December 7, "The excitement has not abated. The tone of the President's [Buchanan's] message will give force to [the secessionists'] resolve. There being no fear of an attempt at coercion they will lose sight of more remote consequences."

The authorities in Charleston began to crack down on all blacks, free or slave. A search was made for runaway slaves; proof had to be produced that a black person was of free status or he or she would be enslaved. Even the brown elite, heretofore safe from this type of witch-hunt, was threatened. Johnson related to his brother-in-law after the secession convention, "Our situation is not only unfortunate but deplorable and it is better to make a sacrifice now than wait to be sacrificed *ourselves*."

On December 11, 1860, Major Robert Anderson, the commander at Fort Moultrie on Sullivan's Island, received oral instructions to hold possession of the forts in Charleston harbor, and if attacked, to defend himself "to the last extremity." The smallness of his force, Anderson was told, would not permit him to occupy more than one of the three forts, but an attack on or attempt to take possession of any of them should be regarded "as an act of hostility, and you may then put your command into either of them which you may deem most proper to increase its power of resistance." Anderson was authorized to take similar steps whenever he had "tangible evidence of a design to proceed to a hostile act."

On December 17, 1860, the secession convention met in Columbia, the capital of South Carolina. Because of a rumor of an outbreak of smallpox, however, it adjourned to Charleston, where it reconvened on December 18. The Northern press was not welcomed to the proceedings. Robert B. Rhett, Jr., the editor of the Charleston *Mercury*, wrote John Bigelow, the editor of the *New York Evening Post*, that he had received his note in regard to the *Post*'s sending a correspondent to observe the proceedings of the convention, but that in Rhett's opinion the reporter "would run great risk of his life, and I am sure would not be allowed to report the proceedings." Rhett told Bigelow that an outsider would be tarred and feathered and made to leave the state, "as the mildest possible treatment consistent with the views of the people here." Fortunately for the people of New York, Rhett said, the *Mercury* and *Courier* would accurately print the story of the proceedings. "No agent or representative of the *Evening Post* would be safe in coming here," Rhett concluded. "He would come with his life in his hand, and would probably be hung. Professionally yours, R. B. Rhett, Jr."

"Major Robert Anderson, U.S.A.," the *Courier* editorialized in December, 1860, "has achieved the unenviable distinction of opening civil war between Americans by an act of gross breach of faith." The Rev. A. Toomer Porter wrote, "I do not think that anyone can portray the scenes of that day. There was no more shouting, but men and women were hurrying to and fro, with an excitement words cannot express at all. The wildest rumors were started, everyone supposed that Fort Sumter was full of shells, and that Major Anderson had trained his guns on the city, and we should soon be bombarded."

When the delegates arrived at the railroad station in Charleston, they were met by a fifteen-gun salute and a parade. The dignitaries were escorted to the Mills House by military units amid great pomp. Only eight months earlier, the Democratic party had brought thousands to Institute Hall to debate the future of the nation. The leaders had stayed at the Mills House and the Charleston Hotel. Now a smaller convention of the people of South Carolina was meeting at the same hall and staying at the same hotels to act out the inevitable result of the failure of that convention.

The convention consisted of 169 delegates, almost all of whom were slaveholders. They were, by all indications, the elite of the state: 5 former governors, 40 former state senators, 100 former state representatives, 12 clerics, and many lawyers. Dr. James H. Thornwell wrote, "It was a body of sober, grave and venerable men, selected from every pursuit in life, and distinguished, most of them, in their respective spheres, by every quality which can command confidence and respect." Almost half the delegates owned fifty slaves or more.

The entrance hall of a Charleston hotel during the Secession Convention. This illustration appeared on the front page of the Illustrated London News.

The secession convention met at Broad Street near Legaré and debated for two days. "The convention," James M. Johnson wrote, "is in full blast." The leaders discussed strategy with delegations from Alabama and Mississippi. Everyone in South Carolina knew in advance what the outcome would be. On December 20, 1860, the state of South Carolina voted to secede from the United States. Mrs. St. Julien Ravenel related in her 1906 history of Charleston that St. Andrews Hall was "the scene of so many joyous entertainments," that the delegates "occupied the gilt, velvet-covered chairs sacred to the chaperons of the St. Cecilia," and that the president of the convention stood under a Sully portrait of Queen Victoria. But she recognized that the "time was too grave for thought of these accessories." There was no debate. The roll call vote—conducted behind closed doors—took eight minutes. It was unanimous. The convention adjourned at 1:15 to celebrate with more parades.

The Ordinance of Secession was signed at Institute Hall on Meeting Street that evening. The larger facility allowed the public to view the signing. The delegates gathered at St. Andrews Hall and marched in procession to Institute Hall, where they were greeted by the members of the General Assembly. The delegates and legislators entered the cavernous hall to the applause of thousands. Dr. John Bachman, a Lutheran minister and noted naturalist, gave the invocation, in which he asked for "wisdom from on high" and besought God to "enable us to protect and bless the humble race that has been entrusted to our care." The signing lasted two hours. There were speeches and celebrations. The Rev. Toomer Porter described the events of that date in his reminiscences:

> The large building was packed, and the throng in the street was immense. It was all one way in Charleston. Judge Magrath was the first speaker. He stood on the left of the stage facing the audience, and began (I give his very words): "Fellow citizens: The time for deliberation has passed." He paused, and started across the stage to the right, walking in slow measured steps. Everyone who remembers Judge Magrath's walk, will recall him as he passed a large handkerchief through his hands, from one diagonal corner to the other. He said not a word more, and the audience waited until, in an impassioned voice and gesture, he added: "The time for action has come." At that moment there went up a universal yell, presage of what has gone into history as "the rebel yell." It died out, and rose for several minutes before the Judge could proceed. And I, fool as I was, yelled with the rest of them, and threw up my hat, and no doubt thought we could whip creation. It was very dramatic in the Judge, a fine piece of acting, but alas, the prologue of what a tragedy!

Edmund Ruffin also described the momentous events in his diary:

> The signing occupied more than two hours, during which time there was nothing to entertain the spectators except their enthusiasm & joy. Yet no one was weary, & none left. Demonstrations of approbation in clapping & cheers were frequent—& when all the signatures had been affixed, & the President holding up the parchment proclaimed South Carolina to be a free and independent country, the cheers of the whole assembly continued for some minutes, while every man waved or threw up his hat, & every lady waved her handkerchief.

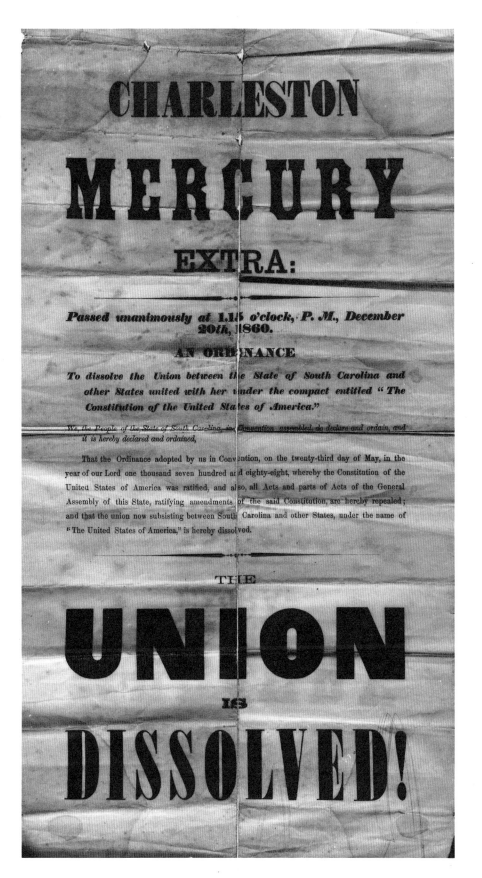

The signing of the Ordinance of Secession, December 20, 1860, at Institute Hall, depicted on the cover for the sheet music of "The Palmetto State Song." A contemporary observer wrote, "It was a body of sober, grave, and venerable men, selected from every pursuit in life, and distinguished, most of them, in their respective spheres, by every quality which can command confidence and respect. . . . In the midst of intense agitation and excitement, they were calm, cool, collected, and self possessed." The signing of the document that proclaimed South Carolina an independent nation lasted two hours, "during which time," Edmund Ruffin recalled, "there was nothing to entertain the spectators except their enthusiasm and joy." Three thousand spectators watched. Later that night Charlestonians celebrated with parades, bonfires, and demonstrations.

The most famous front page in Charleston's history and perhaps in the history of the United States. The Charleston Mercury, long a proponent of secession, had this "extra" on the streets literally within five minutes of the enactment of the Ordinance of Secession. (Rhett gave a copy of the ordinance to his newspaper before it was reported to the convention.) The Mercury announcement appears in virtually every pictorial history of the Civil War.

When the convention adjourned, people filled the streets. There were popular demonstrations from early in the afternoon; military companies paraded, salutes were fired, bonfires were lighted in the main streets, and rockets and small explosive were fired by the young boys. "As I now write, after 10 p.m." Ruffin continued, "I hear the distant sounds of rejoicing with the music of a military band, as if there was no thought of ceasing." Major Anderson may have undoubtedly heard the military music as well. Sitting and waiting at Fort Moultrie, Anderson had to decide what he would do. There were rumors at Fort Moultrie that two thousand of the best riflemen in the state were about to occupy a hill near the fort and the roofs of nearby houses in order to capture the federal troops.

The reaction in the North was varied. Some said, like Horace Greeley, "Erring sisters go in peace." Oliver Wendell Holmes wrote a poem which began, "She has left us in . . . passion and pride," referring to the state of South Carolina. The extreme abolitionists were delighted; they wanted no responsibility for the Slave South. Wendell Phillips, echoing Garrison's earlier comment about the Constitution, exclaimed, "The covenant with death is annulled; 'the agreement with hell' is broken to pieces." But the great majority of Northerners viewed secession as illegal and unacceptable and vowed to preserve the Union. Mary Chesnut wrote in her diary, "We are divorced, North and South, because we have hated each other so."

James M. Johnson concluded that he could "not supinely wait for the working of a miracle by having a chariot let down to convey us away." Hundreds of free black Charlestonians left. "As it regards Emigration," Johnson wrote on December 19, 1860, "your humble servt is on the alert with the whole of our people who are debating where to go. The majority are in favor of Hayti [Haiti]. Some few are leaving here by each steamer."

Petigru, the crusty old Whig lawyer, refused to acknowledge the legality of secession. Mary Chesnut also noted in her diary, "Mr. Petigru alone in South Carolina has not seceded." Stephen A. Hurlbut, President Lincoln's secret emissary, informed the president on March 27 that Mr. Petigru "is now the only man in the City of Charleston who avowedly adheres to the Union . . . the only citizen loyal to the Nation." Later on, when a friend told him Louisiana had seceded, Petigru replied, "Good God, Williams, I thought we had *bought* Louisiana."

On December 23, 1860, the secretary of war sent Major Anderson confidential orders:

> It is neither expected nor desired that you should expose your own life or that of your men in a hopeless conflict in defense of these forts. If they are invested or attacked by a force so superior that resistance would, in your judgment, be a useless waste of life, it will be your duty to yield to necessity and make the best terms in your power. This will be the conduct of an honorable, brave and humane officer, and you will be fully justified in such action. These orders are strictly confidential and not to be communicated even to the officers under your command without close necessity.

On December 24 the secession convention adopted the Declaration of Immediate Causes Which Induce and Justify the Secession of South Carolina, written by Christopher G. Memminger of Charleston. In this declaration, the people of South Carolina rested

Secessionists rally at the Mills House in December, 1860. Speechmaking from the Mills House balcony was common during the secession crisis. Built in 1853, the Mills House boasted Charleston's "first thoroughly Victorian" interior. The present building, constructed in the 1970s, is a replica.

Prior to World War II, at least one fort was the first requirement for a harbor of any importance. Colonial Charles Town from its earliest days was protected by a fort on the western tip of Sullivan's Island. Indeed, Sullivan's Island is named for the watchman Captain Florence O'Sullivan, who fired his small cannon to warn the city's inhabitants when he saw a Spanish ship off the bar. Later a small fort was built and called Fort Sullivan. There in 1776 Colonel William Moultrie constructed a large fort, where on June 28 colonial South Carolinians made their heroic stand against the British navy. Renamed in honor of Colonel Moultrie, this fort played a key role in the beginning of the Civil War.

Fort Moultrie looked across the narrow harbor channel to Fort Johnson on a tip protruding from James Island and Cummins Point on Cummins Island. Of more strategic importance, however, was a shoal, well known in the colonial era, called the Middle Ground, which projected outward from James Island. Fort Moultrie was located just a thousand yards north of this shoal, and the narrow channel forced deep-draft ships to sail very close to Fort Moultrie, well within the reach of her artillery. It was on this shoal that Fort Sumter was constructed.

The fort was a product of the disastrous result of the war of 1812. President James Madison, run out of Washington by the British, was determined to construct modern and effective coastal fortifications. Thus in 1821 the military began surveying the South Atlantic coast, and by 1827 plans were drawn. The obvious location for this second harbor fort was the Middle Ground.

Fort Sumter was, when first built, among the "most spectacular harbor defense structures to come out of any era of military architecture." The present Fort Sumter is not at all the original fort, which boasted three stories and stood fifty feet in height above low water. The parade ground was one acre. Construction began in 1828 but was slow. In the first place, construction on a sandbar proved to be time-consuming and difficult. The fort was built originally on a grillage of continuous square timbers over rock, but later

granite blocks were used as a foundation instead. The granite had to be laid between high and low tides, and at times the water covered the construction site. In the second place, there was a long delay in the 1830s when a question arose as to the legal ownership of the property and had to be resolved by lawyers. Clear title was obtained only in 1841. There were also the typical Charleston construction problems: a work force uneven in ability, unbearable heat, mosquitoes, yellow fever, and especially a lack of readily available materials. Ten thousand tons of granite had to be shipped in from the North, some from the Penobscot River area of Maine. Sixty thousand tons of other kinds of rock were also shipped in. The

local brickyards could not supply enough brick. Landing the material was difficult. In the 1830s the fort was named in honor of the great Revolutionary war hero Thomas Sumter, who lived to be nearly ninety-eight years old.

As unbelievable as it sounds, construction on Fort Sumter was not complete in 1860, when events brought it to the forefront of national consciousness. Samuel W. Crawford, a Union officer and surgeon stationed with Anderson at Fort Moultrie and briefly at Sumter, said that in 1860 it was "in no condition for defense." Only 15 of the planned 135 guns had been mounted. Neither the barracks nor the officers' quarters were finished.

their case for secession on the North's hostility to slavery and its refusal to enforce the fugitive slave laws. In a 4–1 vote, the convention defeated attempts to rewrite the declaration to include other grounds for secession such as the tariff. One delegate, Thomas Jefferson Withers, had written before secession, "The true question for us is, how shall we sustain African slavery in South Carolina from a series of annoying attacks, attended by incidental consequences that I shrink from depicting, and finally from utter abolition? That is the problem before us—the naked and true point." The convention therefore, in the words of Charles E. Cauthen, "explicitly rested disunion upon the question of slavery." In the early morning hours of December 26, Major Anderson removed his federal troops from Fort Moultrie, where the first important military battle of the Revolution had been won, to a new fort built on a sandbar in Charleston harbor. It was called Fort Sumter.

Christmas, 1860. In the wake of South Carolina's secession, Major Robert Anderson decided it was time to move his small command from Fort Moultrie on Sullivan's Island, a position which was indefensible, to Fort Sumter, which could be defended. He spiked the cannons and moved his troops out silently late on the night of December 25, 1860, and into the morning hours of December 26. The Courier editorialized that by moving to Fort Sumter, Anderson had started civil war. Indeed, three commissioners from South Carolina were about to meet with President Buchanan on December 27 when the news of Anderson's move arrived in Washington. The president exclaimed, "This is not only without but against my orders, it is against my policy." But Buchanan never ordered Anderson back to Moultrie.

CHAPTER 4

THE FIRST SHOT:
LINCOLN TESTS THE WATERS
OF CHARLESTON HARBOR

President James Buchanan, whom most Americans justifiably do not remember, was followed by President Abraham Lincoln, whom most Americans venerate. Buchanan, however, was still president in December, 1860, prior to the secession of South Carolina. He gave the distinct impression that the Federal government had accepted secession. For example, he seriously considered ordering Anderson and his men to evacuate Fort Sumter and return to Fort Moultrie. "A President of the United States who would make such an order," his attorney general, Edwin Stanton, thundered, "would be guilty of treason." To which Buchanan replied, "Oh, no! Not so bad as that, my friend! Not so bad as that!" There was even a preliminary agreement to negotiate the ownership of Federal property in South Carolina. Buchanan informed a delegation of South Carolina Congressmen, as he wrote in December, 1860, "that if they [the Federal forts] were assailed this would put them completely in the wrong and making them the authors of the Civil War."

The North was in a state of anticipation. So was the South, and so were the Charlestonians. On January 9 the *Star of the West,* a Union ship laden with supplies bound for Fort Sumter, was turned back by Citadel cadets firing artillery from Morris Island. "The expulsion of the *Star of the West* from Charleston Harbor yesterday morning was the opening of the ball of revolution," the *Charleston Mercury* crowed. "We are proud that our harbor has been so honored. We are more proud that the State of South Carolina, so long, so bitterly, so contemptuously reviled and scoffed at, above all others, should thus proudly have thrown back the scoff of her enemies." An officer on the *Star of the West* with a sense of humor said, "The people of Charleston pride themselves upon their hospitality, but it exceeded my expectations. They gave us several balls before we landed." On February 24 one Charlestonian wrote, "Everybody apprehends that the *crisis* is approaching, that we are on the *eve* of an explosion." Many believed the South was bluffing. Private John Thompson, stationed at Fort Sumter, wrote his father in Ireland, "You need not be in any unnecessary anxiety on my account, for to tell the truth in spite of all their bluster I am almost sure they never will fire a shot at us, indeed I think they are only too glad to be let alone." Mrs. Thomas Smythe informed her son Augustine Smythe in a January, 1861, letter that "the Northerners will have so much to do at home before long, they will be glad to let us alone. It is confidently predicted there will be no fighting of any magnitude in this region, nothing but skirmishing within sight of their boats." Others took the South at its

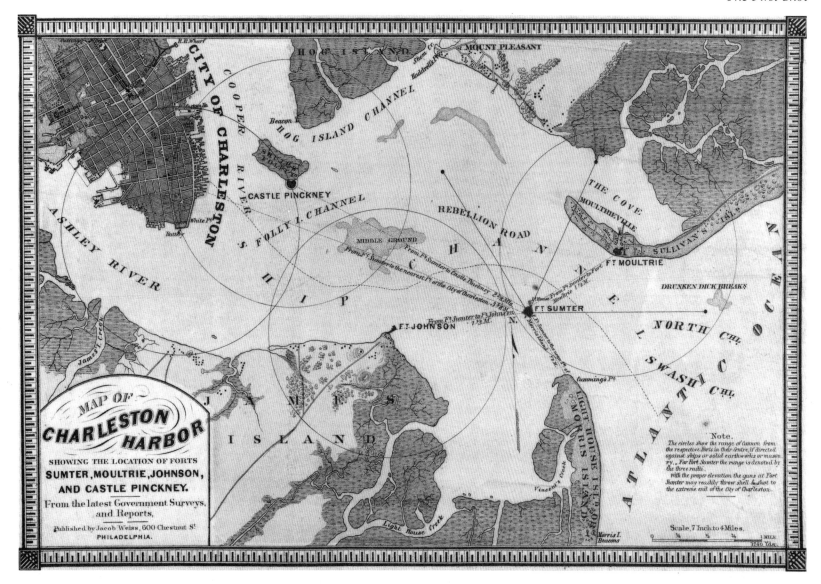

Map of Charleston harbor, 1861. Ships trying to gain access to the harbor were forced to pass through a relatively narrow channel between Fort Sumter and Fort Moultrie. The strategic importance of Sumter is obvious.

Firing on the Star of the West, *January 9, 1861. This drawing by Theodore R. Davis, an artist for* Harper's Weekly, *was made during Davis's tour of Charleston in April and May, 1861, two days after the surrender of Fort Sumter and months after the actual firing on the* Star of the West. *Davis, then twenty-one years old, claimed to be an illustrator for the* Illustrated London News *and traveled with William Howard Russell of the* London Times. *He fooled the Southerners (who would not have cooperated with a Yankee journal like* Harper's Weekly) *and Russell as well. The drawing depicts the Union garrison at Fort Sumter, unable to come to the aid of the* Star of the West, *which is also shown in detail in the insert. Fort Moultrie is to the left, the* Star of the West *is in the center, and Morris Island is to the right.*

February 3, 1861. The women and children of the Fort Sumter garrison leave Charleston aboard the steamship Marion *for New York. The firing on the* Star of the West *convinced Major Anderson and Governor Pickens that war was now a real possibility. Mrs. Anderson, worried about her husband, searched all over New York City for his old sergeant Peter Hart. She convinced Hart to come to Charleston, badgered Governor Pickens into letting Hart go to Sumter, and took Hart to Sumter, where she visited with her husband. She then returned to Washington and collapsed in a fit of nervous exhaustion. The major very much appreciated his wife's concern.*

word and began to prepare for civil war, even in the absence of strong presidential leadership. Senator Simon Cameron of Pennsylvania was told that there was "one great consolidated party in favor of a fight and especially in favor of blotting out the city of Charleston." By then even President Buchanan realized he could not just give away Federal property. "If I withdraw Anderson from Sumter," he said, "I can travel home to Wheatland by the light of my own burning effigies."

The Confederate States of America was established on February 8, 1861. Lincoln was inaugurated on March 4. He promised in his inaugural address not to interfere with slavery but made it clear he would not brook secession: "In your hands, my dissatisfied fellow-countrymen, and not in mine, is the momentous issue of civil war. The government will not assail you. You can have no conflict without yourselves being the aggressors." Most Southerners interpreted Lincoln's address as the Charleston diarist Emma Holmes did: "stupid, ambiguous, vulgar and insolent," a "virtual declaration of war." The unadulterated Southern hatred for the new president knew no bounds. A reporter for the *Mercury* called him "the Ourang-Outang at the White House."

Major Anderson, the Union commander at Fort Sumter, who himself had been a slave owner and was married to a Georgian, gave the Confederates no cause for aggression. Indeed Anderson himself, though loyal to the Union, accepted peaceful secession as inevitable and did all he could, consistent with his duty, to avert a war.

One could argue, as Milby Burton does in *The Siege of Charleston, 1861-1865*, that the first overt act of war was not the firing on Sumter but the seizing of Castle Pinckney, another Federal fort in Charleston harbor. But Federal forts had been taken by the Confederacy elsewhere. Or one could argue that the war started on January 9, 1861, with the firing on the *Star of the West*. Even Buchanan could not help but try to reprovision Sumter.

Occupying Fort Sumter through January, February, March, and the first part of April, 1861, Anderson was a pawn in a larger game. Charleston was the stage, but the decisions were being made in Montgomery, the capital of the Confederacy, and in Washington. When asked by representatives of the Confederacy to surrender, Anderson politely refused. When Brigadier General P. G. T. Beauregard of Louisiana arrived to take charge of the Confederate military command at Charleston, the drama began.

The critical events of March and April, 1861, are both obvious and mysterious. Did Lincoln cynically manipulate the Confederacy into firing the first shot, or did he bumble into the conflict while trying to preserve peace? Who, if anyone, was in control of the situation? What really happened?

In March, 1861, when Lincoln became president, this was the lay of the land. Anderson was at Sumter. The Confederates occupied Fort Moultrie and Castle Pinckney. The *Star of the West* had been repulsed in January. Only seven states (not including the key state of Virginia) had seceded. Three Federally controlled forts lay in seceded territory: Fort Taylor in Key West, Fort Pickens in Pensacola, Florida, and Fort Sumter in Charleston harbor. By general consensus, North and South, Fort Sumter was to be the testing ground because it was a direct threat to Charleston, the Cradle of Secession. It had become the first test of Abraham Lincoln. In fact, as Kenneth Stampp has written, "Ever since December, Fort Sumter had seemed to be the place where war, if it came, would most likely begin."

Dear——: I feel too indignant; I can hardly stand the way in which this little garrison is treated by the heads of Government. Troops and proper accommodations are positively refused; and yet, the commander has orders to hold and defend the fort. Was ever such sacrifice (an intentional one) known? The Secretary has sent several officers, at different times, to inspect here, as if that helped; it is a mere sham to make believe he will do something. In the meantime a crisis is very near; I am to go to Charleston the first of the week. Within a few days, we hear—and from so many sources that we cannot doubt it—that the Charlestonians are erecting two batteries, one just opposite us, at a little village, Mount Pleasant, and another on the end of this island; and they dare the commander to interfere, while they are getting ready to fight sixty men! In this weak little fort, I suppose, President Buchanan and Secretary [of War] Floyd intend the Southern Confederacy to be cemented with the blood of this brave little garrison. These names should be handed down to the end of time.

When the last man is shot down, I presume they will think of sending troops. The soldiers here deserve great credit; though they know what an unequal number is coming to massacre them, yet they are in good spirits and will fight desperately. Our commander says he never saw such a brave little band. I feel desperate myself. Our only hope is in God. My love to all.

Your affectionate sister . . .

—Letter from the wife of an unknown officer stationed at Fort Moultrie, December 11, 1860

P. G. T. BEAUREGARD

Pierre Gustave Toutant Beauregard (1818–1893) was born and raised in Louisiana, near New Orleans. He was a member of the Southern aristocratic class, which later endeared him to the upper echelon of Charleston society; he was foreign and exotic, but not too foreign for a city that was itself home to a substantial French population.

Beauregard graduated from West Point in 1838, second in his class. He became a career military officer and an outstanding military engineer, worked on fortifications in Louisiana, and, like many future Civil War officers, fought valiantly in the Mexican War, during which he served on General Winfield Scott's staff. He participated in many of the key battles of that war and claimed throughout his career, with some justification, that he masterminded the successful attack on Mexico City.

After the war with Mexico, Beauregard returned to New Orleans, where he was chief engineer for a period. In late 1860 he was appointed superintendent of West Point, but because of the imminent secession of Louisiana, he served only five days. Beauregard resigned from the army and accepted the position of brigadier general of the Confederate States of America. "He is," T. Harry Williams wrote, "one of the most frequently described generals in Confederate annals. Significantly, nearly every observer noted that he looked French or foreign. . . . He had dark hair and eyes and a sallow, olive complexion. His features were marked by a broad brow, high cheekbones, a cropped mustache, and a protruding chin." Beauregard cultivated the look of a French marshal and imitated Napoleon, whom many people thought he resembled. In Williams's words, "Because he was French and seemed different, he was the victim of all kinds of rumors, most of them baseless. The charge of immorality was, of course, inevitable. Some soldiers believed that he was accompanied on the march by a train of concubines and wagons loaded with cases of champagne. Even in Louisiana it was said, by non-Creoles, that he was unfaithful to his wife, infidelity being allegedly a Creole characteristic. These accusations were given color by the adoration which the women of the Confederacy lavished upon him from the beginning of the war. He might have critics in some quarters, but he was the favorite general of the ladies. They almost smothered him with letters, flags, scarves, small desks, and flowers. One visitor to his office saw two vases of flowers on his table, flanking his maps and plans, and a bouquet of roses and geraniums serving as a paperweight."

Beauregard was sent by President Jefferson Davis to take command in Charleston in March, 1861, and was to serve there on and off throughout the Civil War.

With the fall of Fort Sumter he became a national celebrity. A Charleston lady wrote on April 15, "Beauregard's treatment of Anderson was generous and noble. . . none of the female part of the community could have been so magnanimous." He courted the press. The English journalist William Howard Russell found the general businesslike, efficient, and commanding.

Beauregard was praised by all for his handling of the firing on Fort Sumter. He was the first genuine hero of the Civil War. Songs were written about him. His picture graced scores of newspapers. He was not humble before the war, and his fame as a result of Sumter did nothing but increase his self-confidence— and, as his detractors said, his arrogance.

In May, 1861, he was transferred to Richmond. He was in command of one of the two Confederate armies at Manassas (or First Bull Run, as the Union army called the battle). He drew up the orders of battle, handled his command well, and had a horse shot out from under him. He was once again a popular hero and was promoted to the rank of general. This early moment was, however, the high point of his Civil War career.

Beauregard was next assigned to the west, where he served as second in command under the legendary Confederate hero Albert Sidney Johnston. When Johnston was killed at the critical battle of Shiloh, Beauregard led the attack against Grant and Sherman. Unfortunately, the Union army, reinforced by General Buell's, turned the tide, and Beauregard led the Confederate retreat to Corinth, Mississippi. Because of illness, he left his army.

Beauregard was severely criticized for his retreat from Shiloh. T. Harry Williams wrote, "His claim that Shiloh was a victory and that the return to Corinth was a planned withdrawal aroused ridicule. A much-quoted newspaper couplet sneered:

> Here's to Toussaint Beauregard,
>
> Who for the truth has no regard,
>
> In Satan's clutches he will cry,
>
> I've got old Satan, Victori."

Whether as a result of the defeat at Shiloh, Beauregard's personality or popularity, or because he had left his army, Jefferson Davis, who had never liked him anyway, removed him from command and transferred him back to Charleston. Beauregard was bitter and despondent about being relieved of his command and being reassigned to Charleston, but he accepted the change with grace.

Beauregard energetically resisted the siege of Charleston. He made fortifications and made speeches, saying at one point, "Whatever happens at first, we are certain to triumph at last, even if we had for arms only pitchforks and flintlock muskets."

The western army's loss was actually Charleston's good fortune. In truth, Beauregard was not a great general, at least when it came to offensive strategy. He was, however, strong in the art of fortification and of unquestionable courage. Perhaps Jefferson Davis knew what he was doing when he gave this excellent engineer and defensive strategist one of the toughest defensive assignments of the war.

Certainly Beauregard did a first-rate job defending Charleston. New Orleans fell early in the war, and Savannah was paralyzed by the blockade, yet Charleston remained open as a major blockade-running port, second only to Wilmington, North Carolina, throughout the war and surrendered only when defeat was certain.

The grateful people of Charleston remembered Beauregard even after his death. He was Charleston's Robert E. Lee. In Washington Park, next to City Hall, there stands a monument to Beauregard erected in 1904. A full-length portrait of the general still hangs in City Hall outside of the City Council Chambers, and another portrait graces the City Council Chambers. There are thus three memorials to Beauregard on the City Hall grounds—more than to Moultrie, Sumter, Washington, or Lee.

Southern belle Susan Smythe during the Civil War. Like many Charleston ladies, she sent General Beauregard a bouquet of flowers. He returned the favor by calling on her and writing her a note.

General Beauregard's note to Miss Susan Smythe. General Beauregard, ever the polite Southern gentleman, wrote to thank Miss Smythe for her bouquet. The entire text of the note is as follows:

Charleston S.C. April 24th
1863

Miss Sue Smythe
Charleston S.C.

Permit me to thank you for the beautiful bouquet you had the kindness to send me last evening. I accept it with the more pleasure as it reminds me of my home, the "land of flowers," from which I have been absent so long, & which is now suffering under the iron heel of Northern despotism! May your own home be forever spared from such a calamity is the fervent prayer of

Resp Your Sincere Friend
G. T. Beauregard

Miss Sue Smythe

P.S. Allow me to send you my Phot. herewith in return for your kind attention—G. T. B.

This was President Abraham Lincoln's dilemma: if he withdrew Union troops from Sumter, he acknowledged the actions of the South and the end of the Union. He was yielding to force. He abandoned his oath to preserve, protect, and defend the Constitution of the United States. If he sent troops to defend Sumter, however, he would be the aggressor in a contest no one—North or South— wanted.

This was President Jefferson Davis's dilemma: if the Union held Sumter, he acknowledged that he headed a government so weak it allowed a foreign government to hold a fort in the harbor of its second-largest city. He would lose the respect and perhaps the recognition of foreign governments. On the other hand, an attack on a small band of soldiers who had given no provocation would be seen as unnecessarily aggressive and even cowardly. He would then be the warmonger. He would fire on the flag and cause millions of Northerners, who did not want war, to rally to Lincoln for a noble cause—the preservation of the Union.

The people of Charleston were looking to their new country and their new president for the right decision. Each side was evaluating the other. The Confederates wanted to take over Fort Sumter peaceably. Lincoln wanted to avoid a confrontation but maintain his position until something could be worked out. Supplies at Sumter were running low. It would take 20,000 Federal troops to hold the fort, according to Anderson. "Evacuation seems almost inevitable," wrote General-in-Chief Winfield Scott. Radical Republicans pushed Lincoln to start the war. Radical Confederates pushed Davis.

Could Lincoln have conceived of a plan during those months to force the issue at Charleston—to bring on the first shot by the Confederates—so that he could unify and rally Northern opinion? The evidence is very strong that he did.

On March 13 Captain Gustavus V. Fox, a former naval officer and a trusted Lincoln lieutenant, presented a plan to Lincoln for a naval expedition to reinforce Fort Sumter. Fox came to Charleston on March 21, visited with Major Anderson, and told him of the possibility of such an expedition. Anderson did not like the idea. Fox also learned (and presumably told Lincoln) that Anderson could hold out only until April 15. Indeed, Anderson had written a letter in February describing how critical his situation was. The president had promised no interference at Sumter because he believed—erroneously— that Anderson could hold out. He had said so in his inaugural address. Now, literally the day after his inauguration, Lincoln read Anderson's letter and learned the truth. Sumter must be sent provisions or evacuated within a matter of weeks. Perhaps Lincoln wanted to wait. But he knew he couldn't wait much longer. Much of what the new president did next is shrouded in secrecy.

On March 21 Lincoln sent two other trusted friends to Charleston: Ward H. Lamon, a former law partner in Springfield and newly appointed federal marshal for the District of Columbia, and Stephen A. Hurlbut, also an Illinois lawyer, and a Charleston native. Lamon wrote in his *Recollections* that he was sent on a confidential mission to "the virtual capital of the state which had been the pioneer in all of this haughty and stupendous work of rebellion." Lamon, described by Shelby Foote as "a good man in a fight," was concerned for his physical safety: "I was about to trust my precious life and limbs as a stranger within her gates and an enemy to her cause." The secretary of state, William Seward, opposed Lamon's going to Charleston. According to Lamon's inflated recollections, Seward told Lincoln,

Jefferson Finis Davis, provisional president of the Confederate States of America. Davis was United States senator from Mississippi when his state seceded. Having graduated from West Point (twenty-third in a class of thirty-two) and having been somewhat of a hero in the Mexican War, Davis believed he would be offered a high military command in the new Confederacy. According to William C. Davis, however, he was shocked and disappointed to be offered the presidency, which he reluctantly accepted. The situation in Charleston harbor became his first presidential problem. Because Davis ignored Robert B. Rhett in his selection of members of his Cabinet, the Mercury took an immediate dislike to Davis. Mary Chesnut wrote in her diary, "They believe SC is going to secede again"—this time from the new Confederacy.

The Union officers at Fort Sumter in April, 1861. Major Robert Anderson is seated second from the left. Captain Abner Doubleday is seated at the far left. He fired the first shot for the Union. After Sumter he became a brigadier general and saw action at Antietam, Fredericksburg, and Gettysburg. He is remembered as the originator of baseball, which he was not. Seated to Anderson's left are Assistant Surgeon Samuel W. Crawford and Captain John G. Foster. Like Doubleday, Crawford became a general; he fought at Cedar Mountain, Antietam, Gettysburg, the Wilderness, and Petersburg and was brevetted for gallantry. After the war he wrote the definitive history of the beginning of the war, The Genesis of the Civil War, The Story of Sumter, 1860-1861 (1887). Foster also became a general. He led a brigade in coastal operations in North Carolina. He ultimately succeeded Quincy Gillmore as commanding officer of the Department of the South and returned to Charleston as a major general in 1864 to assist in the siege of Charleston.

Standing are (from left) Captain Truman Seymour (who led one of the unsuccessful charges at Battery Wagner in 1863); Lieutenant George W. Snyder; Lieutenant Jefferson C. Davis (no relation to the Confederate president, he became a general and later had an extraordinary career including service at Pea Ridge, Chickamauga, and as a corps commander of William T. Sherman); Second Lieutenant Richard K. Meade; and Lieutenant Theodore Talbot.

This photograph of the interior of Fort Sumter was taken shortly after Major Anderson and his garrison left the fort. The Confederate soldiers are posing for the newfangled slow-exposure camera. Note the Stars and Bars, the flag of the Confederacy. The photographer was either F. K. Houston or George S. Cook, both of whom were from Charleston.

Gustavus V. Fox was the brother-in-law of Montgomery Blair, a member of a powerful Maryland political family and Lincoln's postmaster general. In early 1861 Fox argued forcibly to President Lincoln that Fort Sumter could be reprovisioned and reinforced. Fox came to Charleston in March to consult with Anderson and came back with the fleet in April. Later, as assistant secretary of the navy, Fox became obsessed with capturing Charleston.

"I greatly fear that you are sending Lamon to his grave. I fear they may kill him in Charleston. Those people are greatly excited, and are very desperate. We can't spare Lamon, and we shall feel very badly if anything serious should happen to him." "Mr. Secretary," replied Mr. Lincoln, "I have known Lamon to be in many a close place, and he has never been in one that he didn't get out of. By Jing! I'll risk him. Go, Lamon, and God bless you! Bring back a Palmetto, if you can't bring us good news."

When Lamon arrived at the Charleston Hotel, he signed his name below the names of a group of Virginians and placed a long dash after it, giving any reader the erroneous impression that he was from Virginia.

On March 23 Lamon met with the unionist James L. Petigru, who told him that peaceable secession or war was inevitable, that the "whole people were infuriated and crazed, and that no act of headlong violence by them would surprise him." He asked Lamon not to visit him again, "as every one who came near him was watched, and intercourse with him could only result in annoyance and danger to the visitor as well as to himself, and would fail to promote any good to the Union cause." It was now too late, he said.

Lamon also met with Governor Pickens, but not without incident. According to Lamon, the news had spread in Charleston that a "great Goliath from the North," a "Yankee Lincoln-hireling," had come to town uninvited. Thousands gathered at the hotel to catch a glimpse of this strange ambassador. The corridors, the main office, and the lobby were thronged, and the adjacent streets were crowded with people looking for a fight. The mood was ugly. "This was my initiation into the great 'Unpleasantness,'" Lamon recalled. As he pressed his way through the crowd, he was touched on the shoulder by an elderly man who asked him in an authoritative tone of voice, "Are you Mark Lamon?" He replied, "No, sir; I am Ward H. Lamon, at your service."

"Are you the man who registered here as Lamon, from Virginia?" the man asked. "I registered as Ward H. Lamon, without designating my place of residence. What is your business with me, sir?" "Oh, well," continued the man, "have you any objection to state what business you have here in Charleston?" "Yes, I have." Then after a pause, Lamon told the gentleman, "My business is with your governor, who is to see me as soon as he has finished his breakfast. If he chooses to impart to you my business in this city, you will know it; otherwise, not." The old gentleman then said, "Beg pardon; if you have business with our governor, it's all right; we'll see."

Shortly after breakfast, Lamon met with Governor Pickens, who told him in no uncertain terms that reinforcement of Fort Sumter meant war. "Nothing," he said, "can prevent war except acquiescence of the President of the United States in secession, and his unalterable resolve not to attempt any reinforcement of the Southern forts. To think of longer remaining in the Union is simply preposterous. We have five thousand well-armed soldiers around this city; all the States are arming with great rapidity; and this means war with all its consequences." Pickens concluded, "Let your President attempt to reinforce Sumter, and the tocsin of war will be sounded from every hill-top and valley in the South."

Lamon, for reasons which have never been clear, told Governor Pickens that Sumter would, in all probability, be abandoned, though he had no authority to give such assurances. Yet Lamon was as close a confidant and friend as Lincoln had. He had been

Ward Lamon, Abraham Lincoln's close friend, bodyguard, and law partner, came to Charleston on a secret mission in March, 1861.

Lincoln's law partner. It was Lamon who, armed with four pistols and two large knives, acted as Lincoln's personal bodyguard on his middle-of-the-night journey to Washington through Baltimore prior to assuming the presidency. Lamon next went to see a deeply despondent Major Anderson at Fort Sumter. The mob awaited Lamon's return to the Charleston Hotel, where he almost certainly would have been hurt, if not hanged, had it not been for the intercession of former congressman Lawrence Keitt, who happened on the scene.

After meeting with the local postmaster, Lamon took the night train back to Washington. Since he could not bring the president good news, he brought him back a Palmetto branch. "I had ascertained the real temper and determination of their leaders by personal contact with them," he said, "and this made my mission one that was not altogether without profit to the great man at whose bidding I made the doubtful journey."

Lamon had left Governor Pickens with the distinct but erroneous impression that Sumter would be evacuated. Indeed, the whole country believed Sumter would be evacuated. Abner Doubleday later wrote, "Almost every one had persuaded himself that the new President would not attempt coercion." Lamon went even further after he departed Charleston and wrote to Governor Pickens to tell him that he would return to coordinate the evacuation. Either Lamon was part of a well-executed ploy by Lincoln, he acted on orders from Seward, who genuinely wanted to abandon Sumter, or he was simply young and impulsive. We will never know. Professor Charles W. Ramsdell writes, "What had he been sent to Charleston to do? There must have been some purpose and it could hardly have been to prepare the way for Anderson's evacuation. Does it strain the evidence to suggest that it was chiefly to find out at first hand how strong was the Southern feeling about relief for Fort Sumter and that this purpose was camouflaged by the vague intimations of evacuation?" Ramsdell argues that Lamon himself did not understand the real purpose of his visit because Lincoln would not have trusted his "bibulous and impulsive young friend" with such important information.

Stephen A. Hurlbut, later a major general in the Union Army, conducted a quieter and more comprehensive investigation in Charleston for President Lincoln. A native Charlestonian, he came down on the train with his wife and Lamon but stayed with relatives. "On Sunday morning [March 27]," Hurlbut reported to Lincoln, "I rode around the City, visiting especially the wharves and the Battery so as to view the shipping in port and the Harbour. I regret to say that no single vessel in port displayed American Colours. Foreign craft had their National Colors; the Flag of the Southern Confederacy, and of the State of South Carolina was visible every where—but the tall masts of Northern owned Ships were bare and showed no colors whatever. Four miles down the Harbor the Standard of the U. States floated over Fort Sumter, the only evidence of jurisdiction and nationality."

On Monday, March 25, Hurlbut met with Petigru, with whom he had studied law. Petigru told Hurlbut what he had told Lamon, that there was now not a drop of loyalty to the Union in South Carolina. He visited with merchants, businessmen, planters, old friends, and family. He attended church. "From these sources," Hurlbut concluded,

> I have no hesitation in reporting as unquestionable, that Separate Nationality is a fixed fact, that there is an unanimity of sentiment which to my mind is astonishing— that there is no attachment to the Union—that almost every one of those very men

who in 1832 held military commissions under secret orders from Gen'l Jackson and were in fact ready to draw the sword in civil war for the Nation, are now as ready to take arms if necessary for the Southern Confederacy.

Charlestonians, Hurlbut noted, expected to gain a commercial advantage in the event of war. "They expect a golden era, when Charleston shall be a great Commercial Emporium and Control for the South as New York does for the North."

Hurlbut informed Lincoln on March 27, "I have no doubt that a ship known to contain only provisions for Sumpter [*sic*] would be stopped and refused admittance. Even the moderate men who desire not to open fire, believe in the safer policy of time and Starvation. At present the garrison can be withdrawn without insult to them or their flag. In a week this may be impossible and probably will. If Sumpter is abandoned it is to a certain extent a concession of jurisdiction which cannot fail to have its effect at home and abroad."

Thus by March 27, when Lamon and Hurlbut returned to Washington, Lincoln knew that any attempt to relieve Sumter would result in war. He was also aware of a growing inclination in the North to fight for the Union. "I tell you, sir," an irate Republican wrote to one member of Lincoln's cabinet, "if Fort Sumter is evacuated, the new administration is done forever." A friend of John C. Breckinridge wrote, "Lincoln hesitates like an ass between two stacks of hay." Lincoln was also aware of the impatient and headstrong Governor Pickens of South Carolina, who was capable of starting the war with or without the Confederacy.

On March 29 Lincoln met with his cabinet, which was divided on the issue of Fort Sumter. Seward wrote at the time, "I do not think it wise to provoke a Civil War beginning at Charleston and in rescue of an untenable position." Lincoln, however had made up his mind. He issued a secret order to prepare a naval expedition. Its destination was not given, but it was to sail on April 6, "to be used or not according to circumstances." Lincoln also made other preparations, so secret that they were kept from the secretary of war and the secretary of the navy.

On April 4 Lincoln held a meeting with a number of Republican governors known to favor a strong stand at Sumter. No one knows what transpired at that meeting, though some historians conjecture that Lincoln told them of his plan and warned them to prepare for war. On the same day, he also met with John B. Baldwin, a Virginia unionist, who told the president that the only solution was to evacuate Fort Sumter. According to Baldwin's later sworn testimony before a Congressional committee, Lincoln became excited and said, "Why was I not told this a week ago? You have come too late!"

Actually, it was not too late. Still on April 4, Lincoln met with Captain Fox, the commander of the naval expedition to Charleston harbor. Fox got his orders personally from President Lincoln. Anderson would be relieved, Lincoln told Fox, but Governor Pickens would be notified first, before Fox could arrive at Sumter. Members of the Cabinet objected to this notification, but it was a key element in Lincoln's plan. A letter was then sent to Anderson by regular mail notifying him of the relief expedition. That letter, written by Lincoln himself (although it was copied and signed by the secretary of war) reads as follows:

Francis W. Pickens was governor of South Carolina in the fateful months leading up to the firing on Fort Sumter. He was intelligent and scholarly but could be abrasive. He did not invoke strong loyalties in his followers. Bruce Catton described him as a "lawyer and planter who had both inherited and married money." Pickens was a new convert to the cause of immediate secession, and he had all the fire that went with it. He was not a military man, but he had served in Congress and as minister to Russia. He tried to win possession of Fort Sumter by diplomacy but ultimately had to yield to Jefferson Davis to take the fort by force of arms. His tenure as governor was unsuccessful. In fact, an executive council was established to govern the state because of the lack of confidence in Pickens.

At this period grievous complaints were made by the mechants of the city of the utter stagnation of trade. All the business had fled to Savannah. Foreign vessels would not attempt to enter the harbor where civil war was raging, especially as it was reported that obstructions had been sunk in the channel. The Charleston people said that they now fully understood and appreciated the kindness of the people in Savannah in furnishing them with old hulks to destroy the harbor of Charleston.

Abner Doubleday, *Reminiscences of Fort Sumter and Moultrie in 1860–61* (1876)

Washington, April 4, 1861

Sir: Your letter of the 1st instant occasions some anxiety to the President. On information of Captain Fox he had supposed you could hold out till the 15th instant without any great inconvenience and had prepared an expedition to relieve you before that period. Hoping still that you will be able to sustain yourself till the 11th or 12th instant, the expedition will go forward, and finding your flag flying, will attempt to provision you, and in case the effort is resisted will endeavor also to reenforce you.

You will therefore hold out, if possible, till the arrival of the expedition. It is not, however, the intention of the President to subject your command to any danger or hardship beyond what in your judgment would be usual in military life, and he has entire confidence that you will act as becomes a patriot and a soldier, under all circumstances. Whenever, if at all, in your judgment, to save yourself and command, a capitulation becomes a necessity, you are authorized to make it.

On April 6 Lincoln wrote an unaddressed and unsigned message to Governor Pickens in his own handwriting. It was personally delivered to the Governor by a trusted state department clerk, Robert Chew.

I am directed by the President of the United States to notify you to expect an attempt will be made to supply Fort Sumter with provisions only; and that, if such an attempt be not resisted, no effort to throw in men, arms, or ammunition will be made without further notice, or in case of an attack upon the fort.

As numerous historians have pointed out, this crucial message was a masterpiece of ambiguity. Lincoln, the master of the English language, the most eloquent of public speakers, the author of the Gettysburg Address, drafted a message in his own hand because he knew that all parties would read it differently. Let the great Southern historian Charles W. Ramsdell explain:

To the suspicious and apprehensive Confederates it did not merely give information that provisions would be sent to Anderson's garrison—which should be enough to bring about an attempt to take the fort—but it carried a threat that force would be used if the provisions were not allowed to be brought in. It was a direct challenge! How were the Southerners expected to react to this challenge? To Northern readers the same words meant only that the government was taking food to hungry men to whom it was under special obligation. Northern men would see no threat; they would understand only that their government did not propose to use force if it could be avoided.

Late on the night of April 6 and into the morning hours of April 7, one of the most mysterious episodes of all took place. The *Powhatan*, the flagship of the naval expedition, left New York under a new commander, Lt. David D. Porter. Lincoln had given command to Porter, but Secretary of State Seward, after conferring with Lincoln at midnight, wired, "Deliver the *Powhatan* at once to Captain Mercer." Porter apparently had other orders. He replied, "Have received confidential orders from the president and shall obey them." Was Porter under secret orders from Lincoln *not* to go to Sumter and thereby ensure that no attack would take place? Fox could not relieve Sumter without the powerful *Powhatan*. Or was Porter really ordered to proceed to Fort Pickens, not Sumter, because there was a mix-

Plate 1

Conrad Wise Chapman's heroic portrait of a lone
Confederate sentry and tattered Confederate flag at
Fort Sumter in 1863 defying the Federal South
Atlantic Blockading Squadron, one of the largest
fleets ever assembled to blockade a port in wartime.

Plate 2

Charleston in 1831. This painting of East Battery is by S. Bernard. The house with the one-story piazza is the Edmunston-Alston house, now a house museum of the Historic Charleston Foundation. In 1830 Charleston was the South's largest city, with a population of 30,289.

HARPER'S WEEKLY.
A
JOURNAL OF CIVILIZATION.

VOL. IV.—No. 174.] NEW YORK, SATURDAY, APRIL 28, 1860. [PRICE FIVE CENTS.

Entered according to Act of Congress, in the Year 1860, by Harper & Brothers, in the Clerk's Office of the District Court for the Southern District of New York.

Plate 3

A scene outside the Charleston Hotel during the Democratic Party National Convention in April, 1860. The grandest hotel in the city was home to the ultra-Southern, "fire-eating" secessionist delegations. Symbolically, these delegates chose to stay at the opposite end of Meeting Street from the Douglas delegates at the Mills House and Hibernian Hall.

THE DEMOCRATIC CONVENTION.

WE devote the bulk of our space this week to illustrations of the momentous Convention now in session at Charleston, and upon the fruit of whose labors the destiny of the Union may depend. We give below a picture of the Delegates leaving the Charleston Hotel on the morning of 23d; on page 260, a picture of the gathering in the area of the Convention Hall; and on pages 264 and 265, a fine engraving of the Convention in session on 23d April. These pictures explain themselves, and need no verbal description.

ON THE WAY TO CHARLESTON.

No. IV.

From Major Jack Downing, Downingsville, Downing County, Maine; in care of Mr. Harper, who'll send it in print.

CHARLESTON HARBOR, *April* 16, 1860.

HERE I be at last, Uncle Jack, large as life and twice as nattural, with the schunur ankurd rite off agin the city, and the stars and stripes a flyin' from the gaff. Hoorah! ses I, fur the man that wins; and if yeou goes in fur him, Uncle Jack, yeou'll be Postmaster jist so long as yeou pleas.

Furst and foremost, tho', let me tell yeou how I went tew Old Virginny tew help unkivver the marble imurtashun of Henry Clay. I told yeou how Mr. Buchanan had me fixed up, and away I went with them air Natshunol Rifles, feelin' jist as good as eny on 'em. We went down tew Richmond in grate stile, and I told the fellurs heow we went tew Madawaska tew fite the Brittishurs; and a French fellur, who wos a pieurnear with a big and dull axe, told 'em heow he wos a Nashurnal Gard under a Mister Louis Phillips, and sung about "infants of Pat Rie," who was a continnerly a "marchin' on," which he called a Marsells Hymn, but which ben't in the regular 'dishun of Watts & Hopkins. All this tyme we was a goin' it inter Virginny, I tell yeou, and a keepin' the konducter awake by shoin' our tickets.

At last ses he, "Richmond!" and thair we wos, and thair was a cumpeny all reddy to receave us, and didn't they give three cheers for Corporol Downing, I tell yeou! Then they 'scorted us tew our hotel, a reg'lar dubble-barril affair on tew sides ov a street, with a bridge atween the tew sides up stares and know toll tew pay.

Furst we all tuk a julup. An' I kept it up, a puttin' them air julups deown jist so long as I stay'd thair; an' I tell yeou, no wun noes what sweetun'd lickur is till they drinks julups. If I'd a dyed, and bin sent tew Downinville, and berry'd in the gardin, they'd a bin a mint patch thair furever. Mint's a Virginny institushun.

The next day thair was the paraid. Cavalry a prancin' abouet like fun on all sized hosses, and infantry a marchin' arter, and carriges with invited gests, ov which I wos wun. I sot along side ov "Tyler few," who's a rampashus Dimmercrat now, and has a big noes, and axed me tew his farm. The Chefe Marshall was a Mr. Dimmick, frum Cape Cod, an' a pesky spri little chap he is, bein' genurally tew the hed of the Republic Gard—a set ov fellurs who watch the pennurtensherry and keep things sort ov strate.

Thair wos an uncommun lot ov folks tew see the immertashun unkiver'd, and it bete Forth ov July, specially fur ladies in whoops. I tell yeou tu tell Sarah Hale that air set on 'em maid eout ov grapevines I got for her ain't a circumstance. Wa'al, finelly, they all got fixed, and then they prey'd, and a fellur told us all about Mr. Clay, and then they tuk the sheet of, an' thar he stud. It deon't amount tew much, arter awl, and wun't kumpair with Crawford's Washington—a mitey fine peace of brass casting, I tell yeou.

Arter the norgurashun thair wos a dinner, tew wich yeour old frend Mister Brooks maid a phlamin' speech, as did uthers. I, bein' called upon, and totally unprepair'd, drew eout my old Forth o' July oration, oltur'd ovur, and spoke it right eout, lickurty-cnt. Mister Botts wasn't a missed a bit.

The next day the sogers went away, and I sort o' sounded reound, and I writ to Mister Buchanan: "Play Hunter agin Wise, jist as yeou dew the New Yorkers, but go in fur Breckinridge." Neow yeou see if he deon't dew jist so.

Then I went deown tew a plaice they calls Rochetts, whair I feound the old pink-starn schunur a

DELEGATES TO THE DEMOCRATIC NOMINATING CONVENTION LEAVING THE CHARLESTON HOTEL ON THE MORNING OF APRIL 23, 1860.

[FROM A SKETCH BY OUR [ARTIST [CORRESPONDENT.]

Plate 4

*This handsome painting of Fort Sumter (1871)
hangs in the capitol in Washington, D.C. It is one
of three paintings of the fort by Brigadier General
Seth Eastman. The other two depict Sumter after
the Federal bombardment and after the war.
Eastman, acting under special orders of the
president, depicted the nation's principal
fortifications between 1870 and 1875. Sumter is the
only fort depicted more than once, which
demonstrates its symbolic importance to the nation.
Named for South Carolina's Revolutionary War
hero Thomas Sumter, the fort is built on a sandbar
in Charleston harbor.*

Plate 5

*In this painting by Edwin White (1817–1877),
Major Robert Anderson and his officers are depicted
giving thanks for their safe arrival in Fort Sumter in
December, 1860. Abner Doubleday can be seen
fourth to the right of the flag. Anderson, a
Kentuckian married to a Georgian, was deeply
religious and profoundly disturbed about his
predicament. He did his duty, although as he wrote
on April 8, 1861, "my heart is not in the war which
I see is to be thus commenced." He was promoted to
brigadier general after the surrender of Fort Sumter
and was sent to his native Kentucky.*

Plate 6

After the signal shot, numerous batteries on James Island, Morris Island, and Sullivan's Island opened fire on Fort Sumter, as did a battery in Mt. Pleasant. By 5:00 A.M. more than forty cannons were firing on Sumter. The bombardment, depicted in this famous print by the commercial lithographers Currier & Ives, was constant for the first two and a half hours. It was a glorious spectacle, "sublimely grand," according to one contemporary.

Plate 7
The interior of Fort Sumter during the initial bombardment as imagined by an artist for Harper's Weekly. *Obviously the soldiers would stay inside the fort, not stand out in an open field waiting to be killed by a cannonball.*

Plate 8

During the Civil War era the commercial lithography company Currier & Ives made thousands, indeed hundreds of thousands, of prints by a process using stone. The prints were produced initially in black and white and hand-colored by an assembly line of workers. Here the bombardment of Fort Sumter is shown in dramatic detail in a well-known Currier & Ives print. In this picture of the Union garrison returning fire from the lower casemate of Fort Sumter, more realistic than the Harper's Weekly depiction, Major Anderson is seen standing at the left.

Plate 9

*Another view by Currier & Ives of the
bombardment of Fort Sumter, but this one from
Fort Moultrie. Note the Palmetto flag in the upper
left-hand corner.*

Plate 10
Another imaginary contemporary view of the
bombardment depicts a dead soldier (center
foreground). Miraculously, no one was killed
during the two-day bombardment.

Plate 11

Mary Boykin Chesnut, the wife of James Chesnut, Jr., and the author of the Civil War's most famous diary. Originally published as A Diary from Dixie *in 1905, it has now appeared in a definitive edition entitled* Mary Chesnut's Civil War. *Mary Chesnut married Senator Chesnut when she was seventeen, and because her husband was active in both the Confederate Army and government, she was close to many major events of the Civil War. She was also a friend to Jefferson Davis's wife, Varina, as James Chesnut was one of Davis's loyal supporters. This portrait was painted by Samuel Osgood in 1856.*

Plate 12

Brigadier General Pierre Gustave Toutant Beauregard, the hero of Fort Sumter. This portrait of the famous general hangs in the City Council chambers of City Hall in Charleston. Note that Beauregard is wearing a blue uniform, not a gray one. Confederate gray uniforms were not mandated until 1863. Beauregard was beloved in Charleston. The young men of the city sent this telegram to President Lincoln after the fall of Sumter:

> *With mortar, cannon*
> *and petard*
>
> *We tender Old Abe*
> *our Beau-Regard.*

up between Seward and Lincoln? The secretary of the navy, Gideon Welles, later claimed that Seward deliberately ruined Fox's relief expedition because he was embarrassed at having secretly promised prominent Southerners that Sumter would be evacuated and now could not deliver on his promise. We will never know. The great historians who have studied the matter in detail disagree.

On April 8 Lincoln's message was given to Governor Pickens and General Beauregard. At the same time, however, the Confederates already knew from intelligence and even newspaper reports that a large naval expedition was on its way. Theoretically, no one knew the destination of Captain Fox's seven ships, but Lincoln's message had implied that force would be available, and Fox's expedition must be that force. In fact, some of the ships were heading to Pensacola, but that was kept so secret that the Confederates assumed incorrectly that the entire expedition was headed for Charleston. On the same day, Major Anderson began to see the heavy artillery increase around him. A house on Sullivan's Island was torn down, revealing a battery of four powerful cannons.

THE HISTORIANS DISAGREE

There is a vigorous and long-standing disagreement among historians as to how the first shot of the Civil War came to be fired. The version in this text is based primarily on the work of Professor Charles W. Ramsdell of Texas and an eyewitness, Dr. Samuel W. Crawford. They believed Lincoln induced the South to attack Sumter and that other historians have missed Abraham Lincoln's "genius for political strategy." Kenneth Stampp and Richard N. Current, leading historians of Northern sympathies, agree with much of Ramsdell's and Crawford's basic interpretation but believe there was more bumbling and coincidence than does either Ramsdell or Crawford. They say Ramsdell, a Southerner, was trying to portray Lincoln in an unfavorable light, and Crawford would not admit that his own army bumbled into war. But Stampp and Current also portray Lincoln as manipulating the situation so that the start of the war could be blamed on the South.

Many other historians, however, perceive the start of the Civil War differently. David M. Potter, Allan Nevins, and James G. Randall, to name just a few, arrive at a different conclusion from the same facts. They believe Lincoln wanted and expected peace, that war could could have been averted, and that the events leading up to Fort Sumter happened not by design but by error. Potter argues, for example, that the *Powhatan* incident, while "extremely curious," was the result of Secretary Seward's plan to evacuate Sumter and focus on Fort Pickens, that the *Powhatan* was sent to Fort Pickens before Lincoln realized he needed to resupply Sumter, and that Lincoln resupplied Sumter because Northern political opinion kept him from giving away another federal fort. He did not, in Potter's view, intend to start the Civil War. Potter writes, convincingly, "Assuming that Lincoln wanted to avert war . . . it will then appear that his policy offered maximum possibilities of avoiding conflict: a Confederate attack to prevent food from going to Sumter would constitute an offensive act; therefore Lincoln, wishing to save Sumter without a fight, sought to hold it by a policy so purely defensive that the South would hesitate to make an issue of it. The fact that Lincoln's policy resulted in war does not necessarily mean that it was a war policy."

Allan Nevins, the author of the most comprehensive history yet written of the Civil War, *The Ordeal of the Union,* derides Ramsdell's version as only serving the purpose "of comforting sensitive Southerners." The Potter and Nevins school dismisses the *Powhatan* incident as a bungling mishap. It should be noted, however, that only months before the action at Fort Sumter in January, 1861, President Buchanan suffered a mixup in naval strategy. When the *Star of the West* sailed off without an escort, Buchanan tried to countermand the order, could not, and then did not have sufficient time to provide an army escort for the relief vessel. These naval snafus would have been uppermost in Lincoln's mind, and it defies belief that he would make the exact same mistake as his predecessor.

Charlestonians, as was their custom, enjoyed life to the brink of war. On April 12, 1861, two days before the bombardment of Fort Sumter, Mary Boykin Chesnut, the wife of Col. James Chesnut, formerly a United States senator and one of Beauregard's chief lieutenants, attended "the merriest, maddest dinner we have had yet. Men were audaciously wise and witty. We had an unspoken foreboding that it was to be our last pleasant meeting." Mary Chesnut's diary is one of the most important first-hand accounts of the Civil War, and Mrs. Chesnut is quoted often by historians. Her insights, wit, and writing style make her diary a gem. For example: "Why did that green goose Anderson go to Fort Sumter?" Mrs. Chesnut complained to her diary. "Then everything began to go wrong." In many ways Mrs. Chesnut is quite the modern woman. "There is no slave, after all," she wrote, "like a wife."

The decision was now Jefferson Davis's to make. Both alternatives were dangerous. Either Fort Sumter must be captured before the Federal naval expedition arrived or it would be relieved by the Federal fleet. It was a Hobson's choice: if Sumter were attacked, the South would be the aggressor and would be put in the wrong. If Sumter were relieved, Davis's government would lose face. The Confederate secretary of state, Robert Toombs, was against attacking Sumter. On the arrival of the telegram bearing Lincoln's notification to Governor Pickens, Toombs is reported to have said, "The firing upon that fort will inaugurate a civil war greater than any the world has yet seen." He told Jefferson Davis, "Mr. President, at this time it is suicide, murder, and will lose us every friend at the North. You will wantonly strike a hornet's nest which extends from mountains to ocean and legions now quiet will swarm out and sting us to death. It is unnecessary; it puts us in the wrong; it is fatal."

The historian Bruce Catton wrote, "It would be hard to put, in one paragraph, a better explanation of the tactical insight behind Lincoln's decision to send Captain Fox down to Charleston harbor."

But what could Jefferson Davis do? If he allowed Lincoln to reprovision Fort Sumter peaceably, Lincoln might then give him "further notice" that he was throwing in "men, arms, or ammunition." Had not the message clearly said so? On Davis's instruction, Confederate secretary of war Leroy Pope Walker telegraphed Beauregard, "Under no circumstances are you to allow provisions to be sent to Fort Sumter."

On April 9 Beauregard discovered by seizing the mail from Fort Sumter that Anderson had been informed of the arrival of the Federal fleet. Indeed, the public knew all about the so-called secret preparation for war from the New York newspapers, which printed lurid and fairly accurate accounts of various ships' and troops' movements. The *Mercury* printed detailed accounts from the New York papers on April 10. Also on April 10, the Confederate government learned definitely that the naval expedition had left New York, and it decided to act before the fleet could arrive. Time was now a decisive factor. Beauregard was ordered to proceed. "The gage is thrown down," said the *Charleston Mercury*, "and we accept the challenge. We will meet the invader, and God and Battle must decide the issue between the hirelings of Abolition hate and Northern tyranny, and the people of South Carolina defending their freedom and their homes."

Mary Chesnut confided to her diary,

> Companies & regiments come constantly in. Wigfall all night in the harbour. Anderson burning blue lights as signals to the fleet. . . . Mr. Chesnut has gone in some sort of uniform, sash & sword, to demand the surrender of Fort Sumter. Patience oh my soul—if Anderson will not surrender, to night the bombardment begins. Have mercy upon us, Oh Lord! . . . If I could but know the answer of Anderson. They have intercepted a letter from him urging them to let him evacuate—& painting very strongly the horrors likely to ensue. Poor country—with such rulers.—

Beauregard brought in 5,000 more soldiers because he felt that the Yankees were on the way to land troops and attack Morris Island. He determined to build a "circle of fire" around Fort Sumter. Efforts were redoubled. General Beauregard told Confederate secretary of war Walker that "if Sumter was properly garrisoned and armed, it would be a perfect Gibraltar to anything but constant shelling, night and day, from the four points of the compass. As it is, the weakness of the garrison constitutes our greatest advantage, and we must, for the present, turn our attention to preventing it from being re-enforced." Private Thompson described the situation inside Fort Sumter:

> Our supply of breadstuffs was fast giving out and the Carolinians knew it. They had cut off all communication with the shore, and starvation was staring us in the face. We had been on 3/4 rations for a long time and on the 8th of April a reduction to half rations was made and cheerfully submitted to, the hope of being re-enforced or withdrawn having not yet entirely left us. On the eleventh one biscuit was our allowance, and matters seemed rapidly coming to a crisis.

The 2,000 men at Morris Island scurried around in anticipation. More than 6,000 Confederate troops surrounded the small band at Fort Sumter. The *Courier* editorialized: "We are sick of the subject of evacuation. . . . Let the strife begin." The city was crowded with soldiers, wagons, horses, and people waiting for the war to start. The harbor was full of boats transporting troops.

On April 11 Beauregard learned that one of Fox's ships was only a few miles away. That afternoon Colonel James Chesnut, Jr., and Captain Stephen D. Lee went to Sumter to hand Anderson a message from Beauregard. "I am ordered by the Government of the Confederate States," it read, "to demand the evacuation of Fort Sumter." Anderson replied that the demand to evacuate was one with which "I regret that my sense of honor, and of my obligations to my Government, prevent my compliance." When Anderson asked if he would be notified prior to the commencement of firing, he was told that he would. "I shall wait the first shot," Anderson replied, "and if you do not batter us to pieces, we shall be starved out in a few days."

Anderson's remarks were reported to Beauregard, who wired Montgomery for instructions. The instructions were to obtain from Major Anderson a fixed time for his surrender. Still anxious to avoid bloodshed, Beauregard sent his aides out to Anderson again after midnight to inquire as to when Anderson would be "starved out"—and could then honorably surrender. Beauregard had been Anderson's student at West Point, and he showed his former professor every courtesy. Anderson played for time, knowing the fleet was on its way. Finally he replied that he would evacuate on April 15 at noon (as his men would have been without food for three days by then), "should I not receive prior to that time controlling instructions from my Government or additional supplies." But the Montgomery government had already telegraphed Beauregard, "Do not desire needlessly to bombard Fort Sumter. If Major Anderson will state the time at which . . . he will evacuate, and agree that in the meantime he will not use his guns against us unless ours should be employed against Fort Sumter, you are authorized thus to avoid the effusion of blood. If this or its equivalent be refused, reduce the fort."

Colonel Chesnut, Beauregard's aide, knowing also that the fleet was on the way, could not agree to any further delay. He had waited too long already at Sumter for Anderson's reply. Indeed, Chesnut sincerely believed this was all a political charade and that there would be no war. In November he had said that "the man most averse to blood might safely

James Chesnut, Jr., had the distinction of giving the order that started the Civil War and of being married to Mary Boykin Chesnut, the author of the most renowned Civil War diary. Chesnut was an accomplished South Carolinian who had graduated with honors from the College of New Jersey (now Princeton University), studied law with James L. Petigru, and gone into practice in his native Camden, South Carolina. He served in state government and was United States senator from South Carolina when the secession movement was coming to fruition. He was the first United States senator to resign his seat. Chesnut was a delegate to the Montgomery Convention, which created the Confederacy, and was a strong supporter of Jefferson Davis for the Confederate presidency. (A fellow delegate resigned, saying, "Oh, I was tired of seeing Chesnut play rug dog to Jeff Davis.") He became an aide to Beauregard, and it was Chesnut's decision on that early April morning to inform Major Anderson that General Beauregard "will open the fire of his batteries on Fort Sumter in one hour from this time."

drink every drop shed in establishing a Southern Confederacy." As he stood at Fort Sumter, he wrote to Anderson as follows:

> Fort Sumter, S.C., April 12, 1861, 3:20 A.M. Sir: By authority of Brigadier General Beauregard, commanding the Provisional Forces of the Confederate States, we have the honor to notify you that he will open the fire of his batteries on Fort Sumter in one hour from this time. We have the honor to be very respectfully, Your obedient servants, James Chesnut, Jr., Aide-de-camp. Stephen D. Lee, Captain C.S. Army, Aide-de-camp.

It was 3:30 A.M., April 12, 1861. According to Captain Stephen D. Lee, another of Beauregard's aides who accompanied Chesnut, Anderson seemed to realize the importance of the consequences and the great responsibility of his position. He told the Confederate officers, "If we never meet in this world again, God grant that we may meet in the next." The war that no one wanted, that no one really believed would ever happen, was about to begin.

The bombardment of Fort Sumter, a truly glorious spectacle were it not so imbued with tragedy, began at 4:30 on the morning of April 12. It was a cloudy morning. Not a star was visible. A heavy mist covered the harbor and the adjacent islands. Through that gloom, one contemporary eye-witness wrote, "came the brilliant flash of exploding shells from the batteries all around the bay, while the deep hoarse tones of talking cannon echoed over the waters, the scene was sublimely grand, and sensations wildly inspiriting swelled in every heart." Three Union vessels remained outside the bar, unable and to all appearances unwilling to enter the harbor.

Colonel Chesnut and his men had left Fort Sumter and gone to Fort Johnson on James Island. There either Chesnut or Lee gave Captain George S. James the order to fire. The first mortar shot, aimed high into the air so as to form an arch, was the signal to start the Civil War. The second shot was also fired from Fort Johnson, this one by Lieutenant. W. H. Gibbes of Columbia. Tradition has it, incorrectly, that the first shot of the war was fired by Edmund Ruffin of Virginia, the sixty-seven-year-old radical secessionist, ally of Rhett, writer, philosopher, and fanatic. He came to Charleston to avoid being "under his [Lincoln's] government even for an hour." In fact Ruffin jerked a lanyard of a columbiad gun at the Iron Battery on Cummings Point, Morris Island. It was a direct hit against the parapet of Fort Sumter. Abner Doubleday wrote that a shot from Cummings Point "lodged in the magazine wall, and by the sound seemed to bury itself in the masonry about a foot from my head, in very unpleasant proximity to my right ear. This is the one that probably came with Mr. Ruffin's compliments." Ruffin fired the first shot from Cummings Point, but it was Lieutenant Henry S. Farley who yanked the lanyard on the signal shot. Roger Pryor of Virginia, who had urged the Charlestonians to "strike a blow," could not bring himself to fire the first shot of the war when the opportunity was offered to him. In later years, out of respect for Ruffin's age, no one disputed his claim that he had fired the first shot of the Civil War.

All of the forts in the harbor then commenced firing. "At half past four [I heard] the heavy booming of cannon," Mary Chesnut wrote. "I sprang out of bed, and on my knees prostrate, I prayed as I never prayed before." By 5:00 A.M. more than forty cannons were firing on Sumter from two batteries on James Island (including Fort Johnson), Cummings

William Waud, an Englishman who had assisted in the construction of the Crystal Palace, made this sketch at Cummings Point on Morris Island as the Confederate Army prepared to bombard Fort Sumter. It depicts a gang of slaves mounting a cannon. Waud worked for Frank Leslie's Illustrated Newspaper. His brother, Alfred Waud, was the most prolific of the Civil War combat artists.

Sergeant John Carmody mans the battery of Fort Sumter during the bombardment. Carmody was furious that Fort Sumter was being shelled and the Union garrison was not returning fire. Contrary to orders, he sneaked away from his post, ascended to the barbettes at the top of the fort, and fired every cannon (they were already loaded) at Fort Moultrie. "The contest," Sergeant Chester said later, "was merely Carmody against the Confederate States and Carmody had to back down, not because he was beaten, but because he was unable, single-handed, to reload his guns." The drawing is by Theodore R. Davis after the event.

Charlestonians watch the bombardment of Fort Sumter in this famous front-page illustration from Harper's Weekly. A Charleston lady wrote a few days later, "Everybody crowded down to the battery, and stared with all their eyes at the forts and when Anderson's white flag appeared the shout was vigorous. We spent almost all of those two days down on the battery or in Mr. Louis DeSaussure's house at the corner [of East and South Battery] looking with the greatest eagerness for all that could be seen."

Point Battery on Morris Island, a battery in Mt. Pleasant, and four batteries on Sullivan's Island (including Fort Moultrie). Shots were not fired from the Battery in Charleston.

The bombardment was furious. It was constant for the first two-and-a-half hours. "There stands the bold defiant fort," F. L. Parker wrote, "as quiet as death. No light is seen, not a sign of life appears, not even a sentinel can be distinguished, but high above her floats her proud banner, the Stars and Stripes, the flag which for 75 years has never quailed before an enemy."

Private Thompson described the situation inside Sumter: "At 3 o'clock we hoisted our colors the glorious 'Star Spangled Banner' and quietly awaited the enemies fire. Long before daylight, at 4 1/2 A.M., the first shell came hissing through the air and burst right over our heads. The thrill that ran through our veins at this time was indescribable, none were afraid, the stern defiant look on each man's countenance plainly told that fear was no part of his constitution, but something like an expression of awe crept over the features of everyone, as battery after battery opened fire and the hissing shot came plowing along leaving wreck and ruin in their path."

After daybreak, the defenders of Fort Sumter fought back and fought bravely, but they were no match for Beauregard's artillery. Charlestonians climbed onto rooftops to watch the attack and cheer on the Confederacy. The Battery and all the wharves were crowded with spectators. The sounds of the cannon were loud and terrifying. Shot poured into the fort in an incessant stream, causing great flakes of masonry to fall in all directions. Giant mortar shells, after sailing high in the air, landed in the parade ground of Sumter, and their explosion shook the fort like an earthquake. Houses and buildings in the old city rattled. Abner Doubleday claims to have fired the first shot on behalf of the Union forces: "In aiming the first gun fired against the rebellion I had no feeling of self-reproach, for I fully believed that the contest was inevitable, and was not of our seeking." Private Thompson wrote, "Towards mid-day we could distinctly see a fleet of three war vessels off the bay, and we were certain they were an expedition fitted out to relieve us, and the hopes of speedily getting assistance compensated for the lack of anything in the shape of dinner. . . . We confidently expected the fleet to make some attempt to land supplies and re-enforcements during the night, it being as dark as pitch and raining, but we were disappointed. Morning dawned and with appetites unappeased and haggard look, although determined and confident, all took their positions for the days work."

The bombardment continued into Saturday, April 13. Firebombs, or "hot shot," were hurled into Sumter. The troops there continued to fire back. "I witnessed then a scene that I doubt was ever equalled," The Rev. A. Toomer Porter wrote. "The gallantry of the defense struck the chivalry of the attackers, and without a command every soldier mounted the parapet of every battery of the Confederates and gave three cheers for Major Anderson." Beauregard too later reported that the Confederate troops, "carried away by their natural generous impulses, mounted the different batteries, and . . . cheered the garrison for its pluck and gallantry and hooted the fleet lying inactive just outside the bar."

The firebombs had their effect: Sumter exploded and caught fire. "The heat and smoke inside was awful," a Union soldier later recalled. "The only way to breathe was to lay flat on the ground and keep your face covered with a wet handkerchief." Anderson could not hold out, and the fleet led by Fox did not come to his rescue. "Part of the fleet was visible outside the bar about half-past ten A.M. It exchanged salutes with us," a Union officer

Edmund Ruffin, planter, writer, fiery secessionist, and defender of slavery, was also the author of An Essay on Calcareous Manures, which initiated an era of agricultural reform in the antebellum South. Because of his age and fame and the intensity of his devotion to Southern independence, Ruffin was given the honor of firing one of the first shots of the war.

The opening shot of the Civil War was a signal shot fired from Fort Johnson on James Island (far left) which exploded directly over Fort Sumter (center) at 4:30 A.M. on the morning of April 12, 1861. This watercolor by Theodore R. Davis recreates the moment as if the observer is standing at the Confederate battery on Cummings Point, Morris Island. The city of Charleston is to the left. Fort Moultrie is to the right of Sumter.

wrote, "but did not attempt to enter the harbor, or take part in the battle. In fact, it would have had considerable difficulty in finding the channel as the marks and buoys had all been taken up."

On April 14 Anderson surrendered. Remarkably, there were no deaths and only a few wounded. The local news reports were thrilling: "The advantage was unquestionably upon the side of Fort Moultrie. In that fort not a gun was dismounted, not a wound received, not the slightest permanent injury sustained by any of its defenses, while every ball from Fort Moultrie left its mark upon Fort Sumter.... The last two or three hours before dark, Major Anderson devoted himself exclusively to Fort Moultrie, and the two fortresses had a grand duello. Game to the last, though much more exposed, Fort Moultrie held her own, and it is believed, a little more than her own. Towards night, several rounds of red-hot shot were thrown into the barracks of the enemy." Beauregard sent over a fire engine from the city. The Stars and Stripes were lowered. Captain Doubleday made preparations to fire a salute to the American flag. It was a dangerous thing to attempt as sparks of fire were floating around everywhere, and there was no safe place to deposit the ammunition. Unfortunately, a pile of cartridges under the muzzle of one of the guns went off prematurely and blew off the right arm of the gunner, Daniel Hough, killing him almost instantaneously. He was the first man to die for the Union in the Civil War.

"About eighteen hundred shots had been fired into Fort Sumter," wrote Doubleday, "and the upper story was pretty well knocked to pieces. To walk around the parapet we had constantly to climb over heaps of debris." The fort was taken. The *Mercury* exalted,

> The rest is briefly told. Col. Wigfall returned and notified the captains of the several companies to inform their respective commands that the fort was unconditionally surrendered. The scene that followed was altogether indescribable. The troops upon the hills cheered and cheered again. A horseman galloped at full speed along the beach, waving his cap to the troops near the lighthouse. These soon caught up the cry, and the whole shore rang with the glad shouts of thousands.

Charleston and the Confederacy celebrated. The harbor was soon filled with boats. Charlestonians wanted to see the result of the first battle of the Civil War.

Yet in truth the victory belonged to a man far away from Charleston, Abraham Lincoln. His strategy had worked. He had forced the Confederacy to fire at Fort Sumter, thereby electrifying the North. The "time before Sumter was like another century," wrote a New York woman. "It seems as if we never were alive till now; never had a country till now." Public opinion in the North, once divided, now united behind the president. "The first gun that spat its iron insult at Fort Sumter," declared Oliver Wendell Holmes in an 1863 Fourth of July oration in Boston, "smote every loyal American full in the face." The president had only tried to send food to loyal starving soldiers. The rebels had opened fire on a federal fort for no reason. On May 1 Lincoln wrote to Fox,

> You and I both anticipated that the cause of the country would be advanced by making the attempt to provision Fort Sumter, even if it should fail; and it is no small consolation now to feel that our anticipation is justified by the result.

Lincoln's two secretaries, John G. Nicolay and John Hay, wrote later,

> President Lincoln in deciding the Sumter question had adopted a simple but effective policy. To use his own words, he determined to 'send bread to Anderson'; if the

The bombardment of Fort Sumter as depicted in Le Monde Illustré of Paris. The start of the war was big news in Europe. Sumter is in the foreground; Sullivan's Island and Fort Moultrie are to the right. The town of Mt. Pleasant is at the upper right, and Charleston is at upper left.

Conquering Confederates at Fort Sumter soon after its capture

The inhabitants of Charleston had now for more than three months followed the develop ment of secession and rebellion with unflagging zeal and daily interest, until they began to regard the affairs of Sumter as their own pet and exclusive drama. It had afforded them excite-ment upon excitement—speeches, meetings, drills, parades, flag-raisings, bonfires, salutes, music, and banners; reaching into their social and family life, it had carried their fathers, sons, brothers, and friends away into the camps and trenches. Sumter had been their daily talk and nightly dream. . . . To the beholders [of the bombardment of Fort Sumter] it was the inauguration of the final scene in their local drama; to the nation and world at large, it began a conflict of such gigantic proportions and far-reaching consequence, that it will forever stand as one of the boldest landmarks in history.

—John G. Nicolay, President Lincoln's Private Secretary, *The Outbreak of Rebellion* (1881)

The formal evacuation of the fort took place on the 14th, the garrison withdrawing with the honors of war, and being transferred to one of the Federal vessels lying in the offing. A vast concourse of people witnessed it from the shores of the harbor, and the waters of the bay were alive with boats and sightseers. Thus fell Fort Sumter. In a military point of view its defense was contemptible—to realize how contemptible one need only look to the ruins of the same work held later in the war by Rhett, Elliott and Mitchell, without a gun to reply to Gillmore's 200 Parrotts, or a casement to shelter them, save such as they themselves tunnelled in the debris, working under merciless fire. The tenacity of purpose which could avail itself of passive resistance and fight for time had no place in their defense. A formidable fleet lay idly by and witnessed the bombardment and surrender without an effort either by force or stratagem to aid the garrison.

—Johnson Hagood, Brigadier-General, C.S.A., *Memoirs of the War of Secession* (1910)

A drawing of the interior casemates of Fort Sumter in ruins. The fort's flagpole is in the foreground and was a favorite subject for wartime photographers. The drawing was made by Walton Taber, who was probably a longtime staff artist for Century, *a national magazine which years later produced the monumental* Battles and Leaders of the Civil War. *Taber, like many Civil War artists, produced engravings drawn from contemporary photographs.*

STEAMSHIP BALTIC, off SANDY HOOK,
Thursday, April 18, 1861.

Hon. S. Cameron, Secretary of War, Washington, D.C.:

S IR:—Having defended Fort Sumter for thirty-four hours, until the quarters were entirely burned, the main gates destroyed by fire, the gorge wall seriously injured, the magazine surrounded by flames, and its door closed from the effect of the heat, four barrels and three cartridges of powder only being available, and no provisions but pork remaining, I accepted terms of evacuation, offered by General Beauregard, being the same offered by him on the 11th instant, prior to the commencement of hostilities, and marched out of the fort, Sunday afternoon, the 14th instant, with colors flying and drums beating, bringing away company and private property, and saluting my flag with fifty guns.

ROBERT ANDERSON,
Major First Artillery.

rebels fired on that, they would not be able to convince the world that he had begun the civil war.

And Lincoln himself told his trusted friend Orville H. Browning of his plan later that year, in July. Browning recorded his conversation with Lincoln as follows:

> He himself conceived the idea, and proposed sending supplies, without an attempt to reinforce giving notice of the fact to Gov. Pickens of S.C. The plan succeeded. They attacked Sumter—it fell, and thus, did more service than it otherwise could.

A former Union officer stationed at Fort Sumter in April, 1861, Dr. Samuel W. Crawford, later wrote a history of the events he had witnessed, *The Genesis of the Civil War*. He concluded that Lincoln had indeed maneuvered the Confederacy into firing the first shot: "The action of the Montgomery Cabinet was unavoidable and, in a manner, forced upon it. The current of events had set manifestly towards the near commencement of hostilities, but it was hoped by those in favor of a peaceful settlement that something might yet be gained by delay. A large number of influential men had not yet defined their position. In the harbor of Charleston the preparations for an attack were not complete, and the Confederate Commissioners were yet in Washington. But the communication of the President precipitated the issue and forced it to an unavoidable conclusion. The temper of South Carolina was well known."

In the days following the fall of Fort Sumter, Stephen A. Douglas went to see Abraham Lincoln. The former opponents met so that Douglas's support—and therefore the support of the Democratic Party—could be enlisted in the war effort. Douglas told Lincoln he had best call out 200,000 men, not the 75,000 he originally called for in his proclamation. Why? the president asked the senator from Illinois. Remembering the battering he had taken at the Charleston Democratic National convention just a year before, Douglas replied, "You do not know the dishonest purpose of those men as well as I do."

Charlestonians were ecstatic at the fall of Fort Sumter. William Howard Russell of the London Times *reported that the streets of the city "present some such aspect as those of Paris in the last revolution [1848]."*

CHAPTER 5

WAR: THE EARLY YEARS AND THE BLOCKADE

"The streets of Charleston present some such aspect as those of Paris in the last revolution," William Howard Russell wrote in *My Diary, North & South* on April 17, 1863. "Crowds of armed men singing and promenading the streets. The battle-blood running through their veins—that hot oxygen which is called 'the flush of victory' on the cheek; restaurants full, revelling in barrooms, club-rooms crowded, orgies and carousings in tavern or private house, in taproom, from cabaret—down narrow alleys, in the broad highway. Sumter has set them distraught; never was such a victory; never such brave lads; never such a fight."

Charlestonians—no matter how excited—now settled in for the war. Troops came and went. Men from other Southern states who had never traveled more than a few miles from home now took up residence in military camps in and about the city. Fortifications were built all over the area: on James Island, on the Charleston neck, and on the islands around the city. John Berkley Grimball wrote in his diary, "Nearly all the Houses on Sullivans Island have been taken possession of by the Soldiers. Martial Law now there, and no one can go on the Island without a permit."

Shortly after the firing on Fort Sumter, the Union Navy sent warships to form a blockade to prevent goods, food, and war matériel from entering or leaving Charleston harbor. "Old Abe has at last fulfilled his threats of blockading us by sending the *Niagara* here," Emma Holmes wrote in her diary. The *Niagara* carried nine guns and was manned by 600 men. Charlestonians thought she was the fastest ship in the Navy. Grimball noted in his diary in May, 1861, "The War Steamers have again appeared for a Blockade and to day they stopped a British [schooner] going out and ordered her back." The overall goal of the Union Navy was simple: to stop both the import and export trade of the South's few deepwater ports. Charleston was high on the list because it was the South's second-largest port, had good railway and steamboat connections, and was the Cradle of Secession.

The blockade had an immediate effect on Charleston's economy: why, after all, should American or European ship owners risk sending a ship through a naval blockade? The solution for the Confederacy was to use ships to run the blockade. But this was not a simple matter. Ships had to be rebuilt and fitted for fast travel. The risk was enormous, but the profits were great. Blockade running became a major industry, a lifeline for the South.

Charleston was the center of privateering, an activity in which ships privately owned by Southerners could legally attack and bring in private Northern ships. The Confederacy issued letters of marque granting citizens this right provided they posted a bond and

*Charlestonians formed many and varied
organizations of troops with a variety of names.
Here are a group of well-dressed young officers with
their troops at Castle Pinckney, a small fort in
Charleston harbor.*

Charlestonians believed Cotton was King and that, in the words of Senator James H. Hammond, "no power on earth dares to make war upon it." Thus in 1861 cotton was not exported to either Great Britain or France, in the hope that the great European powers would recognize Southern independence. This photograph shows cotton piling up on Charleston's wharves during the early years of the Civil War.

William Howard Russell, the famed reporter from the *London Times,* was in Charleston in April, 1861. He heard all the "Cotton is King" talk, that Great Britain would use her navy to protect the Southern coast and the cotton crop, and that the South could win a modern war against the more industrialized North. After all, it had been a United States Senator from South Carolina, James Henry Hammond, who had spoken those famous words "You dare not make war on cotton. No power on earth dares to make war upon it. Cotton *is* King." Russell found this belief to be alive and well in 1861. He also found it "remarkable" and the King Cotton theory to be a "grievous delusion." To the Charlestonians it was "a lively all-powerful faith" that cotton would win the coming war.

"I inquired of a fine, tall, fair-haired young fellow whom they expected to fight," Russell wrote. " 'That's more than I can tell,' quoth he. 'The Yankees ain't such cussed fools as to think they can come here and whip us, let alone the British.' 'Why, what have the British got to do with it?' 'They are bound to take our part: if they don't, we'll just give them a hint about cotton, and that will set matters right.' This was said very much with the air of a man who knows what he is talking about, and who was quite satisfied 'he had you there.' "

In 1859 the South exported 78 percent of its cotton crop to Great Britain, where four to five million Britons were employed in the textile industry. Yet there were other forces at work. "Our Carolinians are very fine fellows," Russell later wrote, "but a little given to the Bobadil style—hectoring after a cavalier fashion, which they fondly believe to be theirs by hereditary right. They assume that the British crown rests on a cotton bale, as the Lord Chancellor sits on a pack of wool."

Some of the British aristocracy were delighted to see the American democratic experiment fail. Many were cynical about both sides. The famous historian Thomas Carlyle wrote that the Americans were "cutting each other's throats because one half of them prefer hiring their servants for life, and the other by the hour."

divided their booty with the Confederate government.

Charlestonians excelled in the enterprise of blockade running. The leading figure in this business was George Alfred Trenholm, senior partner in three trading companies that had been established before the war: John Fraser & Company in Charleston; Fraser, Trenholm and Company in Liverpool; and Trenholm Brothers in New York. The Confederate government soon employed John Fraser & Company to bring in war supplies, and Trenholm and his partners made millions in the early years of the war. Thus, while the blockade made the importation of goods into Charleston difficult, it never stopped it completely.

A young Union sailor, Alvah F. Hunter, recalled, "The vigilant picketing of the channel leading to the inner harbor was kept up because of complaints which had reached Washington that extra-venturesome blockade runners were now and then succeeding in getting into or out of Charleston in spite of the blockading vessels outside the bar and the large fleet at anchor in the outer harbor." A good blockade-running captain could enter Charleston harbor by sailing close to the shore of Sullivan's Island, aided by signal lights flashed from the shore. He could succeed in running past the Federal squadron blockading the channel if the vessel was fast and light enough.

The blockade did, however, make life unpleasant for Southerners generally and Charlestonians in particular. Mary Chesnut wrote in July, 1861, "Already the blockade is beginning to shut [ammunition] out." Early in the war a merchant wrote that the "blockade is still carried on and every article of consumption particularly in the way of groceries . . . [is] getting very high."

Charlestonians maintained their social activities. Parties were held at Fort Sumter complete with band, dancing, and refreshments. Guests arrived by private rowboats and by steamboat. Occasionally, when the tide went out and the partygoers stayed too late, the boats got stuck in the mud and the ladies had to sleep aboard ship in their shawls. To many, the war brought excitement and glamour; new faces appeared at Charleston parties, including foreigners, diplomats, and soldiers. One young Charleston lady recalled that the winter of 1861–62 was "very gay in the beleaguered city. There was no thought of anything but speedy triumph, and the spirit of the land was high with courage and hope." A young Middleton recalled her Italian cousin Bentivoglio Middleton's coming from Italy to aid the Confederate cause and appearing at a party late:

> But the hero of the occasion was Benti. He was off on a leave-of-absence visit to Middleton Place, and so missed his invitation which had been sent to him at Fort Sumter. I suppose some faithful comrade had forwarded it to him, for in the middle of the evening he arrived, booted and spurred, in his regimentals (that most becoming of uniforms, Confederate gray) somewhat bespattered with mud, his bronzed cheeks glowing with his ride of over twenty miles, saying as he looked down at his boots, with many apologies, he was so afraid he would be too late, he did not stop to dress. In a moment he was in the midst of the dancing.

One of the more exotic foreigners to appear in Charleston was Ambrosio José Gonzales, a Cuban soldier of fortune whose family fought for three generations for Cuba's independence from Spain. Gonzales came from a prominent family and was sent to school in New York, where he met and became close friends with P. G. T. Beauregard. He had

Thomas Lockwood, the most successful of many Charlestonians engaged in blockade running. He captained numerous vessels owned by John Fraser and Company, George A. Trenholm's shipping company and a virtual Confederate States bank in Europe. Lockwood's favorite was the Kate. "The Kate's ability to slip past blockaders became legendary," Stephen R. Wise concludes in Lifeline of the Confederacy.

Margaret Mitchell, the author of *Gone with the Wind*, researched her facts before she created the character Rhett Butler. In 1936 she wrote a letter explaining his origins: "I made him a Charlestonian because I had to make him a blockade runner, and there was little or no blockading done from Savannah." She came up with the name Rhett because she was looking for a "one-syllable South Carolina Coast first name." Butler was a "Georgia Coast last name."

been a part of the Cuba Libre movement of the 1840s and had fought with Narciso López in abortive attempts to win Cuban independence and annex Cuba to the United States. Many of the Cuban freedom fighters were plantation owners, so an alliance with Southern slaveholders made perfect political sense to them. In 1856 Gonzales married the daughter of William Elliott, a wealthy Lowcountry planter. Thus in 1861, when the war started and his old friend Beauregard arrived in Charleston, Gonzales had his chance to fight for independence again—this time for the South. Jefferson Davis called Gonzales "a soldier under two flags but one cause."

Gonzales devoted himself to the Confederate cause with the same passion he had brought to the cause of Cuba. He served as an aide to Beauregard during the firing on Sumter and became a colonel in the Confederate Army, the only Cuban among foreign-born Confederate officers. He was Beauregard's chief of artillery and then inspector general in the Charleston theater. He cut quite a figure in Confederate Charleston and Richmond. Mary Chesnut said of him in her diary, "There is here a handsome Spaniard, or rather a Cuban, leader of a rebellion there, too. He is said to be so like Beauregard as to be mistaken for him." The war was a disaster for Gonzales, as it was for all South Carolinians, but his sons were raised in postwar South Carolina and went on to found the (Columbia) *State* newspaper in 1891.

The remains of a blockade runner on the beach at Sullivan's Island, near Charleston.

Early in the war, Port Royal, which was fifty miles from Charleston and situated near Beaufort, was occupied by the Union Army and Navy. The Federal fleet was commanded by Samuel F. Dupont and the troops by General Thomas W. Sherman. The Union fleet, described by E. Milby Burton as "the most formidable armada ever assembled under the American flag," sailed into Port Royal Sound in November, 1861, and captured the area. Thirty-six transport ships carrying nearly 13,000 troops arrived with fourteen men-of-war. It was the first significant Union victory of the Civil War, and, as it turned out, two Charleston brothers, Thomas and Percival Drayton, fought in it— on opposite sides. According to a family legend, the Drayton brothers met before the war at St. Michael's Church, prayed for guidance, shook hands, and parted, one to fight for the Confederacy and the other for the Union. Thomas became a brigadier general in the Confederate Army and commanded the Confederate forces at Port Royal. Percival commanded the gunboat *Pocahontas*, which hurled very effective shots at the Confederate forts. "To think of my pitching here right into such a nest of my relations, my brother, nephews, Tatnell and others," Percival confided soon afterward to a New York friend. "It is very hard, but I cannot exactly see the difference between their fighting against me and I against them except that their cause is as unholy a one as the world has ever seen and mine just the reverse." Percival Drayton joined the South Atlantic Blockading Squadron off Charleston in 1862 and went on to command the U.S.S. *Passaic*, a monitor, in the siege of Charleston in 1863. He became fleet captain under Admiral Farragut, who said to him during the naval attack on Mobile those famous words "Damn the torpedoes! Full speed ahead."

A little-known general, Robert E. Lee, was briefly in charge of the defense of Charleston. The successful Union assault on Port Royal, which shocked Charleston, caused grave concern in Richmond, the capital of the Confederacy. The Union attack brought Lee to Charleston the day after the fall of Port Royal to head up a new military department of South Carolina, Georgia, and East Florida. "The announcement that Lee had been chosen to command on the threatened southeastern coast of the Confederacy was not received with general favor," Douglas Southall Freeman has written. "Granny Lee, whom tenderness of blood had brought failure in western Virginia, was not the man, in the opinion of many, to conduct a vigorous campaign for the defense of Charleston and Savannah." After some controversy, however, Lee proved the doubters wrong.

Lee arrived in Charleston on November 7, 1861, and proceeded during November to reorganize the entire defense system of the Georgia and South Carolina coast. The Union forces had the advantage of a vastly superior navy, now entrenched in the Beaufort area. Lee made his headquarters at Coosawhatchie, on the line of the Charleston and Savannah Railroad. His strategy was to concede the immediate coast (a move that did not sit well with the planters of the area) except for the forts guarding Charleston and Savannah, which he greatly improved; to obstruct all the waterways between the two cities not already occupied by the Union navy; and to protect the railroad. In this manner Lee created a mobile defense, using the railroad to move and concentrate his troops—he had only 14,000 men to garrison Charleston and Savannah—where they were most needed. His reports to the Confederate War Department were not optimistic. He felt that the Union, having control of the water and inland navigation, commanded all the islands on the South Carolina coast and threatened both Savannah and Charleston. The Union ships could come within four miles of Lee's headquarters. The Confederacy had no guns

"My brother," Percival Drayton wrote in 1862, "thinks I am not quite sound on the constitutional rights of slave owners and thinks that they [slaves] cannot be looked upon as persons. My answer to him was that when a poor [fugitive slave] woman comes crying to me of the loss of her children whom she could rejoin [only] by returning to a state of slavery, she has at least two of the distinctive attributes of the rest of the human race, love of liberty and offspring."
— Quoted in Ashley Halsey, Jr., *Who Fired the First Shot?* (1963)

Percival Drayton, born into a large South Carolina family, was a career naval officer who made his home in Philadelphia. When the war came he fought for the Union, even though it meant fighting literally against his brother, Thomas Drayton, at Port Royal, South Carolina, in 1861. He participated in the siege of Charleston in April, 1863, and fought with Farragut in the Battle of Mobile Bay.

Thomas Drayton graduated from West Point in 1828 and was a lifelong friend of Jefferson Davis. A planter, legislator, and railroad director prior to the war, he was commissioned as a Confederate brigadier general in 1861. He lost Port Royal to a Union fleet early in the war.

On 8th November, 1861, General Robert E. Lee took command of this military department. My uncle, Mr. Allen Smith Izard, had been his classmate at West Point, and I saw him quite often as a visitor at my grandmother's house. I suppose I must have been bothering my mother a good deal about enlisting in the army, at the age of fifteen, for one evening as General Lee got up to say good-night, my mother led me up to him and asked him to tell me how foolish I was. In answering my mother, he patted me on the head, saying, "You are quite right, Mrs. Smith, we should spare the Confederacy her seed-corn!"

—D. E. Huger Smith,
A Charlestonian's Recollection (1913)

to resist the Union batteries. "I fear," Lee reported, "there are but few state troops ready for the field. The garrisons of the forts at Charleston and Savannah and on the coast cannot be removed from the batteries while ignorant of the designs of the enemy. I am endeavoring to bring into the field such light batteries as can be prepared."

Major General George B. McClellan considered a major assault on Charleston, hoping to capture the city and use it as a base against Augusta and Atlanta, a key railroad junction. McClellan wrote General Sherman that "the greatest moral effect would be produced by the reduction of Charleston and its defenses. There the rebellion had its birth; there the unnatural hatred of our Government is most intense; there is the center of the boasted power and courage of the rebels." But Lincoln was preoccupied with an attack on Richmond; Charleston was never at the top of his agenda. Lee's strategy therefore succeeded, as it turned out, until Sherman's march in 1865. Lee made major changes in the command, placing General Roswell S. Ripley over the Charleston district. Ripley, a native of Ohio, served Charleston and the Confederacy gallantly as brigadier general in command of the Department of South Carolina and its coastal defenses for much of the war.

Robert E. Lee. This portrait hangs in the mayor's office at Charleston's City Hall.

Roswell S. Ripley was born in Ohio, graduated from West Point (seventh in his class of thirty-nine), served in the Mexican War (about which he wrote a history), and was brevetted for gallantry. Prior to the Civil War, he married a Charlestonian, moved to South Carolina, and joined the South Carolina militia. Ripley was among the first to volunteer to fight for his adopted state and commanded an artillery unit at Fort Moultrie in the April, 1861, bombardment of Sumter. He later became a brigadier general and served under General Lee and General Pemberton in the defense of Charleston.

The poet Paul Hamilton Hayne caught a glimpse of Lee at Fort Sumter:

> In the midst of the group topping the tallest by half a head was, perhaps, the most striking figure we had ever encountered, the figure of a man seemingly about 56 or 58 years of age, erect as a poplar, yet lithe and graceful, with broad shoulders well thrown back, a fine justly-proportioned head posed in unconscious dignity, clear, deep, thoughtful eyes, and the quiet, dauntless step of one every inch the gentleman and soldier. Had some old English cathedral crypt or monumental stone in Westminster Abbey been smitten by a magician's wand and made to yield up its knightly tenant restored to his manly vigor . . . we thought that thus would he have appeared, unchanged in aught but costume and surroundings.

While at his command in the Charleston area, Lee covered an extraordinary number of miles on horseback traveling to inspect fortifications. He had seen a particularly handsome horse in western Virginia. His name was Jeff Davis. He had won two first prizes at the Greenbrier county fair and had seen action in Virginia, where Lee first sought to purchase him.

As luck would have it, the horse—now named Greenbrier—came to South Carolina with his owner, Captain Brown. Lee tried to purchase Greenbrier; Captain Brown offered to give him to Lee as a gift, which Lee declined; and Lee finally bought the horse for $200. "The strength and endurance of this fine animal won him the reputation of being a 'fine traveller,'" Freeman wrote, "and ere long his old name was dropped and he became simply Traveller."

Apparently General Lee grew his white beard while he was stationed in South Carolina. In a letter from Charleston to his youngest daughter, Mildred, dated November 15, 1861, he wrote, "I have a beautiful white beard. It is much admired. At least, much remarked on." Like other fathers, he cautioned, "I have told you not to believe what the young men tell you." He was very concerned about his prospects, as he related to his daughter: "Another forlorn hope expedition. Worse than West Virginia. I have much to do in this country. The enemy is quiet after the conquest of Port Royal Harbor, and his whole fleet is lying there. May God guard and protect you, my dear child, prays your Affectionate father, R. E. Lee."

A few thoughtful Charlestonians were already fearful of coming events. "Everything looks very dark and gloomy," Jacob Schirmer confided to his diary in November, 1861. "Our enemies appear to be increasing their forces all around us." The next month, Schirmer was even more depressed. "There has not been any year of our life that has passed, that has been fraught with so many events which will ever be remembered and which should indelibly imprint on our minds the instability and uncertainty of all our hopes and expectations." The acerbic Emma Holmes wrote, "The fiercest wrath and bitterest indignation are directed towards Charleston, by 'our dearly beloved brethren of the North.' They say 'the rebellion commenced where Charleston *is*, and shall *end*, where Charleston *was*.'" Other Charlestonians worried about the city they loved. In May, 1862, Harriott Middleton wrote to her cousin Susan, "Do you not hope that Charleston may be saved. I don't mind our house but I can't bear to give up the old streets and buildings, and the churches. I feel such a strong personal love of the old place." Harriott Middleton, however, left town for the safety of Flat Rock, North Carolina.

As the fire rose, so did the wind, showering sparks & flakes around or bearing them far aloft in the air where [they] floated like falling stars . . . hour after hour of anxiety passed, while flames raged more fiercely and the heavens [were] illuminated as if it were an Aurora Borealis—it was terrifically beautiful. . . . Throughout that awful night . . . the flames leaped madly on with demoniac fury, and now the spire of our beautiful Cathedral is wrapped in flames. There it towered above everything the grandest sight I've ever beheld; arch after arch fell in and still the cross glittered and burned high over all. At five A.M. the city was wrapped in a living wall of fire.

—Diary of Miss Emma Holmes, December 16, 1861

As early as June, 1861, the Union Navy attempted to close the port of Charleston by sinking a large number of obsolete ships in the harbor. By December a "Stone Fleet" of old ships had been brought down to Charleston from Northern ports, loaded with rock and sunk in the entrance to the harbor. Nature had other ideas, however, and the current carried the stones out to sea. Within four months the harbor was open again.

Robert E. Lee was appalled by this crude attempt to ruin Charleston harbor by "those people," the term he invariably used for Yankees. He wrote Judah P. Benjamin, the secretary of war, "This achievement, so unworthy of any nation, is the abortive expression of the malice & revenge of a people."

Charles Cowley, a lawyer and Union officer who served as judge advocate on the staff of Admiral Dahlgren, wrote of the Stone Fleet in his memoirs, *Leaves From A Lawyer's Life Afloat And Ashore*:

> Sixteen vessels loaded with stone were sunk in the Main Channel. But two or three spring tides (those flood tides which attend the full moon), washed the "stone fleet" out of the way.

> Harper's History states that, "in a few weeks, the Ashley and Cooper Rivers made for themselves a new channel, better than the previous one." Greeley thinks "the partial closing of one of the passes, through which the waters of the Ashley and Cooper rivers find their way to the ocean, was calculated to deepen and improve the remaining." But the fact is, there never was a partial closing of the ship channel. The sixteen old whalers, loaded with stone and sunk checkerwise there, disappeared like phantom ships.

On December 11, 1861, the city experienced one of the most tragic fires in its history, "a Hurricane of Fire," according to Jacob Schirmer. At 8:30 in the evening alarm bells sounded. The fire spread from Hasell Street at East Bay to the market, to Meeting street, and eventually to the Ashley River along Tradd Street. It destroyed the Circular Congregational Church, the Art Association, and whole sections of Meeting Street and Queen Street. Ironically, it destroyed both St. Andrews Hall on Broad Street, where secession had been debated and enacted, and Institute Hall on Meeting Street, where the Ordinance of Secession had been signed. Some said the fire had been deliberately set by African Americans; others, that slave refugees from the Sea Islands had been careless about a campfire. In later years, pictures of burned-out portions of Meeting Street would be used to illustrate the destruction of the war, but in reality the damage was done by what came to be called the Great Fire of 1861. Five hundred forty acres had burned, and 575 homes had been destroyed. "All the insurance companies except the 'Elmore,'" Schirmer noted, "have become perfectly bankrupt." "I may say," James L Petigru wrote his daughter, "in general that the whole space in S. W. direction from the foot of Hasell street on the Cooper River side to the Ashley River at a point between Tradd and Gibbs street is one smoking ruin." Petigru's home on Broad Street was destroyed. "It is far easier to bear what comes from the hand of God than that which proceeds from the folly or wickedness of man," he commented. Like many of his fellow Charlestonians, he was devastated by the fire. "I shall never recover [from] it," he wrote his daughter, but "you may comfort yourself, dear child, with the assurance that I will bear it with resignation."

Meeting Street, looking south toward Broad Street, in 1865. The damaged Circular Church is surrounded by scaffolding. St. Michael's Church, in the background, was painted black to make it more difficult for Union artillery to spot. The Mills House is to the right. Most of this damage was done by the Great Fire of 1861, not the Union bombardment.

THE CHARLESTON JEWISH COMMUNITY AND THE CONFEDERACY

The Charleston Jewish community gave its enthusiastic support to the Confederacy. Having found in South Carolina from colonial times a haven from religious persecution, a freedom to practice their religion, and the freedom to engage in all forms of commerce, the Jews of Charleston showed great devotion to the Confederate cause.

Many Jewish Charlestonians simply enlisted in the Confederate army. While Charleston produced no Jewish war heroes or famous generals, a sizeable number of Jews became ordinary soldiers. Indeed, as a percentage of the population, Jews showed a remarkable loyalty to the Confederacy. Rabbi Barnett A. Elzas, in his 1905 history, *The Jews of South Carolina,* quotes "The Sunday News" as follows:

> The list of South Carolina Jews who remained true to their country and to their country's cause in the darkest hours and who proved their fidelity and patriotism by laying down their lives upon the field of battle could be greatly extended. . . . When the history of South Carolina's part in the great struggle is written and the books are finally posted, we are sure that the Hebrew soldiers of this State who wore the grey will have their full meed of praise.

There were Jewish infantrymen at Secessionville. Gustavus Poznanski, Jr., the nineteen-year-old son of the rabbi at the Jewish temple, K. K. Beth Elohim, was killed in that battle. They served in the cavalry and artillery. William Fox was a first sergeant in the Irish Volunteers and was wounded at Gettysburg. Julius Hoffman enlisted in April, 1861, fought at Manassas and the Wilderness, and surrendered at Appomattox. Others served with Hampton's Legion and Hagood's Brigade. Captain Jacob Valentine, a veteran of the Mexican War (and the youngest member of the Palmetto Guards), served at Fort Moultrie. Private Moses E. Lopez participated in the bombardment of Fort Sumter.

The Mordecai family was in the forefront of support for the Confederacy. Benjamin Mordecai donated the then substantial sum of ten thousand dollars to the state of South Carolina for the war effort as soon as the Palmetto State seceded. The secession convention passed a resolution acknowledging Mordecai's "liberality and patriotism . . . and very generous donation." Mordecai went on to organize the successful Free Market of Charleston, which provided for the families of soldiers at the front. He invested everything he owned in Confederate bonds and lost it all. Moses Cohen Mordecai, whose house still stands at 69 Meeting Street, was a prominent and successful shipowner and state senator. His blockade-running activities during the war included the use of his steamer, *Isabel,* named for his wife, and his schooner, *J. W. Ladson.* He too lost his fortune in the war. In 1870, having moved to Baltimore, Mordecai and Company subsidized the removal to South Carolina of eighty-four bodies of South Carolina soldiers killed at the battle at Gettysburg.

The Jewish women of Charleston were as fervent in their support of the Southern cause as their legendary non-Jewish counterparts. In fact, the two most famous female Jewish Confederates, Eugenia Levy Phillips and Phoebe Yates Pember, were sisters and Charlestonians. They were daughters of Jacob Clavius Levy and Fanny Yates, a native of England. According to Bell Irvin Wiley, the Levys were "a prosperous and cultured" Charleston family. Eugenia Phillips was born and raised in Charleston. She married Philip Phillips, one of the South's outstanding lawyers and in his early years a member of the South Carolina General Assembly. He was later a lawyer in Alabama and Washington, D.C., and served as a congressman from Alabama from 1853 to 1855. When the war began in 1861 the Phillipses were detained in Washington for weeks by Federal authorities. They were eventually allowed to leave Washington and cross the border. Eugenia, a friend of the renowned (or notorious) Confederate spy Rose Greenhow, brought with her from Washington, in code, sewn in her corset, a secret battle plan and other information. The Phillipses were hailed as heroes on their return. While in Union-occupied New Orleans in 1862, Eugenia Phillips was imprisoned by General Benjamin "Beast" Butler for laughing on her balcony during the funeral procession of a Union officer. Thomas Cooper DeLeon, a friend of Eugenia's, wrote in his memoirs, *Belles, Beaux and Brains of the 60's.*

> But in truth it was Mrs. Phillips's contempt of the general and her cool sarcasm that caused her imprisonment. Haled before him, she laughed equally at the charge and at his authority to war on women. When told that she would be sent to Ship Island, she blandly replied: "It has one advantage over the city, sir; you will not be there!"

> When told that it was a yellow fever station, she laughed: "It is fortunate that neither the fever nor General Butler is contagious."

She later refused to take the oath of allegiance to the United States.

Eugenia Phillips's sister, Phoebe Pember, was similarly devoted to the Confederacy. When her husband, Thomas Pember of Boston, died in 1861, she left her home in Aiken and went to live with her parents in Georgia. She soon went to Richmond, Virginia, where through the influence of Mrs. George W. Randolph, wife of the secretary of war of the Confederate states, Mrs. Pember was appointed matron at the Chimborazo Hospital, the largest facility in the South for wounded soldiers. Chimborazo was to become one of the largest hospitals in the world and, according to Bell I. Wiley, Mrs. Pember encountered "considerable opposition when she entered into what at that time was regarded as a domain reserved for males." She proved to be quite tenacious, however, and was given high marks on her performance. Indeed, she once pulled a pistol on soldiers trying to steal whiskey. When the Union troops captured Richmond in 1865, Mrs. Pember stayed on to care for the sick and wounded. She wrote her memoirs, *A Southern Woman's Story* (1879), after the war.

As it happened, Robert E. Lee and several of his staff were guests at the Mills House that fateful night of December 11. "General Lee remarked that as the fire seemed beyond control and was advancing toward the hotel it would be necessary to prepare to leave at a moment's notice," a staff officer later recalled. In order to get a better view of the fire, Lee and some other officers went to the roof of the Mills House, which towered over the adjacent houses. From this position they saw a scene of horror. More than a third of the city was engulfed in a sea of fire. On returning to the parlor, the officers found a number of ladies preparing to leave with baggage and babies. As the heat was closing in, General Lee took one baby in his arms, Major Long took another, and they went down a back stairway, through the cellar, and emerged outside to the glare and heat of the burning buildings. They were, one officer recalled, "driven off amid a shower of sparks and cinders to the house of Mr. Charles Alston on the East Battery which in the absence of the family was kindly put at General Lee's disposal by young Mr. Alston." This house, at 21 East Battery, is now known as the Edmonston-Alston House.

The decision was made that Charleston would, in the words of an 1862 resolution of the governor and council, "be defended at any cost of life or property." Lee thought that Charleston should never be surrendered. He instructed his successor to defend the city even if that entailed fighting "street by street and house by house as long as we have a foot of ground to stand upon."

Lee was replaced by Major General John C. Pemberton in March, 1862. Pemberton was never popular with the people of Charleston. He was a Northerner by birth and was therefore distrusted, although his loyalty to the Confederacy was total. He relieved the popular General Ripley of his command and never could get along with Governor Pickens. Within a short time, the city began to change for the worse. Stores were closed. "Gambling saloons were opened and drove a thriving business; both officers and men were swept away by the same current of dissoluteness and vice," a resident wrote. Martial law was declared from May to August, 1862. Fortunately, Johnson Hagood was appointed provost marshal. A lawyer and planter from Barnwell, South Carolina, Hagood had graduated from the Citadel and had the respect of both the business community and the army. He was colonel of the 1st South Carolina Volunteers; distinguished himself at Secessionville and was promoted to brigadier general; served in the Army of Northern Virginia (he was in the trenches at Petersburg), the Army of Tennessee, and in North Carolina. After the war Hagood was governor of South Carolina and served as chairman of the board of visitors of the Citadel for fourteen years. Johnson Hagood Stadium is named for him.

The First South Carolina Regiment furnished an infantry guard, complete with guard tent, in Washington Park, next to City Hall, and posts in various parts of the city. Major Frank Hampton's Battalion of Cavalry (afterward part of the Second South Carolina Cavalry Regiment) furnished a mounted patrol which was on duty day and night. From sunset until sunrise a boat guard patrolled the rivers which bordered the city.

Charleston became an armed camp. There were numerous complaints, especially from the *Courier*, about martial law. Colonel Hagood later recalled in his *Memoirs of the War of Secession*: "*The Courier* blazed out indignantly at the first pinch in the working of the system, characterizing the limited time for granting passports daily 'as a grievous and intolerable oppression—an unreasonable and tyrannical measure.'"

The feeling here against Yankees exceeds anything I could imagine, particularly among the good Christians. I spent an evening among a particularly pious sett [*sic*]. One lady said she had a pile of Yankee bones lying around her pump so that the first glance on opening her eyes would rest upon them. Another begged me to get her a Yankee Skull to keep her toilette trinkets in. All had something of the kind to say. At last I lifted my voice and congratulated myself at being born of a nation and religion that did not enjoin forgiveness on its enemies, that enjoyed the blessed privilege of praying for an eye for an eye, and a life for a life, and was not one of those for whom Christ died in vain, considering the present state of feeling. I proposed that till the war was over they should all join the Jewish Church, let forgiveness and peace and good will alone, and put their trust in the sword of the Lord and Gideon. It was a very agreeable evening, and all was taken in good part. I certainly had the best of the argument, and the gentlemen seconded me ably.

—Phoebe Pember in a letter to her sister, Eugenia Phillips

> The sins of the people of Charleston may cause that city to fall; it is full of rottenness, every one being engaged in speculations.
>
> —Joseph Gorgas, Chief of Ordnance of the Confederate States of America, July, 1863

In May, 1862, a slave and harbor pilot, Robert Smalls, stole a Confederate steamer, the *Planter,* and sailed it out to the Union blockade. This is Smalls's own account of the incident, which sparked national attention and proved to some Americans, at least, that slaves would fight for their freedom:

> Although born a slave I always felt that I was a man and ought to be free, and I would be free or die. While at the wheel of the 'Planter' as Pilot in the Rebel service, it occurred to me that I could not only secure my own freedom but that of numbers of my comrades in bonds, and moreover, I thought that the 'Planter' might be of some service to 'Uncle Abe.' I was not long in making my thoughts known to my associates, and to my dear wife. . . .
>
> I reported my plans for rescuing the 'Planter' from the Rebels' Captain to the crew (all colored) and secured their secrecy and cooperation. On May 13, 1862 we took on board several large guns at the Atlantic Dock. At evening of that day the Captain went home, leaving the boat in my care, with instructions to send for him in case he should be wanted. As I could not get my family safely on board at the Atlantic Dock, I took them to another dock, and put them on board a vessel loading there, 'The Ettaone.'
>
> At half past 3 o'clock in the morning of the 14th of May 1862 I left the Atlantic Dock with the 'Planter,' went to the 'Ettaone,' took on board my family, and several other families, then proceeded down Charleston River slowly. When opposite Fort Johnson I gave the signal and on reaching Fort Sumter at 4 A.M. I gave the signal which was answered from the fort, thereby giving permission to pass. I then made speed for the [Union] blockading fleet. When entirely out of range of Sumter's guns, I hoisted a white flag, and at 5 A.M. reached a Union blockading vessel, commanded by Capt. Nichols, to whom I turned over the 'Planter.'

The secretary of the navy reported to President Lincoln, "From information derived chiefly from the contraband Pilot, Robert Smalls, who has escaped from Charleston, Flag Officer Du Pont, after proper reconnaissance, directed Commander Marchand to cross the bar with several gun-boats and occupy Stono. The river was occupied as far as Legareville, and examinations extended further to ascertain the position of the enemy's batteries. The seizure of Stono Inlet and river secured an important base for military operations, and was virtually a turning of the forces in the Charleston harbor."

The Union forces advanced from Port Royal to the Stono Inlet, to Edisto Island, to Seabrook Island, and then to Johns Island. The large rivers were a weakness in the defense of the city because they allowed Federal ships numerous entrances which were difficult to protect. Indeed, General Pemberton abandoned Cole's Island at Stono Inlet, which the evenhanded historian John Johnson described as "an unwise order." It ultimately allowed the Federal forces to dig in on Folly Island and create a staging area for the assault on Morris Island. General Beauregard, writing after the war, declared that a Union assault by James Island "was unquestionably the one to be most apprehended. The Confederate troops stationed there were insufficient in number and had to defend 'a long, defective and irregular line of works.'" Beauregard greatly feared a massive infantry attack, the erection of artillery batteries on the island, and an attack on the inner harbor defenses.

Union troops making camp on Seabrook Island. The Union Army and Navy moved up the South Carolina coastal islands from Hilton Head to Edisto to Kiawah to Seabrook to Folly and finally to Morris Island.

Young artillerists of the Confederacy, 1863. This rare photograph shows a group of Charlestonians, some of them mere boys, constituting a home company—probably Company I, Palmetto Battery, Charleston Light Artillery—at Fort Pemberton, James Island. The Stono River is in the background.

A rare 1861 Confederate photograph of the officers of Charleston's own Washington Light Infantry.

The Planter, *the steamer taken by Robert Smalls in 1862 and piloted by him for the remainder of the war.*

ROBERT SMALLS

Without any doubt the most famous African-American Charlestonian of the Civil War, Robert Smalls was born in Beaufort, South Carolina, in April, 1839. His parents were slaves of the McKee's, and Robert was a favorite of the family. He was given opportunities other slaves were not, and when he was twelve, he was taken to Charleston, where he could be hired out. He excelled in various jobs, working as a waiter, a driver, and a rigger and ultimately a sailor.

Smalls married Hannah, a slave, in the 1850s and worked to buy her freedom. He was allowed to keep a portion of his wages, with the greater part going to his master. When the war started, Smalls was the pilot of the *Planter,* a small dispatch and transportation side-wheel steamer which plied the waters of Charleston harbor. It had the capacity to carry 1,400 bales of cotton. The Confederate army pressed the boat into military service along with its civilian crew, including Smalls. The *Planter* became the dispatch boat and flagship for General Ripley, the commanding officer in charge of Charleston's defenses, who used it inspecting forts, transporting officers and troops, and charting the whereabouts of the enemy. Smalls led a group of slaves to freedom aboard the *Planter* when he made his famous escape in the early hours of May 13, 1862.

After delivering the *Planter* to the Union navy, Smalls and his crew were taken to Port Royal and presented to Commodore Dupont, who called Smalls's act "one of the coolest and most gallant naval acts of the war." Smalls and his crew were awarded prize money for having commandeered an enemy vessel. Smalls received $1,500, the others $400 apiece. It was too low a figure. Years later, in 1897, Congress rectified this wrong by providing Smalls a special pension of $30 a month, a U.S. navy captain's pension at that time. In 1900 he received $5,000 minus the $1,500 he had already been paid.

Smalls's career had only begun. He served the remainder of the war on board the *Planter* and other vessels, although he never actually joined the army or navy. He was of great value to the Union navy because he knew Charleston harbor well and knew where many of the obstacles, mines, and torpedoes were located, since he had helped to place many of them. He aided the Union by providing information about the Stono River area and participated in seventeen engagements. In the April, 1863, siege of Charleston he piloted the ironclad *Keokuk. The Dictionary of American Biography* recounts Smalls's greatest moment under fire: "In 1863, while the *Planter* was sailing through Folly Island creek, the Confederate batteries at Secessionville opened such a hot fire on her that the captain deserted his post and took shelter in the coal bunker. Smalls entered the pilot house, took command of the boat, and carried her safely out of reach of the enemy's guns." For this act of courage he was made captain of the *Planter.* Surrender of the vessel would, of course, have meant certain death for Smalls and the other black crew members. He therefore defied his superior and saved his ship—and himself.

Smalls became a political symbol early in the war. In August, 1862, he was sent to Washington by General Rufus Saxton to meet with President Lincoln and Secretary of War Stanton to seek permission to arm African Americans and allow them to join the army. Smalls traveled to New York to raise funds to aid the freed slaves in the Port Royal area. A *New York Times* headline called him "The Hero of the *Planter.*" The African Americans of New York City cheered him and presented him with a medal picturing the *Planter* sailing out to the blockade past Fort Sumter.

Smalls continued to pilot the *Planter* until 1866. He assisted in the support of Sherman's army and transported Saxton to Charleston after the fall of the city in 1865. He took part in the April 14 ceremony at Fort Sumter when General Anderson raised the old flag over the fort. "Almost central in interest," one Northerner wrote, "the *Planter,* crowded almost to suffocation" with former slaves, was piloted by Smalls, "a prince among them, self-possessed, prompt and proud."

At the end of the war Smalls returned to Beaufort, where he was active in Republican party politics. "His moderate views and kindness toward the family of his former master," one historian wrote, "made him to the whites the least objectionable of the freedmen with political aspirations." He served in the state House of Representatives from 1868 to 1870 and in the Senate from 1870 to 1874. From 1875 to 1887 (except 1880–81) he served in Congress. In 1889 he was appointed collector of the Port of Beaufort, in which capacity he served until 1913 (except during Grover Cleveland's second term).

He died in 1915. He had purchased his former master's home in Beaufort in 1865 and lived there the rest of his life. There are several monuments to him, but the most eloquent is at Robert Smalls Junior High School in Beaufort. In May, 1862, Smalls had been a twenty-three-year-old slave who could not read.

Robert Smalls became one of the first African-American heroes of the Civil War. A slave and an accomplished harbor pilot, Smalls commandeered the Confederate steamer the Planter in May, 1862, and with his wife, two small children, and twelve other slaves, sailed it out to the Federal fleet. He captained the Planter for the Union Navy throughout the war.

David Lopez was born in Charleston in 1809, the tenth of twelve children of David and Priscilla Moses Lopez. He grew up in Charleston and became a successful businessman and a prominent member of the Jewish community. Lopez was an innovative builder and, according to Charleston's leading authority on local Jewish history, Solomon Breibart, was "largely responsible for building Institute Hall, where the Ordinance of Secession was signed in 1860", as well as other important Charleston buildings, such as the Farmers and Exchange Bank (1854) on East Bay Street and Zion A.M.E. Church. His home still stands at 18 Wentworth Street.

In February, 1862, Governor Pickens ordered James Chesnut, Jr., "to get Lopez, if necessary, to superintend our repair of arms in this state." Lopez was asked to serve as general superintendent of state works, and in that capacity he developed facilities throughout the state for the manufacture and repair of weapons and parts.

Lopez's most memorable contribution to the war effort was in building one or more of the innovative torpedo boats which attacked the Union ships blockading Charleston. The boats were the idea of Theodore Stoney and were designed by Dr. St. Julien Ravenel of Charleston. (Dr. Ravenel's home stands at 5 East Battery.)

Harry Simonhoff claims in *Jewish Participants in the Civil War* that one of the torpedo boats, the *David*, was named for David Lopez. Solomon Breibart contends that this was "wishful thinking" on Simonhoff's part.

Extensive defensive batteries were therefore erected on James Island. Batteries were also built to the east and west of Fort Moultrie on Sullivan's Island: Battery Beauregard was built to the east of Moultrie and Battery Marshall was built at the eastern end of Sullivan's Island on Breach Inlet. Battery Bee was built at the west end of the island and was named in honor of Brigadier General Barnard Elliott Bee, a well-respected Charlestonian killed at First Bull Run. It was Bee who rallied his brigade by shouting "There is Jackson standing like a stone wall," thereby giving to history Jackson's well-known sobriquet. Battery Marshall was also named for an officer killed in Virginia, Colonel J. Foster Marshall.

Young Augustine (Gus) Smythe, a Confederate soldier from a prominent Charleston family, wrote in May, 1862, "The gun boats had been coming up the river higher every day, so that at last we erected a masked battery on the banks, where we could get a good shot at them." The hidden battery failed to deter the Union advance. Finally the Union forces landed on James Island just outside Charleston. "People are moving in crowds from the city. Carts are passing at all hours filled with furniture," William Grayson observed. "The talk in the streets is when do you go; where are you going. Every one take care of himself and the enemy take the hindmost, seems to be the prevailing maxim. My younger folks are gone; some to Newberry; some to Anderson. My wife and I remain. I am adverse to play the vagabond at seventy-four. Besides if Charleston falls what part of the country can be safe from the marauding parties of the enemy." Gus Smythe wrote a member of his family, "I am not at all surprised to hear of the stampede in town, for I think that Charleston will soon be in the hands of the enemy, together with all our seaport towns." Many free blacks fled also; within a year of the firing on Fort Sumter, a thousand of them had left Charleston. Reduced financially by the war just as their white neighbors were, many of the brown elite remained in the city and later became important leaders in the Reconstruction era.

A vigorous and decisive battle was fought on James Island at Secessionville in June, 1862. Major General David Hunter, who had replaced General Thomas Sherman in April, wanted to capture Charleston and make a name for himself. On June 2, with naval support, Union troops landed at Grimball's plantation on the southwesternmost tip of James Island. The ultimate object of the Federal offensive was to capture Fort Johnson, a key to the defense of the inner harbor. On June 14 General N. G. ("Shanks") Evans, the hero of First Bull Run, arrived to take command of the Confederate forces on the island. The battle was joined at Secessionville, so named for the secession of a group of younger planters from an older group, not for any political reason. Robert Smalls helped to guide the Union troops. In hand-to-hand combat, the Union lost 700 men; the Confederates, 200. It was a bitter and bloody battle. A Confederate soldier wrote poignantly,

> One poor fellow who had evidently been wounded, had crawled to the edge of the bushes, & there taken off his clothes, viz : pants, coat & shoes, & laid them by his side, then folded his hands across his breast & died. Poor fellow, had he been attended to & had *food*, he might have lived. He must have heard horrible stories of having his clothes torn off him after death, & wished not to have his body disturbed. —Awful!

Milby Burton concluded, "If the Battle of Secessionville had been a Union victory, and if the victorious troops had pushed forward . . . there is no telling what would have happened to Charleston. Had Charleston fallen in 1862, the entire course of the war could have been changed." Brigadier General Hagood always regarded it as one of the decisive battles of the Civil War. Ultimately the Union troops withdrew to Port Royal, proving that the overland approach to the conquest of Charleston would not work. In 1862, when Union troops were withdrawn from James Island by order of General Hunter, Captain Percival Drayton wrote, "I for one do not believe that Charleston can be taken except through James Island, and trust that the rebellion cannot end until its cradle is in our possession."

Despite his victory, General Pemberton proved unpopular and was replaced by the more popular Beauregard in September, 1862. After leaving Charleston, Pemberton went west, where, as luck would have it, he was assigned to the defense of Vicksburg. He was the commanding officer who surrendered to General Grant there on July 4, 1863. It was one of the largest capitulations of an army in American history.

From their base at Port Royal, the Union Army and Navy built a war machine to either capture or destroy Charleston.

Sullivan's Island, across the Cooper River from the city and formerly a pleasant summer resort, became a virtual island fortress. Gus Smythe wrote his aunt in November, 1862, "All of the houses nearly up to the church have been torn down, and batteries erected on their sites. These are very heavy; their armament consisting of ten 10-in Columbiads, of which seven are mounted & the other three are lying there, ready to be put on their carriages. There is also a new & very heavy battery from the Moultrie House, extending along the beach, & bearing directly on Moffett's Channel, consisting for the most part of heavy Columbiads. In Ft. Moultrie we have fourteen eight-in. Columbiads mounted, and in Ft. Sumter there is scarcely a casemate without its gun." Gus's mother, Mrs. Thomas Smythe, had written him earlier, "I have several times expressed a desire to spend this summer on the Island & so have your Aunts. It would suit very well in many respects. . . . The whole Island is under Martial Law, now, & it is said the houses are being broken into, robbed & pillaged by the troops. There may not be much of it left by next summer."

Between the Battle of Secessionville and the beginning of the real siege of Charleston in April, 1863, there was relative calm interspersed with some Confederate victories, one of which was the capture of the Union gunboat *Isaac P. Smith* with its crew in January,

The Battle of Secessionville, James Island (June 16, 1862), was a key battle because of what failed to happen. Had the Union Army successfully crossed James Island and captured Charleston, the entire course of the Civil War could have been changed.

1863. General Beauregard, a daring and inventive commander, ordered a sneak attack on the gunboat in the Stono River off James Island by land forces and artillery. Acting under command of Lieutenant Colonel Joseph Yates, First South Carolina Artillery, the Confederates took all hands prisoner (11 officers and 108 men). The boat became the *Stono* and was handed over to the Confederate Navy. Yates received the thanks of the Confederate Congress.

It was now becoming clear that this war would not end quickly. Emma Holmes wrote in late 1862, "My heart grows sick and sad at the fearful array of killed and wounded which comes slowly in . . . old Charleston mourns her gallant dead at each new battle." Colonel Chesnut's quaint remark, that one would be able to drink from a thimble all of the blood spilled in the war, now seemed very distant—and very cruel indeed.

Christopher G. Memminger, a key moderate in South Carolina politics, originally opposed secession but was persuaded in its favor by 1860. He authored the Declaration of the Immediate Causes of Secession and was one of the architects of the Confederate Constitution. He was chosen by Jefferson Davis to be secretary of the treasury of the Confederacy, a thankless and—as it proved—impossible job.

CHRISTOPHER G. MEMMINGER

Christopher Gustavus Memminger was born on January 9, 1803, in the duchy of Württemberg, Germany. His father, a soldier, was killed in the Napoleonic wars when Memminger was just a child; the boy was brought to Charleston by his mother and her parents. When he was four, his mother died and he was placed in the Charleston Orphan House. Seven years later he went to live with Thomas Bennett, a trustee of the orphanage and a future governor of South Carolina. The young Memminger was extremely bright. He attended South Carolina College, studied law, and became a successful lawyer.

In the 1830s he opposed nullification, and his opposition to secession did not end until late in the 1850s. He was elected to the General Assembly as a representative in 1836, became chairman of the finance committee, and became an expert on banking laws and finance.

In January, 1860, in the aftermath of John Brown's raid, Memminger was chosen a commissioner to address the legislature of Virginia. He was chosen, no doubt, because he was the exact opposite of Robert Barnwell Rhett: he was extremely conservative and not a hothead. He was, in fact, the leader of the "cooperationists," whom Rhett detested. His address, however, hardly inspired the state of Virginia to secede and was generally viewed as a failure. "The Virginia General Assembly," Emory Thomas has written, "listened politely to Memminger's plan and cordially told him that Virginia would wait and see a while longer."

By this time Memminger was convinced of the necessity of secession. He was active in the secession movement both in South Carolina and throughout the South. He wrote the Declaration of the Immediate Causes of Secession, which recognized the threat that was posed to the continuation of slavery. His report to the convention was copied in the Ordinance of Secession, which he, as much as anyone else, authored. He was chairman of the Committee of 12, which wrote the first constitution of the Confederate States of America.

Memminger was perceived as cool-headed, "a tactician instead of an ideologue," according to Thomas. "Memminger," T. R. R. Cobb wrote his wife, "is as shrewd as a Yankee, a perfect—metamorphosed into a legislating lawyer."

Memminger was one of six South Carolina delegates to the convention in Montgomery, where the Confederacy was born. Jefferson Davis had the support of Robert Woodward Barnwell, the dean of the South Carolina delegation, and offered him the position of secretary of state. Barnwell did not accept but recommended that Davis appoint Memminger secretary of the treasury. This infuriated Rhett and his allies, as Rhett was passed over for any cabinet post. The *Richmond Examiner* wailed that Davis "added to his own deficiencies [in finance] by an almost inexplicable choice of his Secretary of the Treasury."

Memminger's task of handling the finances of the Confederacy was probably an impossible one. He worked hard. He was thoroughly honest. But his was a difficult job at best, and creativity and imagination were not his strong suits. He hoped and believed there would be no war. The Confederate Congress had no plan, would enact no tax, and refused to raise sufficient revenue for the war, although Memminger urged it. The Confederacy's strategy was to borrow funds by selling bonds and hope. As a result, Memminger's department was in serious difficulty as early as 1862.

After the war, a great debate raged in the memoirs of the participants as to whether or not Memminger was at fault in the early years of the war for arguing against a plan to sell millions of tons of cotton quickly. Burton J. Hendrick wrote in *Statesmen of the Lost Cause,* "In every post-mortem on the reason for defeat, the failure to use their strength in cotton took a leading place." While held as a prisoner in Fortress Monroe, Jefferson Davis blamed Memminger as much as anyone for the defeat of the Confederacy. "South Carolina placed Mr. Memminger in the Treasury," Dr. Craven, Davis's doctor, quoted Davis as saying, "and while he respected the man, the utter failure of Confederate finance was the failure of the cause."

The generally accepted view of Memminger is that he was weak. Merton Coulter, for example, describes him in *The Confederate States of America* as "a man of sound instincts but weak willpower, though antagonistic enough to make his dealings with others difficult and largely futile." Coulter also acknowledged that Memminger had "an impossible task" and that the Confederate Congress failed to enact Memminger's program, failed to tax sufficiently for war, and failed also to use cotton effectively.

Memminger was a pretty good scapegoat. He was unassuming, not a military officer, and not much of a political leader. The *Richmond Whig* described him in 1863 as "a second rate lawyer in Charleston, famous for the energy and persistence with which he collected small bills and dunned petty debtors" and averred that "his elevation to the head of the Treasury was a stroke of fortune which must have astonished the good man very much. He has done his best, but he has been overtaken—that is all."

Memminger resigned as secretary of the treasury in June, 1864, amid the collapse of the Confederate currency and retired to his home in Flat Rock, North Carolina. He was booted out of office. When the war ended, he was still in Flat Rock.

Three years later Memminger resumed his law practice in Charleston, where he was once again active in civic affairs. His former home at the corner of Wentworth and Smith streets, which had been seized by the Freedmen Bureau for use as an orphanage for black children, was restored to him in 1867. He died in 1888 and was buried in Flat Rock.

Because Memminger had been active in the educational reforms of the 1850s, such as the introduction of the grade-school system and public education for young women, a school was named for him. The present Memminger Elementary School was erected in 1953. It stands on the site of Memminger Normal (women's) School (1858–1932) and Memminger High School (1933–1950). Memminger was remembered in the 1880s as "the author of the present common school system of Charleston." A marble bust of him graces the chambers of City Council.

After the war, Rev. A. Toomer Porter wrote of Mr. Memminger, "I look back now and consider how it all could have been as it was. Many years afterwards I was in Mr. C. C. Memminger's office, and I said to him: 'Mr. Memminger, I am now as old as you were when this city and State went wild; why did not you older men take all of us young enthusiasts and hold us down?' 'Oh!' he replied, 'it was a whirlwind, and all we could do was to try to guide it.' "

CHAPTER 6

THE SIEGE OF CHARLESTON

The Civil War was far from over in the early months of 1863. The North certainly had the momentum. New Orleans had fallen. The Union had won major victories at Shiloh and Antietam. With the Emancipation Proclamation, President Lincoln had transformed the war from a war simply to preserve the Union to a war to save the Union *and* end slavery. In Allan Nevins's memorable phrase, "war became revolution." In the eyes of Charlestonians, the president was a hypocrite. A Democratic writer sneered,

> *Honest old Abe, when the war first began,*
> *Denied abolition was part of his plan;*
> *Honest old Abe has since made a decree,*
> *The war must go on till the slaves are all free.*
> *As both can't be honest, will some one tell how,*
> *If honest Abe then, he is honest Abe now?*

Victory seemed far from certain in the main theater of the war, Virginia, where General McClellan would not fight. Northern troops had done badly at Fredericksburg, where, Nevins wrote, in "a short winter's day the Union army suffered the cruelest defeat in its history." There was an outcry in the North at the great losses, and renewed determination to strike a dramatic blow.

The idea of a grand naval siege of Charleston, described by the Northern press as the "nursery of disunion" and "the cradle of rebellion," was born from these military setbacks. The political climate in Washington and especially the desire of the Navy Department to win a great victory with its new ironclad warships (without the help of the army) added a sense of urgency. Gustavus Fox, now assistant secretary of the navy, still smarting from his ignominious failure at Fort Sumter in April, 1861, pressed the attack. He was obsessed with capturing this "hotbed of secession." He had, he said, two responsibilities: "First to beat our Southern friends; second, to beat the Army." Fox had even testified before a congressional committee that the monitors were invincible and that a fleet of monitors could compel the surrender of Charleston. Charleston was not of any great strategic importance; Lincoln was not optimistic; but as the place where "rebellion first lighted the flame of civil war," the city had great symbolic value at a time when the Union needed a symbolic victory. Admiral DuPont's chief of staff wrote, "The desire was general to punish that city by all the rigors of war." Gideon Welles, the secretary of the navy, wrote, "A desperate stand will be made at Charleston, and their defenses are formidable. Delay has given them time and warning, and they have improved them. They know also that there is no city so culpable, or against which there is such intense animosity." The *New York Tribune* had written even earlier, "Doom hangs over wicked Charleston. If there is any city deserving of holocaustic infamy, it is Charleston."

From the Confederate point of view, of course, Charleston was the ultimate symbol of the right of the Southern people to be free. It was the very place where Southern nationhood was first begun—politically and militarily. It had to be defended at all costs.

The assault on Vicksburg and the siege of Charleston were part of the overall Union strategy. The siege of Vicksburg commenced in early February, 1863; the fleet which besieged Charleston began concentrating in Port Royal in February and March of the same year. "The ironclads," the great Civil War historian Shelby Foote has written, "might indeed be invincible; some said so, some said not; but one thing was fairly certain. The argument was likely to be settled on the day their owners tested them in Charleston harbor."

Slaves are depicted building fortifications on James Island under the direction of General Beauregard in an effort to repel the Union siege of 1863.

A map of Charleston harbor in 1863. There were sixty-three forts and batteries in the Charleston area during the war. They ranged from eleven batteries on Sullivan's Island alone to batteries ringing the peninsula of Charleston and crossing James Island.

Welles wrote to Rear Admiral Samuel F. DuPont,

> It has been suggested to the Department by the President, in view of operations elsewhere and especially by the Army of the Potomac, that you should retain a strong force off Charleston, even should you find it impossible to carry the place. You will continue to menace the rebels, keeping them in apprehension of a renewed attack, in order that they may be occupied, and not come North or go West to the aid of the rebels with whom our forces will soon be in conflict. . . . There is intense anxiety in regard to your operations.

The siege of Charleston began in early April, 1863. The most powerful armada of the Civil War—or indeed of *any* war to that date—had assembled at Port Royal, and when it arrived in Charleston, it consisted of the deadliest ships of the Union Navy: seven ironclad monitors, flat ships with "cheesebox" turrets on top (the *Passaic, Montauk, Patapsco, Weehawken, Nantucket, Catskill,* and *Nahant*); the experimental *Keokuk;* the *New Ironsides,* a large armored frigate; and other vessels. The *New Ironsides* weighed 3,500 tons; it carried sixteen Dahlgren guns and two Parrott rifles. It was the heaviest artillery afloat—indeed, "the most powerful battleship in the world" according to Foote. The *Keokuk* was an ironclad but had five feet of slanting hull above the water. The *Courier* reported that "the Abolitionists [have] been gradually marshalling their naval forces in front of the harbor." John Johnson wrote in *The Defense of Charleston Harbor,* "In point of both armament and power of resistance, it was to be the most formidable naval attack hitherto made in this or any other country." In the world's great naval battle at Sebastopol in 1854-55, during the Crimean War, the British fleet had less firepower.

Bird's-eye view of Charleston from the 1866 Harper's Pictorial History of the Civil War.

The South was in constant need of ordnance, as it lacked the capacity to manufacture rifles, guns, and especially cannons. Thus when the *Keokuk* sank in April, 1863, General Beauregard was anxious to salvage the two large Dahlgren cannons on board. Union and Confederate naval officers agreed that it was "positively impossible" to retrieve the guns, but Beauregard found a way. He hired civilian shipriggers, the LaCoste brothers, who took a volunteer crew out to the sunken wreck. Diving underwater and working quietly a mile from the enemy for two and a half weeks, the LaCoste brothers and their crews succeeded in retrieving the two cannons. One was used by the Confederate army in defense of Fort Sumter; the other, in defense of Fort Moultrie. Some years after the war the Moultrie Dahlgren fell from its carriage and was covered by sand. When discovered in 1897 it was mounted at White Point Gardens, the Battery. It now has finally come to rest at the corner of East and South Battery.

John Johnson thought the retrieval of the guns of the *Keokuk* so important that he devoted a chapter to the episode in *The Defense of Charleston Harbor.* He closed with this remark: "And it will be only a degenerate race in future years that will let it be forgotten."

The Keokuk Gun. Called by Warren Ripley "Charleston's most historic cannon," this 11-inch Dahlgren now rests at the corner of East and South Battery. It was salvaged by the Confederates from the wreck of the U.S.S. Keokuk, an ironclad warship which sank in Charleston harbor in April, 1863.

Beauregard had established excellent defenses for the city: obstructions in the harbor, seventy-seven guns and cannons of various sizes, mines, torpedoes, and well-placed fortifications described by one Union officer as "a porcupine's quills turned outside in." It was General Beauregard and his brilliant chief engineer, Colonel D. B. Harris, who created the defenses on the coast which attained, as Johnson wrote, "the high degree of excellence for which they became distinguished." (Two of the Columbiad cannons which constituted the bulk of Sumter's artillery firepower in 1863 stand today at the Battery.) The harbor was full of rope obstructions designed to catch the propellers of the Union ships and mines to blow them up. The Confederate command had taken full advantage of the peculiar geography of Charleston harbor. The *Palmetto State* and the *Chicora,* two ironclad steamrams similar to the famous *Merrimac,* were on hand. Beauregard had even given the order for the creation of the first submarines to be used successfully in warfare. The Confederacy did not have much of a navy; torpedo boats and submarine warfare were its only real hope on the sea. The first submarine-type vessel, *David,* was semisubmersible with a torpedo attached to a pole 30 feet in length. It was to be used successfully against the *New Ironsides* in October. Similar boats, called Little Davids (because they were designed to fight the Union Goliaths), were soon in production. The defenders of Charleston also experimented with other torpedo boats of various sizes and descriptions.

The Union fleet's attack on Fort Sumter began on the afternoon of April 7, 1863, when Rear Admiral DuPont, nephew of the illustrious Delaware powder maker, ordered his powerful fleet to enter Charleston harbor. DuPont, described by Welles as "a skillful and accomplished officer [but] . . . a courtier with perhaps too much finesse," had grave doubts about the siege. Unlike Fox, who admired the monitors, DuPont was a sailor of the old wooden navy. He had little faith in the newfangled monitors, doubting their ability to win a decisive battle with a fort. The Navy Department, DuPont said, had a "morbid appetite" to capture Charleston, and he was threatened with being relieved of his command if he did not attack. The armada was led by the monitor *Weehawken,* pushing a large raft to explode torpedoes, followed by three other monitors, the *New Ironsides,* and then four more monitors. They sailed into the harbor believing they could successfully storm one of the great fortresses of the South. The *Passaic* was under the command of Percival Drayton, the Charleston native whose brother was a Confederate officer.

The siege turned out to be a debacle for the Union Navy. DuPont's worst fears were realized. Steering was a problem for the monitors and for the *New Ironsides* because of the strong currents. The ships took a severe battering from Beauregard's well-placed artillery on Sumter, Wagner, and Moultrie. "Sublime infernal, it seemed as if the fires of hell were turned upon the Union Fleet," one eyewitness recounted. The Confederates fired 2,200 shots to the warships' 139. The *Keokuk*, piloted by Robert Smalls, was hit 90 times at point-blank range by the guns at Fort Sumter. "Riddled like a colander" and "the most severely mauled ship one ever saw," witnesses reported. It later sank off Morris Island. The officers of the *New Ironsides* refused to bring the vessel within range of Sumter.

"Well, . . . The Monitors have been met and have been driven back," Gus Smythe wrote. "Sure to you in the city it seemed but a skirmish, but the walls of Sumter as well as her garrison bear testimony to the terrible conflict in which they were engaged. It lasted only two hours, but if they would have stood it for two hours longer the whole east, or seaface, of Sumter would have been cracked."

President Lincoln sent Admiral DuPont the following message:

> Executive Mansion, April 13, 1863. Hold your position inside the bar near Charleston; or if you have left it return to it, and hold it until further orders. Do not allow the enemy to erect new batteries or defenses on Morris Island. If he has begun it drive him out. I do not order you to renew the general attack. That is to depend upon your discretion, or a further order.

The president had urged DuPont for months to attack Charleston and told Gideon Welles that DuPont's excessive caution reminded him of General McClellan.

As Alvah Hunter, a young Federal seaman aboard the monitor *Nahant*, observed, "The President is, of course, the Commander-in-Chief of the Army and Navy of the United States, and, consequently, his word is law. Undoubtedly his order that our position in the outer harbor of Charleston be held was wise, and if that order had been obeyed, the guns of the *Keokuk* would not have been salvaged by the Confederates, nor would Fort Wagner have been strengthened into the hard nut to crack which the combined forces of the army and navy found it to be three months later."

The monitors took a terrible beating. John Ericsson, the Swedish inventor of the *Monitor*, had in fact warned that they were not the panacea the navy sought. "A single shot may sink a ship," he had told Gustavus Fox, "while a hundred rounds cannot silence a fort." Inside the monitors "the nuts that secured the laminated plates flew wildly, to the injury and discomfiture of the men at the guns." The shots, one reporter wrote, "literally rained around them, splashing the water up thirty feet in the air, and striking and booming from their decks and turret." During the two-and-a-half-hour battle, only one ironclad got within 900 yards of Fort Sumter. Five of the monitors were seriously damaged. The *Weehawken* was hit fifty-three times. DuPont lost his desire to continue the fight when he saw the damage done to his monitors. Fortunately for him, the worst had not happened. The *New Ironsides* at one point floated directly over a 3,000-pound mine, which the Confederates were unable to detonate. Thus technology failed both sides. The ironclads had failed to defeat the forts, Beauregard's "circle of fire."

DuPont was despondent and called off the attack. "I attempted to take the bull by the horns, but he was too much for us," he later wrote. "These monitors are miserable failures where forts are concerned." DuPont was to be relieved of his command for this defeat, which stunned the North, but his officers defended him. "The Federal admiral," A. Toomer Porter later recalled, "has been blamed for not steaming in and taking the city. He knew better than his critics. The harbor was magnificently fortified, the channel was filled with torpedoes, and on every spot in it one hundred guns of the largest calibre could be concentrated. No vessel afloat could have been above water a quarter of an hour." Secretary Welles and President Lincoln, however, were both furious with DuPont. Welles wrote in his diary that DuPont imparted "all his fears and doubts to his subordinates, until all were impressed with his apprehension." Welles felt that DuPont should not have quit after "a fight of 30 minutes and the loss of one man." The Navy Department was to suppress the truth of that battle in Charleston harbor for eight months. Congress had to demand the report three times.

Beauregard was ecstatic. He wrote in his official report that "these engines of war, after all are not invulnerable or invincible, and may be destroyed or defeated by heavy ordnance, properly placed and skillfully handled"—in other words, as Beauregard had handled the situation. "The Navy Department heads did not realize," Allan Nevins concluded, "how energetically Beauregard had ringed Charleston with formidable guns and impediments." Augustine Smythe wrote his aunt that the Yankee prisoners said their "opinion of the Monitors has fallen very much and they regard the Ironsides as worth the whole of them." Yet the Confederate military experts realized that something new and terrible had happened. The sheer power of the new and larger Union cannons had done terrific damage to Sumter when these weapons did hit their target. "The powerful shocks given by these projectiles to the solid masonry of the fort," Johnson concluded, "was

Frank Vizetelly of the Illustrated London News *drew this handsome sketch of Charlestonians watching the April 7, 1863, ironclad attack on Fort Sumter from the Battery. Vizetelly sympathized, as many Britons did, with the Confederacy. Note the relaxed attitude of the black Charlestonians depicted in this drawing.*

Colonel Alfred Rhett was the son of Robert B. Rhett, editor of the Mercury. *He was also the commander at Fort Sumter during the April, 1863, siege.*

A RHETT VERSUS A CALHOUN

The commander at Fort Sumter during the first siege of Charleston, April to early September, 1863, was Colonel Alfred Rhett, as tough a soldier as the Confederacy ever produced. The son of Robert Barnwell Rhett, the editor of the *Charleston Mercury,* Alfred Rhett began his service to the Confederacy at the bombardment of Fort Sumter. He served as a first lieutenant in the First South Carolina Regular Artillery at Fort Moultrie.

Rhett cordially disliked Colonel W. Ransom Calhoun, a kinsman of John C. Calhoun. The origin of their quarrel apparently was Calhoun's promotion over Rhett by a fellow West Pointer, Roswell Ripley, then commandant of Fort Moultrie. (Robert Toombs, the Confederate secretary of state, quipped that "Died of West Point" would be a proper epitaph for the Confederate Army.) In the original bombardment of Fort Sumter, Calhoun ignored Rhett, gave orders directly to Rhett's company, and cursed Rhett in the presence of his men. Rhett retaliated by publicly ridiculing Calhoun. Within a matter of months, Calhoun challenged Rhett to a duel.

In what was undoubtedly the most infamous duel fought in Charleston during the Civil War, Major Rhett and Colonel Calhoun faced each other at ten paces. There was a strict adherence to the Code of Honor, or *code duello.* There were prominent seconds and spectators, including three state senators, the speaker of the House of Representatives, and surgeons. The seconds reported the event in a signed statement. This was their conclusion: "The pistols were then placed in the hands of the principals, and the word given, both parties fired almost simultaneously, Colonel Calhoun firing first. Colonel Calhoun fell. . . . [We] declare the duel to have been fairly and honorably fought."

Calhoun died within the hour. Even though the press said little about the incident (the *Mercury* never mentioned it), it became a quiet scandal. Many in the South detested duels, and it was reported to Richmond, where proceedings were started against Rhett but soon dropped. Rhett not only was not punished, but he became colonel of the regiment previously commanded by his rival. Charlestonians were bitterly divided over the duel. Gus Smythe's aunt wrote him, "Last evening Mrs. Middleton . . . sat awhile & talked over the duel. She is a strong friend of Calhoun's. This morning we went to the Depository for a little while, & there Miss Blamyer, a strong friend of the Rhetts, talked on the other side. Calhoun & Rhett had both resigned from the army in order to fight this duel. What a shame."

Rhett went on to fight valiantly for the Confederacy. He commanded Fort Sumter during two concentrated Federal bombardments (including the attack on Wagner) which destroyed the walls of the fort. While Rhett was in command, 6,878 shells struck Sumter, and the colonel was commended for his bravery. Johnson Hagood later recalled that Rhett and "his brave garrison endured a long and terrific bombardment."

Rhett survived the war and later became chief constable of the state. He also wrote a forty-page defense of dueling.

something new and could never be forgotten." It was a portent of the devastating bombardment to come.

The Union Navy brass was disappointed. "I am by no means confident," Gideon Welles said in his diary, "that we are acting wisely in expending so much strength and effort on Charleston, a place of no strategic importance." There were eventually eleven major and minor bombardments of the fort, attacks by small boats, and shelling from land and sea. Fort Sumter never surrendered. It was held tenaciously until it was abandoned in February, 1865, when the end of the war was certain.

In the spring and summer of 1863, however, Charlestonians still thought they might win the war. They and the Confederacy determined that Charleston would never surrender. It was apparent to the Confederates that *some* major future bombardment of Sumter would occur, so a massive military and civilian effort took place to shore up the fort for the inevitable attack. Tons of sand were brought in to reinforce Sumter's walls, as were hundreds of bales of cotton. The siege of Charleston, which began in April with the attack on Fort Sumter, continued. General Quincy A. Gillmore's ultimate goal was Morris Island, which he perceived to be the key to taking Fort Sumter, thus gaining control of Charleston harbor and thence the city itself. James Island was strongly fortified; while the army could have invaded Charleston by that route, the cost, Gillmore believed, would have been higher even than storming Morris Island. The bloody Battle of Secessionville on James Island in 1862 had convinced the Union commanders that their only option was an assault on Fort Sumter and the harbor. An officer of the 54th Massachusetts, Luis F. Emilio, remembered James Island this way:

> James Island is separated from the mainland by Wappoo Creek. From the landing a road led onward, which soon separated into two: one running to the right through timber, across low sandy ground to Secessionville; the other to the left, over open fields across . . . low ground . . . ; Fort Pemberton, on the Stono, constituted the enemy's right. Thence the line was retired partially behind James Island Creek, consisting of detached light works for field-guns and infantry.

> General Beauregard, the Confederate Department commander, considered an attack on Charleston by way of James Island as the most dangerous to its safety. He posted his forces accordingly, and on July 10 had 2,926 effectives there, with 927 on Morris Island, 1,158 on Sullivans Island, and 850 in the city. . . . Had Beauregard's weakness been known, Brigadier General Alfred Terry's demonstration in superior force might have been converted into a real attack, and James Island fallen before it, when Charleston must have surrendered or been destroyed.

Beauregard had to divide his forces between James Island and Morris Island, and Gillmore chose Morris Island for the assault. A diversion on James Island was the opening scene of the next chapter of the siege of Charleston.

In July, 1863, after weeks of secret preparations on Folly Island and Cole's Island, the Union Army attacked Morris Island. "We have heavy batteries that have been secretly constructed near the edge of Folly Island," Captain Alfred Marple wrote in his wartime diary, "which when they open will surprise the enemy terribly. The prospect seems very fair for our being successful." General Gillmore and Admiral John A. Dahlgren had taken up the sword reluctantly laid down by DuPont. In Gillmore, the Union had sent its best engineer (he was first in his class at West Point), the hero who had destroyed Fort Pulaski in Savannah. In Dahlgren it had sent an expert in ordnance, the inventor of the bottle-shaped Dahlgren gun, and an intimate friend of Lincoln.

The Morris Island fortifications protected both Fort Sumter and Charleston harbor. The island was really a sandbar, but in terms of lives, it was an extremely valuable piece of real estate in the summer of 1863. It was to become, in Bruce Catton's words, "the deadliest sandpit on earth." The ultimate goal of the attack on Morris Island was Battery Wagner (called Fort Wagner by the Union), a fortification near the tip of Morris Island which commanded part of the island and part of the harbor and the main ship channel. It was an engineering marvel planned by Charlestonians Captain Francis D. Lee and Langdon Cheves of the Confederate Engineers and originally called the Neck Battery. It was later named Wagner in honor of Lieutenant Colonel Thomas M. Wagner of the First Regiment of South Carolina Artillery, who died from the bursting of a gun at Fort Moultrie in July, 1862. If Battery Wagner remained in Confederate hands, the Union Army would have no base from which to launch an attack against Charleston. Gillmore brought in 10,000 more troops and all the cannons and ammunition he could locate.

A plan was devised in Washington to move troops from Folly Island to Morris Island, then to Wagner, then to Sumter, and on to Charleston. On July 10 most of Morris Island fell within hours. In a brilliant surprise attack led by Brigadier General George C. Strong, a Union brigade crossed Lighthouse Inlet between Folly Island and Morris Island. Strong was so anxious to lead the attack that he leapt into water over his head and had to be helped out, losing his boots and hat in the process. The Confederates fought back gallantly but were overwhelmed. The Union had forty-seven guns and mortars on land and eight on board the monitors. A number of prominent Charleston officers were killed, including Captain Charles T. Haskell, Jr., who died in a rifle pit urging his men on. His last words were "Tell my mother that I died for her and my country."

The Union assault was quite successful at first. But Battery Wagner held. Rowena Reed wrote in *Fighting for Time*, "An enclosed earthwork mounting twelve heavy guns and extending completely across Morris Island near its northern end, Wagner was much more formidable than Gillmore had supposed. Its narrow approaches were protected by rifle pits, mines, and a wet ditch. Constructed of fine quartz sand by Colonel D. B. Harris of the Confederate engineers, with its guns in embrasures and its quarters bombproofed, the work was extremely resistant to bombardment." Both the fleet and Gillmore's artillery bombarded Battery Wagner for eleven hours. Confederate Brigadier General William B. Taliaferro held Wagner with 1,300 men from North Carolina and South Carolina, including the Charleston Battalion.

The direct assault of Battery Wagner lasted from July 10 to July 18, 1863. The Union plan was to bombard the battery with heavy cannons and then make a direct frontal assault on the fort, which proved to be deceptively strong. "When I learned what we were to do," a Union private wrote, "my knees shook so that I thought I should drop." At daybreak on July 11, an infantry charge was made up the narrow beach against Wagner. "Aim low and put your trust in God," General Strong told his lead regiment. Confederate sharpshooters backed up by expert artillery loosed a hail of fire. There were 339 Union soldiers killed to only 12 Confederates. Gillmore should have realized at once that Charleston was not Savannah and Fort Sumter was not Fort Pulaski. But he did not. Neither did his men.

Captain Marple wrote his wife, "I feel certain that Gillmore will take Fort Sumpter, Wagner and Charleston. He is a live General."

Gillmore decided to pound Wagner and Sumter with artillery and then make another frontal attack. The bombardment went on all week, and then on July 18, he determined to send all he had against Wagner. He chose Brigadier General Truman Seymour, who had served with Major Anderson at Fort Sumter, to lead the assault. Seymour asked General Strong to lead the first attack, and Strong chose the Massachusetts 54th, a black regiment led by white officers, to spearhead the charge. Seymour is alleged to have told Gillmore, "Well, I guess we will let Strong put those d——d negroes from Massachusetts in the advance, we may as well get rid of them, one time as another."

Two sons of Frederick Douglass, the famous African-American abolitionist, were members of the 54th, as was Garth W. James, a brother of the novelist Henry James and the philosopher William James. (Another James brother was a member of the Massachusetts 55th, a sister regiment.) The 54th had been organized in the wake of the Emancipation Proclamation in 1863 by Governor John A. Andrews of Massachusetts, a zealous abolitionist who urged the then unpopular idea of the use of black troops. It was to be "a model for all future Colored Regiments." The 54th was commanded by the Boston Brahmin Robert Gould Shaw, only twenty-five years old but a battle-seasoned veteran of Cedar Mountain and Antietam. The regiment departed Boston's flag-draped streets in May, arrived in Hilton Head in June, and arrived on James Island in July. It saw fierce action in a small encounter on James Island on July 16, 1863, its first taste of battle. The men marched from James Island to Cole's Island that night through a terrific thunderstorm

The time may come, when the opposite sections of our restored Union will unite to erect here a monument to the memory of the heroes of both races, who fell on either side. Such a shaft would swell the heart and fill the eye of every departing and returning sailor. Pilgrims from afar would come to gaze upon it, and to lift their hats to it, and walk around it, and to be consecrated by meditating on its glorious memories. Of such a monument who would not say, with Webster at Bunker Hill, "Let it rise to meet the sun in his coming. Let the earliest light of the morning greet it, and parting day linger and play upon its summit."
—Charles Cowley, Esquire, Judge Advocate, South Atlantic Blockading Squadron, *Leaves from a Lawyer's Life Afloat and Ashore* (1879)

This is a rare photograph of Confederate soldiers at Battery Wagner. They are members of the 25th South Carolina, formerly the Washington Light Infantry.

Neither Henry James, the renowned novelist and author of *The Americans, Daisy Miller,* and *The Bostonians,* nor his brother William James, the famed philosopher and psychologist, fought in the Civil War. They did, however, have two younger brothers, Garth Wilkinson (Wilky) James and Robertson (Bob) James, who enlisted and fought in the siege of Charleston. Indeed, New Englanders flocked to the units participating in the siege of Charleston. The Massachusetts 54th, Henry James wrote, seemed "to bristle with Boston genealogies."

Wilky James took part in the murderous charge on Battery Wagner and was standing by the side of the regiment's commander, Robert Gould Shaw, when he was killed. James was badly wounded, a bullet shattering his ankle bone and a fragment hitting him in the back. Instantly sent home to rest and recuperate, he became a hero to his family. His recovery was slow and painful. The patriarch of the James clan, Henry James, Sr., described him as "manly and exalted in the tone of his mind. . . . It is really quite incomprehensible to me to see so much manhood so suddenly achieved." The senior James wrote to a friend, "We all feel profoundly for the Shaws. Wilky was by him when he fell, but had no time to ask him anything. He supposes the wound to have been instantly fatal."

One can only imagine the emotions Henry James felt on his trip to Charleston in 1906 as he gazed out at Fort Sumter and Morris Island, where his younger brothers had served. He wrote in *The American Scene* that "everything differed, somehow, from one's old conceived image. . . . It was a blow even to one's faded vision of Charleston viciously firing on the Flag; the Flag would have been, from the Battery, such a mere speck in space that the view of the act lost somehow, with the distance, to say nothing of the forty years, a part of its grossness. . . . The Forts, faintly blue on the twinkling sea, looked like vague marine flowers; innocence, pleasantness ruled the prospect."

and were tired, hot, and hungry when they arrived. The next day they were transported to Morris Island amid another thunderstorm.

The 54th led the charge on the night of July 18th. Lieutenant Garth W. James recalled the moment: "General Strong, mounted on a superb gray charger, in full dress, white gloves, a yellow bandanna handkerchief coiled around his neck, approached Colonel Shaw to give the final orders." Strong spoke with emotion to the men of the 54th, and pointing at a color-bearer, he asked, "If this man should fall, who will lift the flag and carry it on?" "I will," Colonel Shaw replied. "I want you to prove yourselves," Colonel Shaw told his troops the night of the battle. "The eyes of thousands will look on what you do tonight." "To many a gallant man these scenes upon the sands were the last of earth; to the survivors they will be ever present," Luis F. Emilio later recalled in his history of the regiment:

> Away over the sea to the eastward the heavy sea-fog was gathering, the western sky bright with the reflected light, for the sun had set. Far away thunder mingled with the occasional boom of cannon. The gathering host all about, the silent lines stretching away to the rear, the passing of a horseman now and then carrying orders,—all was ominous of the impending onslaught. Far and indistinct in front was the now silent earthwork, seamed, scarred, and ploughed with shot, its flag still waving in defiance.

Six thousand Union troops stormed the Battery, some invading the fort itself before being repulsed. Fifteen hundred Union troops, including Colonel Shaw, were killed. Two hundred seventy-two men of the 54th were killed or wounded; four officers were killed. Six hundred had charged Wagner. The Confederates believed the casualties were even higher. William H. Carney, a young black private, wrote that "the shot—grape, canister and hand grenades—came in showers, and the columns were leveled." Carney was to become the first African American to be awarded the Medal of Honor, which he was given for bringing the American flag back from the bloody battlefield after being twice wounded himself. Iredell Jones, a Confederate lieutenant, recalled, "The dead and wounded were piled up in a ditch together sometimes fifteen in a heap, and they were strewn all over the plain for a distance of three-fourths of a mile. . . . One pile of negroes numbered thirty. Numbers of both white and black were killed on top of our breastworks as well as inside. The negroes fought gallantly, and were headed by as brave a colonel as ever lived. He mounted the breastworks waving his sword, and at the head of his regiment, and he and an orderly sergeant fell dead over the inner crest of the works. The negroes were as fine-looking a set as I ever saw,—large, strong, muscular fellows." The ill-planned attack utterly failed. Strong's brigade and Colonel Putnam's regiments, coming up the beach after the 54th, also failed to take the tough little Confederate battery. Harriet Tubman, an eyewitness, described to the historian Albert Bushnell a battle that must have been the assault on Wagner: "And then we saw the lightning, and that was the guns; and then we heard the thunder, and that was the big guns; and then we heard the rain falling, and that was the drops of blood falling; and when we came to get in the crops, it was dead men that we reaped."

Historians and contemporaries disagree about the effectiveness of the 54th. General Seymour was later investigated by a congressional committee for sending such a relatively small force against a superior entrenched force. Benjamin Quarles depicts their valor.

My Dear Amelia: I have been in two fights, and am unhurt. I am about to go in another I believe to-night. Our men fought well on both occasions. The last was desperate[;] we charged that terrible battery on Morris Island known as Fort Wagoner [*sic*], and were repulsed with a loss of [many] killed and wounded. I escaped unhurt from amidst that perfect hail of shot and shell. It was terrible. I need not particularize the papers will give a better than I have time to give. My thoughts are with you often, you are as dear as ever, be good enough to remember it as I no doubt you will. As I said before we are on the eve of another fight and I am very busy and have just snatched a moment to write you. . . . Should I fall in the next fight killed or wounded I hope to fall with my face to the foe. . . .

This regiment has established its reputation as a fighting regiment not a man flinched, though it was a trying time. Men fell all around me. A shell would explode and clear a space of twenty feet, our men would close up again, but it was no use we had to retreat, which was a very hazardous undertaking. How I got out of that fight alive I cannot tell, but I am here. My Dear girl I hope again to see you. I must bid you farewell should I be killed. Remember if I die I die in a good cause. I wish we had a hundred thousand colored troops we would put an end to this war.

—Lewis Douglass, the son of Frederick Douglass, to Amelia Loguen, his future wife, July 20, 1863

Lewis Henry Douglass, the first black sergeant major of the 54th Massachusetts Volunteers. He served on Morris Island in 1863. Douglass was the son of the most famous African American of the Civil War era, the fiery abolitionist Frederick Douglass.

> wo months after marching through Boston half the regiment was dead.
> —Robert Lowell, "For the Union Dead"

Harriet Tubman, who came to be known as the Moses of Her People, was herself a runaway slave and a leader of the Underground Railroad. She returned to the South during the war to serve the Union Army as a cook, laundress, nurse, scout, and spy. She is said to have served Colonel Robert G. Shaw his last dinner, on Morris Island in July, 1863.

Milby Burton decries their disorganized retreat. One contemporary wrote later that "the greater part of them followed their intrepid colonel, bounded over the ditch, mounted the parapet, and planted their flag in the most gallant manner upon the ramparts, where Shaw was shot dead; while the rest were seized with a furious panic, and acted like wild beasts let loose from a menagerie." But the loss at Battery Wagner had an impact in the North far out of proportion to its military value. "Hardly another operation of the war," Dudley T. Cornish has written in *The Sable Arm,* "received so much publicity or stirred so much comment. Out of it a legend was born. As a result of it Robert Gould Shaw came as close to canonization as a New England Puritan can." In death Shaw became a symbol of lost youth; forty poems were written in celebration of his heroism, including those by Ralph Waldo Emerson and James Russell Lowell.

The significance of the charge of the 54th Massachusetts was in demonstrating that African-American troops could and would fight and die for their country. It was a simple proposition but one which most whites—North and South—did not believe before that battle. "It is not too much to say that if this Massachusetts 54th had faltered when its trial came," said the *New York Tribune,* "two hundred thousand troops for whom it was a pioneer would never have put into the field. . . . But it did not falter. It made Fort Wagner such a name for the colored race as Bunker Hill has been for ninety years to the white Yankees." Years later the Shaw Memorial Committee defined its mission as being to "commemorate the great event . . . by which the title of coloured men as citizen-soldiers was fixed beyond recall."

Colonel Shaw was buried by the Confederates on Morris Island with the dead of his regiment, or, as the press described it, in a ditch "with his niggers." Susan Middleton wrote her cousin that she heard from an officer on Morris Island that "our officers refused to let the Yankees have his body, but buried him first in the trench, filling it with negroes, and sent word he should 'lie with his brethren.'" Emma Holmes had it that Colonel Shaw "was buried with eleven negroes over him." Northern reaction was indignant, and some insisted that Shaw's body be buried with dignity elsewhere, but Colonel Shaw's father wrote General Gillmore that he did not wish his son's grave disturbed. "I take the liberty to address you," Francis Shaw said, "because I am informed that efforts are to be made to recover the body of my son, Colonel Robert Shaw of the Fifty-Fourth Massachusetts Regiment, which was buried at Fort Wagner. My object in writing is to say that such efforts are not authorized by me or any of my family, and they are not approved by us. We hold that a soldier's most appropriate burial-place is on the field where he has fallen. I shall therefore be much obliged, General, if in case this matter is brought to your cognizance, you will forbid the desecration of my son's grave, and prevent the disturbance of his remains or those buried with him."

There is no question but that the Confederate soldiers intended to desecrate Colonel Shaw's corpse. Instead of being returned in a proper fashion pursuant to the military code of the times, it was stripped of its uniform and buried in a common ditch with the bodies of his soldiers. No other officer of either side was treated this way. Captain H. W. Hendricks, a Confederate officer who was present, confirmed the condition of Colonel Shaw's body. "This desecration of the dead," he later wrote, "we endeavored to provide against; but at that time . . . our men were so frenzied that it was next to impossible to guard against it." Brigadier General Johnson Hagood, commander of the Confederate forces at

Col. Robert Gould Shaw led the Massachusetts 54th in a suicidal attack on Battery Wagner in July, 1863. "Never during the war," Harper's Weekly said, "was an assault made in the face of such opposition."

There are monuments to Robert Gould Shaw in both Charleston and Boston. On the Boston Common there is a statue of Colonel Shaw and his men by Saint-Gaudens with this inscription:

THE WHITE OFFICERS taking life and honor in their hands cast in their lot with men of a despised race unproven in war and risked death as inciters of servile insurrection if taken prisoners besides encountering all the common perils of camp march and battle.

THE BLACK RANK AND FILE volunteered when disaster clouded the Union Cause. Served without pay for eighteen months till given that of white troops. Faced threatened enslavement if captured. Were brave in action. Patient under heavy and dangerous labors. And cheerful amid hardships and privations.

TOGETHER they gave to the Nation and the World undying proof that Americans of African descent possess the pride, courage and devotion of the patriot soldier. One hundred and eighty thousand such Americans enlisted under the Union Flag in MDCCCLXIII–MDCCCLXV.

In present-day Charleston, at 22 Mary Street, there is a community center for black youths named the Robert Gould Shaw Boys Center. The center is the successor to a free school for black children established by funds raised for a monument at the site of Fort Wagner. The enlisted men of the 54th contributed $2,832, a substantial sum in the 1860s, but the memorial was abandoned because of local hostility from whites and the erosion of Morris Island. The funds were then used to establish a free school for black children.

Johnson Hagood, lawyer, planter, and soldier, was a brigadier general in the Confederate Army and later governor of South Carolina. He fought at Bull Run but served during most of the war in his native South Carolina.

Wagner on the day in question, allegedly said, "I knew Colonel Shaw before the war, and then esteemed him. Had he been in command of white troops, I should have given him an honorable burial; as it is, I shall bury him in the common trench with the negroes that fell with him." Hagood denied these remarks, which were reported to him nearly twenty years later. "Colonel Putnam's body was asked for and delivered," he wrote. "Colonel Shaw's body was not asked for." Hagood gave an order to bury the dead immediately because of the heat. "It thus occurred that Colonel Shaw, commanding negroes, was buried with negroes." The Northern press reported Hagood's statement as "He is buried with his niggers." The historian Shelby Foote told the *New York Times* in an interview about the movie *Glory*, "I have no doubt that he said it, though he later denied it."

The Confederates, though victorious, suffered losses as well. As John Berkley Grimball described it in his diary, "There was a desperate contest last night at Wagner Battery.... Col. Simkins was killed—as was also Capt. Ryan, of the Irish—the latter it is said by our own men, by mistake, after he had with great bravery driven the enemy off and was returning." The conditions in the battery were too horrible for words. William V. Izlar wrote in his memoirs after the war that the siege of Battery Wagner "was the most fearful experience of the four years of war.... No water; no sleep, very little to eat.... The mangled dead lay thick on every side." In a lighter vein, young Pickney Lowndes told Emma Holmes that if he thought "hell was half as hot and dreadful as Fort Wagner, he would try to be good."

Sixty African-American soldiers of the 54th Massachusetts were captured and faced the distinct possibility of death, since they were not viewed as prisoners of war. On May 1, 1863, the Confederate Congress had enacted a formal declaration that black men

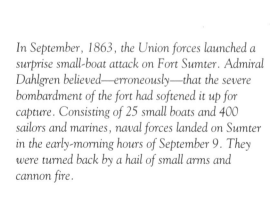

In September, 1863, the Union forces launched a surprise small-boat attack on Fort Sumter. Admiral Dahlgren believed—erroneously—that the severe bombardment of the fort had softened it up for capture. Consisting of 25 small boats and 400 sailors and marines, naval forces landed on Sumter in the early-morning hours of September 9. They were turned back by a hail of small arms and cannon fire.

The captured African-American soldiers of the 54th Massachusetts made the best of their plight. One white Union officer, also a prisoner, left this recollection:

At the close of the day the negro prisoners made a practice of getting together in the jail, and singing their plaintive melodies till late in the evening. The character of their songs was universally mournful, and it was often affecting to listen to them. . . . The harmony and the rich melody of their voices are rarely surpassed. . . . One song, which appeared to be a special favorite with them, was written by Sergeant Johnson, whom I have before mentioned. He intended it as a parody on "When the cruel war is over." I give this song as he furnished it to me:—

When I enlisted in the army,
    Then I thought 't was grand,
Marching through the streets of Boston
    Behind a regimental band.
When at Wagner, I was captured
    Then my courage failed;
Now I'm dirty, hungry, naked,
    Here in Charleston Jail.

CHORUS

Weeping, sad and lonely,
Oh, how bad I feel!
Down in Charleston, South Carolina,
Praying for a good, square meal.

II.

If Jeff Davis will release me,
    Oh, how glad I'll be!
When I get to Morris Island,
    Then I shall be free.
Then I'll tell those conscript soldiers
    How they use us here;
Giving us an old corn dodger,—*
    They call it prisoners' fare.

CHORUS

III.

We are longing, watching, praying,
    But will not repine,
Till Jeff Davis does release us,
    And send us in our lines.
Then with words of kind affection
    How they'll greet us there!
Wondering how we could live so long
    Upon the dodger fare.

CHORUS

Then we will laugh, long and loudly.
    Oh, how glad we'll feel
When we arrive on Morris Island
    And eat a good, square meal!

---

* A corn dodger was a hard-baked corncake, a hoecake, like a modern day hush puppy.

bearing arms would be subject to the laws of the state where they were captured and could be treated as insurrectionary slaves and put to death. In retaliation, on July 30, 1863, President Lincoln signed an order requiring that "for every soldier of the United States killed in violation of the laws of war, a rebel shall be executed."

The first test case under Confederate law arose in Charleston in fall, 1863, with regard to the men of the 54th. "They received no tender treatment," a Charleston newspaper wrote. "The prisoners believe they are to be hung." Indeed, the survivors of the assault on Battery Wagner were taken to the old Charleston jail, which still stands near Beaufain Street. A gallows was erected in the jailyard.

While white Union soldiers were exchanged for Confederate soldiers held by the Federal Army, the black troops of the 54th were not exchanged. General Beauregard sought instructions from Richmond, but, in the meantime, Governor Bonham ordered the provost marshal's court for the Charleston district to be convened to try the black troops. The attorney general, J. W. Hayne, and A. P. Aldrich prosecuted. Nelson Mitchell and Edward McCrady, "lawyers of eminent ability," were appointed to defend the prisoners. One soldier of the 54th, Daniel States, later wrote,

> A lawyer named Mitchell came to the jail and offered to defend us before the court. He did a good deal for us, and talked with Sergeant Jeffries and Corporal Hardy, who went to trial as the two test cases. Mitchell did this without pay, and was very kind to us at all times. He worked hard and won the case, coming to us at midnight and called up to Jeffries, "All of you can now rejoice. You are recognized as United States soldiers."

Despite the heroism of the 54th Massachusetts and men like Colonel Shaw, the Union Army was not about to march into Charleston. Peter M. Chaitin concluded in *The Coastal War*, "In ten days on Morris Island, General Gillmore had lost one third of his men, and the capture of Fort Wagner, his immediate goal, seemed as remote as ever." The Union sailor Alvah Hunter wrote,

> Following the disastrous assault upon Fort Wagner on July 18th, General Gillmore resorted to regular siege operations and approaches. His batteries were located for steady and severe pounding, and the approaches went steadily forward by zig-zags; this was a comparatively easy task in the soft sand of Morris Island. A severe fire of shells was kept up by his guns both day and night. The naval vessels kept at work upon the sea-face of the fort nearly every day. On some days the firing by the ships would be very severe and on other days few or no shells whatever would be fired from the fleet.

> The objective of the descent upon Morris Island was the capture or destruction of Fort Sumter. As the capture looked decidedly difficult, the destruction of that work was determined upon, and some experimental shots were fired from Parrot rifled guns located in batteries that were six or eight hundred yards south and west of Fort Wagner. The few trial shots revealed decided effectiveness in this fire and satisfied General Gillmore that he could destroy Sumter from where he was then located. Possibly the enemy would not hold Wagner so stoutly once Sumter was well on the way to destruction! Special batteries mounting heavy rifled guns were erected, the chief effort of those guns to be the battering down of Sumter.

The best ordnance available was brought in, and a new calcium floodlight was used to illuminate Wagner. This was the first such use of a floodlight in warfare.

Many others came to serve on Morris Island, including Clara Barton, dubbed the Angel of the Battlefield, and Harriet Tubman, one of the leaders of the Underground Railroad and later referred to as the Moses of Her People. Tubman, a former slave who had escaped slavery, came down to Hilton Head to work in the Union Army as a cook, laundress, nurse, scout, and spy. She served Colonel Shaw his last dinner and helped bury the dead and care for the wounded after the battle.

At dawn on August 17, 1863, one of the fiercest bombardments in the history of warfare commenced against Fort Sumter. It went on without interruption for seven days. The breaching batteries erected by General Gillmore were named for famous Union generals—Rosecrans, Meade—and officers killed in action. Four were named for Union generals killed at Gettysburg. They contained two 80-pounder Whitworths, nine 100-pounder Parrotts, six 200-pounder Parrotts, and one 300-pounder Parrott: "in all, eighteen rifle-guns in eight batteries, throwing a ton of metal in the aggregate at each discharge," concluded Johnson in *The Defense of Charleston Harbor*. The power of the Union artillery was immense—a precursor, really, of that of World War I. Never before in history had man been able to bombard a fort with such precision at such long range. By August 24 Gillmore

Nelson Mitchell, the chief lawyer for the African-American soldiers of the 54th Massachusetts, remained loyal to the Union. But unlike James L. Petigru, he became an outcast in Charleston society. He died before the war ended, leaving a widow and two children. He had to the last the gratitude of the men he had helped save. One officer later wrote, "Their admiration for this devoted friend of the Union was so great that the mere mention of his name is sufficient to bring tears to the eyes of the swarthy sons, who have thus far had so little to be grateful for."

The Union Army took over Morris Island in 1863 and turned it into a Federal Fort. Buildings were built and tons of ammunition were brought in. This photograph shows an ordnance depot.

These photographs show the Union headquarters on Morris Island (top left) and a Union bunker (right); Union soldiers, cavalry, and artillery. Morris Island also boasted a forage house for the storage of food for horses, a blacksmith shop to repair equipment, a gas manufacturing plant, a carpenter shop, an ice house, and boat building and repair facilities. After the war the buildings were abandoned and vandalized. They no longer exist.

CLARA BARTON

Clara Barton was born in Massachusetts in 1821. She was an eccentric and nervous child, but as she matured, she overcame her disabilities and became a successful teacher. She later moved to Washington, D.C., where she was employed in the United States Patent Office. When the Civil War began, Barton became a one-woman relief agency, bringing food, medicine, and supplies to the sick and wounded men of the Union Army. Although she had no official position with the army and did not belong to any charitable organization, she became well known and widely respected for her philanthropic work.

Barton left New York by boat on April 2, 1863, and arrived in Hilton Head on the day the siege of Charleston began, April 7, 1863. "When I left Washington everyone said it boded no peace, it was a bad omen for *me* to start," she wrote in her journal. "I had never missed of finding the trouble I went to find, and was never late." In July she accompanied the army when it began its assault on Morris Island. She wrote her cousin Vira a detailed description of what she saw:

> We made our way to the decks and there sure enough was our shell bursting in the enemies sand batteries for the space of a mile along the beach of Morris Island. Our boats crowded with troops but hidden by the bushes and thickets waiting the orders to land or spring upon them.... At seven we discerned some moving objects among the trees, and lo! our troops were leaping from the boats like wild cats and scarce waiting to form on they went in one wild charge, across the marsh and up the banks, and into the entrenchments, and almost in one breath, up rose the *Old Flag,* and the ground was ours with from fifty to a hundred presences from almost under the *guns of Sumpter* [*sic*].

Barton was on Morris Island the night the Massachusetts 54th made its devastating assault:

> I watched the first boat near the coast of Morris Island, and saw the first man leap out upon its glistening sands. One week later, and the flash of a hundred guns and ten thousand muskets lit up the darkness of our desert island, and the thunders of Wagner and "Sumpter" shook it to its center; and on those bloody "parapets" freedom and slavery met—and wrestled hand to hand, and the false flag and the true swelling in the same breeze stood face to face while warriors met and fought, and martyrs died; through the long, dark terrible hours, we gazed and hoped and prayed, and at length—must I write it?—turned back in despair to comfort our wounded and bury our dead.

Morris Island was very rough duty for all involved— Confederate defenders of Battery Wagner, Union soldiers unused to heat and mosquitoes, and Barton. She suffered in her entrenchments from "the unyielding fire of Fort Johnson" as shells frequently burst within a quarter of a mile of her tent. It was blazing hot in the July and August Charleston sun, a very different climate from that of New England. Decent food was hard to obtain and impossible to keep fresh. Barton, along with the soldiers, ate " 'salt junk' old beef of such hardness and saltness as you never dreamed of, lean bacon, and hard crackers, both buggy and wormy."

Even the highest ranking officers got sick. The men worked sixteen hours a day, and Barton worked along with them. As a result, she became ill in August and had to leave Morris Island. She returned to Hilton Head, where she almost died. Barton gradually recuperated and went back to Morris Island, where she continued to nurse and tend the troops.

After she left Hilton Head and Morris Island, Barton recalled "eight months of weary siege— scorched by the sun, chilled by the waves, rocked by the tempest, buried in shifting sands, toiling day after day, in the trenches, with the angry fire of five forts hissing."

In later years, after working with the International Red Cross in Europe, Barton agitated to have the United States become a party to the Geneva Convention, which made the Red Cross possible. After many rebuffs, she finally persuaded the president and Congress to sign the necessary treaty so that the American Red Cross could be created. She was to come to Charleston again, on behalf of that organization—first to aid in the aftermath of the 1886 earthquake and then in 1893, at the age of seventy-one, to help the victims of a disastrous hurricane. Thirty years after her service to the enemies of Charleston, the *News & Courier* praised and thanked the former Angel of the Battlefield: "Miss Clara Barton . . . and her staff left Charleston yesterday. . . . The story of their undertaking . . . is known throughout the country and throughout Christendom." After a tumultuous twenty-three-year tenure with the American Red Cross, Barton retired. She died at the age of ninety-one in Glen Echo, Maryland, just outside Washington, D.C.

Clara Barton, often called the Angel of the Battlefield, spent many hot, weary months on Morris Island nursing Union troops. The future founder of the American Red Cross was on Morris Island the night the Massachusetts 54th made its suicidal charge. She later wrote, "On those bloody 'parapets' freedom and slavery met."

reported that "Fort Sumter is today a shapeless and harmless mass of ruins." Shapeless maybe, but Sumter was far from harmless, as the Federal forces would soon learn. Stores and ammunition were removed to Fort Moultrie.

The siege of Charleston would be bloodier still. Although the symbolic capture of Charleston was far less urgent after the fall of Vicksburg and the Battle of Gettysburg, the desire to punish Charleston had not diminished. On August 21, 1863, General Gillmore sent a message to General Beauregard demanding "the immediate evacuation of Morris Island and Fort Sumter" within four hours or else "I shall open fire on the city of Charleston." Beauregard wrote a blistering reply:

> Among nations not barbarous the usage of war prescribes that when a city is about to be attacked, timely notice shall be given by the attacking commander, in order that noncombatants may have an opportunity for withdrawing beyond its limits. . . . It would appear, sir, that despairing of reducing these works, you now resort to the novel measure of turning your guns against the old men, the women and children, and the hospitals of a sleeping city, an act of inexcusable barbarity.

Augustine Smythe's sister Sue wrote him on August 22, "Our last news from town was very gloomy and discouraging. The wall of Fort Sumter breached, & its destruction inevitable. Some insist this does not necessitate the fall of Charleston, then others think differently, but Gus, what will become of you?" The Smythe family decided about this time that the women and old men should leave Charleston for the country. Twenty-year-old Gus was therefore left in charge of the family homes, "old No. 12" Meeting Street (18 Meeting Street in the present street-numbering system); 36 Meeting Street, the home of Gus's uncle and aunts, the Adgers; and his uncle Robert Adger's home on Legare Street. He wrote his Aunt Janey on August 23, "I think winter will find us fighting here if the

The Bombardment of Fort Sumter. *The artist is probably John Ross Key, a kinsman of Francis Scott Key, but some attribute the work to Albert Bierstadt. Admiral John A. Dahlgren, like General Beauregard, wanted a record of the siege and commissioned the painting, which shows the action in 1863. Confederate ironclads are to the left, Fort Johnson in the foreground, Sumter in the center with battered walls, and Union monitors to the right, as well as Cummings Point and Battery Wagner.*

Yanks don't hurry up, tho' in the meantime they may destroy the city by their shells. Here's a chance for your house to have a hole made thro' it by a Yankee ball, & render it historical. They are very particular now, & will not allow any officer to leave the ship, as we do not know at what moment we may be summoned to action."

On August 29 General Gillmore began the bombardment of the city of Charleston at the order of President Lincoln. In fact, the president was quite interested in and knowledgeable of weapons technology. One historian has described him "in his own person as the Union's closest approach to a weapons research and development agency." Formerly a surveyor and an amateur inventor as well as a lawyer, Lincoln had long been interested in incendiary shells and Greek fire. "Such shells, he thought, would be especially valuable in siege operations, as at Vicksburg and Charleston," Richard N. Current wrote in *The Lincoln Nobody Knows*. "Vicksburg surrendered before a thorough test could be made, but behind Fort Sumter the City of Charleston remained exasperatingly out of reach. After a long range, 200-pounder Parrott gun (the 'Swamp Angel') had been set up on Morris Island, Lincoln himself gave the order to shoot into the city with incendiary shells."

Alvah Hunter recalled the origin of the Swamp Angel this way:

> When the first great bombardment of Sumter began it occurred to some officers in the battery furthest west to try a few shots in the direction of Charleston. These shots so nearly reached the city, the officers were satisfied that they could reach Charleston if they could mount a gun a mile farther west. The subject was much discussed, the marsh was explored, and a spot was found about three-quarters of a mile west of the left battery where it was believed a gun could be mounted if it could be brought to that spot, and the work was begun by constructing a causeway out there. The battery was erected, a 150-pounder [actually a 200-pounder] Parrot rifled gun was brought to it and mounted, and on the night of August 21–22, fire was opened upon the city at a range of about 7,000 yards [with] the gun at an elevation of 35 degrees.

In early 1863 there was still some social life for the remnants of the Charleston aristocracy. The Middleton girls wrote letters from January to May about parties in downtown Charleston: "round dancing" had become "alarmingly prevalent" and "a very gay party" was held at the Manigaults'. By the summer, the morals of the young ladies had declined considerably, and there were "no parties, but plenty of visitors." Harriott Middleton wrote her cousin in July that "the officers said they have but to open their arms and the Charleston ladies rush to them—that it is very delightful to have them in their arms but it would be much more convenient on the sofa. . . . Now don't repeat this to the girls!" Emma Holmes agreed. She confided to her diary that she was "mortified at the disgraceful character the Charleston girls have acquired—once considered so modest and refined." As reported to Miss Holmes, the foreigners were saying that "they have met fast girls, but not equal to those in Charleston."

Charleston society was now badly battered, suffering from deprivation, war fatigue, and constant death. Funerals became a common social event. James L. Petigru, aged, ill, and nearly driven to despair by the war, died in March, 1863. The old social norms were gone. Some Charlestonians continued to dine, give balls, and act as if nothing had happened, but most of those remaining in the city were subdued. Emma Holmes severely

Conrad Wise Chapman grew up in Rome. His parents were Virginians who had moved there so that Chapman's father, the accomplished painter John Gadsby Chapman, could enjoy his calling and work in peace. (The elder Chapman had been harshly criticized for his work *The Marriage of Pocahontas,* in the capitol rotunda.) Chapman's sons grew up as loyal Southerners, though they lived in Italy.

When the war began, young Chapman decided to join the Confederate Army. He served in the famous Orphan Brigade and fought at Shiloh. In September, 1863, he was assigned to Charleston to participate in General Beauregard's plan for a history of the siege of Charleston. Beauregard, as Ben Bassham has pointed out in the *South Carolina Historical Magazine* (January, 1988), "liked and recognized the power of pictures." From September 16, 1863, to March 5, 1864, Chapman produced at least thirty-five magnificent paintings depicting the siege, as well as many black-and-white sketches. It was a dangerous assignment because shells were exploding everywhere the artist painted, at all hours of the day and night. A friend recalled Chapman sitting "on the ramparts of Fort Sumter and other forts under the heaviest kind of artillery fire. Chapman held cannon balls and shells in great contempt." Another soldier remembered Chapman this way: "Often he sat under a heavy cannonade. He minded it no more than if he had been listening to the post band."

The Swamp Angel was the name Union soldiers gave a Parrott rifle which fired 150- to 200-pound shot into the city, approximately four and a half miles away. It was located at a battery situated literally in the marsh on James Island and called Marsh Battery. The bombardment reached its disgraceful nadir when the Union artillery officers began using St. Michael's spire as a marker. The cannon is now a monument in Trenton, New Jersey.

Charleston Under Fire—August 1863, by Theodore R. Davis. This view is from an upper story of the Mills House. St. Philip's Church is to the far right; the ruins of Institute Hall and the Circular Church are to the right; the "German Church" (St. Matthew's Lutheran Church) is to the far left; Citadel Square Baptist Church is to the left.

criticized the Rhetts, Alstons, Middletons, Ropers, "and all that set of worldly, heartless fashionables" for forgetting the dead and making themselves "conspicuous." Widows attended parties in black. Even Miss Holmes went to "musical soirees" she thought appropriate. In July, 1863, she still reported "some very good music," and in August she was present at a supper at which the latest books were discussed.

Life in the city was totally disrupted. Entire sections of town were vacant. Schools closed, as did most churches. The social class and caste distinctions which had marked antebellum Charleston began to blur long before the end of the war. By 1863 the makeup of the city's population had changed dramatically. Confederate soldiers from out of town—most of them uncouth and uneducated by Charleston society standards—were everywhere. When Emma Holmes went for a walk on the Battery, she went to view the "'mobocracy' which turned out in great strength, utterly regardless of taste & expense. We were almost ashamed to be seen in such a common crowd." Slaves began to disappear, and it was difficult and expensive to procure a maid or housekeeper. Many Charleston ladies who were used to having slaves found themselves without. Women who had never before washed the first article of clothing or mopped a floor now learned about housekeeping. By August, 1863, Holmes wrote in her diary that she was becoming an accomplished chambermaid. Many of the old civilities were gone. People's homes were damaged and could not be repaired. Men might now visit in a lady's bedroom—previously a social taboo—because it was the only liveable room in the house.

The lower part of the city was bombed and shelled and the victim of mortar attacks on and off until its surrender a year and a half later. (Four of the mortars which bombarded Charleston from James Island stand today at the Battery.) Fires abounded as the regular firefighters were now in the service of the Confederacy. To some degree, the present existence of any old Charleston homes is due to the free black population. While free blacks were not allowed by law to carry arms, they served the cause in a number of capacities, including as volunteer firemen. James H. Holloway, a prominent member of the brown elite, later wrote that "members of the [Brown Fellowship] society, not as an organization, but as individuals," saved the city from the fires caused by the Federal bombardment.

Most of those who could do so left Charleston for Columbia or the upcountry. Others removed themselves north of Calhoun Street, where the shells generally could not reach. Downtown Charleston became a ghost town. "Poor dear old Charleston!" Susan Middleton wrote her cousin in December, 1863; "I hear the desolation in the lower part of town is appalling." The city was decimated, though there were few military casualties among civilians; the number killed is disputed. In his memoirs, Reverend Porter placed it at eighty. "By 1864, the town presented the most extraordinary appearance," wrote Mrs. Ravenel. "The whole life and business of the place were crowded into the few squares above Calhoun Street, and along the Ashley, where the hospitals and the prisoners were and the shells did not reach. . . . No one can tell what those wartime babies and their mothers endured. Some were born under fire; some by the roadside;—it was awfully biblical! . . . To pass from this bustling, crowded scene to the lower part of the town was . . . like going from life to death."

The Union Army bombarded the city even on Christmas, using church spires as targets. This "Christmas will long be remembered," the *Mercury* reported on December 28,

1863. "At one o'clock a.m., the enemy opened fire upon the City. Fast and furious the shells rained upon the City. The shelling was more severe that any former occasion." Mrs. Ravenel wrote,

> As long as possible the churches were kept open, but the steeples were used as targets, and they were greatly damaged. At St. Philip's the rector, Mr. (afterward Bishop) Howe, was in the middle of his sermon, when a shell passed over the roof and burst in the western churchyard. The congregation remained seated until the service reached its proper close, and after a peculiarly fervent blessing dispersed quietly. The Episcopalians left in the town united, after that, for worship in St. Paul's Radcliffeborough, the rectors taking it by turns to officiate. Other denominations made similar arrangements.
>
> Ten shells passed through St. Philip's, its chancel was wrecked, its organ demolished; St. Michael's suffered in the same way, the other churches likewise; many tombstones were shattered by falling shells.

William Gilmore Simms wrote an angry poem published in the *Mercury* in December, 1863. It began,

> Ay, *strike, with sacrilegious aim*
> *The temple of the Living God;*
> *Hurl iron bolt, and seething flame,*
> *Through aisles which holiest feet have trod;*
> *Tear up the altar, spoil the tomb,*
> *And, raging with demoniac ire,*
> *Send down, in sudden crash of doom,*
> *That grand, old, sky-sustaining spire.*

The Northern public, of course, was delighted by the bombardment of Charleston. "She deserves it all," George Templeton Strong, a prominent New Yorker, wrote in his diary. "Sowing the wind was an exhilarating chivalric pastime—Resisting the whirlwind is less agreeable."

The Union Army built a fortress on Morris Island, complete with a blacksmith shop, a boat repair facility, and a large munitions depot. But it was never a comfortable place to be. Captain Marple wrote his wife, "We are annoyed unmercifully by the mosquitos, and have intolerable water to drink. I go without water as long as I can stand it rather than drink the foul stuff. It is about the color of tea."

The end, however, was in sight. In September, 1863, Battery Wagner was evacuated in the face of an overwhelming Union military presence. Major John Johnson wrote in his monumental work, *The Defense of Charleston Harbor*:

> Thus terminated the siege of Battery Wagner, memorable for its duration of fifty-eight days, for the persevering skill displayed in the attack, and for the sturdy resistance of the defence. History will promote it from a battery to a fort, but it was always known to the Confederates as "Battery Wagner." In conjunction with Battery

Charlestonians fleeing the city during the Union bombardment of August, 1863.

Gregg at Cumming's Point, it had repulsed three assaults of the enemy, and stood without any serious damage to the last one of the heaviest bombardments on record. . . . The highest compliments were paid to the commander of the Union forces by his superiors at Washington. And yet the Confederates were not without their satisfaction also in having made a stand for the protection of Charleston that availed them to the end of the war. For the conquest which they left to the enemy was fruitless; the barren island was but a barren trophy.

Gus Smythe explained the retreat to his aunt this way:

I suppose you have seen by the papers of the evacuation of Morris Isld. It was a heavy blow to us, but it was a matter of necessity admitting no compromise. The Yankee flag on Sunday morning, was flying within 40ft of the ditch of Wagner, & the garrison could hear the voices of the men working in the mines. No one dared to show his head over the parapet, but at a risk of a bullet from the Yankee sharpshooters. Tho' the round shell fell harmlessly against the ramparts, the heavy Parrotte would penetrate into the middle of them, & there burst, tearing up the breast works & exposing the woodwork of the bomb-proofs, whilst the fire, continuous night & day, kept our men in their holes, & prevented any attempt even to repair the damages. Communication with them was next to impossible, much less forwarding supplies; the water was *putrid*, the corpses buried in the sand hills around, were torn up by the shells & exposed to the sun; the sick & wounded were unable to be cared for in a place where a sound man could scarcely care for himself, & at last a virtue was made of necessity, & the place was evacuated. It was better to do so while we could remove our men, than to wait until all their places of refuge were destroyed, & the Yankee miners were in the fort by underground passage and our men were forced to retreat in the face of a pursuing enemy.

The Union claimed a victory. Writing after the war, Major Robert C. Gilchrist exclaimed, "Victory! Victory! Seven hundred forty men driven out of a sand-hill by eleven thousand five hundred! Two months to advance half a mile toward Charleston!" Writing twenty years later, he concluded, "For fifty-eight days, Wagner and Gregg, with a force never exceeding sixteen hundred men, had withstood a thoroughly equipped army of eleven thousand five hundred men, the Ironsides, eight monitors, and five gunboats. For every pound of sand used in the construction or repairs of Wagner, its assailants had expended two pounds of iron in the vain attempt to batter it down. At the close of the bombardment it stood, sullen, strong, defiant as ever."

Fort Sumter lay in ruins but was still occupied by Confederate soldiers living underground like moles. The Union Army and Navy had lost 2,300 men so far, but the stalemate continued. The loss of both Wagner and Battery Gregg had proven not to be decisive. Dahlgren, however, assumed that Sumter was now sufficiently softened up for an attack or had even been abandoned. The possibility of raising the American flag over Fort Sumter was more than Dahlgren or Gillmore could resist. Dahlgren, however, was anxious to have the navy garner the glory and, although he knew the army was making plans to attack, he decided to send in the marines. "You have only to go in and take possession," Dahlgren told Commander Thomas Stevens, "You will find nothing but a corporal's guard." A small-boat attack by the marines on the morning of September 8–9, however, utterly failed. One hundred and twenty five Union Soldiers were taken prisoner. Fort Sumter was now held by 320 Confederate infantrymen under the command of Major Stephen Elliott, Jr. General Beauregard's orders to Elliott had been as follows: "You are to be sent to a fort deprived of all offensive capacity, and having but one gun—a 32-pounder—with which to salute the flag. But that fort is Fort Sumter, the key to the entrance of this harbor. It must be held to the bitter end, not with artillery, but with infantry alone; and there can be no hope of reinforcements." When Dahlgren had demanded Sumter's surrender, Beauregard replied, "Inform Admiral Dahlgren that he may have Fort Sumter when he can take it and hold it."

But the bombardment continued. "The fort is a complete mass of ruins to look at it," Gus Smythe wrote "but, don't worry, there is many a safe nook." The young soldier added a postscript: "Sumter seems destined to be a thorn in the flesh of the Yankees. Even in her ruins she is game. Hurrah for her." Sumter, ironically, became stronger. It was reveted with baskets of sand, palmetto logs, and earth which had to be brought out to the fort at great risk. Smythe wrote his mother that he had "heard several times from other sources, that Lee's army will be sent here, and Richmond left, rather than allow Sherman to devastate this state as he has done Georgia. The City here is in a very lawless condition, robberies and assaults every night. It is horrible and dangerous to go out after dark, especially down town where there is no light on the streets."

A second major bombardment of Fort Sumter began on October 26 and continued unabated until December 6. Gillmore was now Major General Gillmore, having earned his promotion from brigadier by conquering Morris Island. Battery Wagner, now in the possession of the Union Army, was renamed Fort Strong in honor of the Union general, and Battery Gregg was renamed Fort Putnam in honor of the deceased colonel who led the charge on Wagner after Colonel Shaw fell. The Confederates continued miraculously to withstand the assault. On one October night thirteen members of Charleston's Washington Light Infantry died when a shell destroyed the roof of a barracks on Fort Sumter. Major Elliott had constructed a remarkable series of interior defenses, but in December a powder magazine exploded, killing eleven men. The fire was eventually put out. Peter Chaitin writes in *The Coastal War:* "The garrison's commander, hoping to rebuild the morale of his stricken force, summoned the band to the parapet, and the musicians struck up 'Dixie.' As the music drifted across the water to Morris Island, the Federal gunners, in a rare display of sympathy between the opposing forces, suspended their bombardment and raised a cheer for Fort Sumter's brave defenders."

Charleston's defenders became younger. Military school cadets were now joining the Confederate ranks. One of these was William R. Cathcart, age nineteen, who arrived in Charleston from North Carolina's Hillsborough Military Academy in December, 1863, to man the telegraph at Fort Sumter. Involved with telegraphy from the age of twelve, William became a telegraph operator in one of the underground "safe nooks" described by Gus Smythe. The Confederates had installed a telegraph line in 1862, and it joined Sumter and Moultrie to headquarters in Charleston. During the December bombardment, the telegraph line remained open. According to Robert L. Hart, when "the telegraph key itself was knocked out during the shelling, attempts were made to establish visual contact with neighboring Confederate signal stations, but to no avail. Finally, young Cathcart resorted to receiving messages by pressing the ends of the wires to his moist tongue, literally feeling the signals rather than hearing them!" Following the shelling, Cathcart and other members of the signal corps went into the freezing-cold harbor looking for breaks in the line and remained until they found them.

Desperate attempts by the Confederate defenders of Charleston to strike a blow at the Union Navy came in fall, 1863, and early 1864. The novel torpedo boat *David* rammed the *New Ironsides* in October, 1863, and the world's first successful submarine attack occurred on February 17, 1864, when the *H. L. Hunley* (also known to contemporary Charlestonians as "The Fish" and "The Porpoise") sank the *Housatonic*. One Confederate soldier later recalled,

> On February 17, 1864, Lieutenant Dixon, with a crew of six men, made their way with the boat through the creeks behind Sullivan's Island to the inlet. The night was not very dark, and the Housatonic easily could be perceived lying at anchor, unmindful of danger. The "Fish" went direct for her victim, and her torpedo striking the side tore a tremendous hole in the Housatonic, which sank to the bottom in about four minutes. But as the water was not very deep her masts remained above water, and all of the crew, except four or five, saved themselves by climbing and clinging to them. But the "Fish" was not seen again. From some unknown cause she again sank, and all her crew perished.

Dramatic as these attacks were, they were too little, too late.

Both sides were exhausted by the stalemate. The Union Army and Navy had been totally frustrated. Gideon Welles concluded that Charleston had been the "most invulnerable and best-protected city on the coast, whose defenses had cost immense treasure and labor." Union troops and ships were reassigned to other theaters, as were the Confederates. D. E. Huger Smith recalled in his memoirs,

> During the campaign of 1864 this coast was almost denuded of troops in order to reinforce the main armies of Lee and of Johnston, and consequently the duties that fell upon us were many more than those of a field Battery. For a part of that year we held John's Island with the help only of a troop of cavalry, and mounted on our battery horses we did the advanced picket and scouting duty. One picket post was at Haulover Cut, and at daylight each morning we had to scout Seabrook's Island and to count the enemy's vessels as they lay in Edisto Inlet. Also at the extreme point we climbed a very tall sand-hill and counted the ships in sight, noting their courses. These reports we sent in by a courier daily to some point where they could be telegraphed to Headquarters in Charleston. Another advanced picket post which we held, was on the Stono River at Grimball's. Here we were to watch the river, and to fire into anything that came up, sending off a courier with the alarm. If the enemy landed we (three of us in all) were to fall back to a hedge, which we were to "hold" with as much noise as possible until the enemy "eat us up."

The Union Army was guilty of unspeakable cruelty toward Confederate prisoners on Morris Island, where it kept 600 of them in conditions approaching those of concentration camps. They were held in a prison pen situated between Batteries Wagner and Gregg "in exact line of the guns of Fort Sumter," one survivor recalled. The prisoners had been taken to Morris Island in August, 1864, from Fort Delaware to be used as human shields in the line of fire. The Federal troops did this because they contended that Union prisoners were being used as human shields in Charleston.

The whole Charleston area was a desolate armed camp. In November, 1863, Gus Smythe wrote of Sullivan's Island,

> Our house has been pulled down, & all the others on the front beach, from the cove up to the Fort, have shared the same fate, while their place is supplied by batteries. . . . The church is down. The Episcopal one is used for a Commissary, & the Catholic one stands, but is shut up. The whole Island, or rather, that part of it comprising the village, looks desolate & rather the worse for wear. . . . Many of the houses are riddled with cannon balls, & but very few I fear, will ever be habitable again. The Island is full of soldiers, & the whole face from the Fort to the Cove is one long battery mounting the heaviest guns. I do not think now that I shall ever live there again.

The Old City Jail, part of a municipal governmental complex which included the jail (to the left), the work-house (to the right), the Marine Hospital (not shown), and old Roper Hospital (now destroyed). The jail was a military prison during the Civil War. Here Federal prisoners were housed, as were "felons, murderers, lewd women," and deserters from both armies.

In November, 1863, despite the bombardment, President Jefferson Davis paid a visit to Charleston. He arrived by train and to the firing of guns in his honor. Meeting him at the train station were three of his most fervent critics: Beauregard, whom he disliked intensely; Colonel Thomas Jordan, Beauregard's aide; and Robert Barnwell Rhett, one of his chief political enemies. Davis proceeded through the streets of Charleston "thronged with people anxious to get a look at the President. The men cheered and the ladies waved their handkerchiefs in token of recognition." The city had been decorated in honor of his visit. The local press described the festivity:

> The Mills House, Charleston Hotel, Pavilion, and many public and private residences, hung out the State and Confederate flags. From the City Hall to the Court House a garland of laurels had been extended, with a banner in the center, bearing the following inscription: "The Ladies of the Soldiers' Relief Association welcome President Davis to Charleston." On arrival of the procession at the City Hall, President Davis alighted from the carriage amid the cheers of the citizens, and was introduced by Judge MAGRATH to Mayor MACBETH. The Mayor received the President in a short but eloquent address, and extended a cordial welcome to the city.

In a letter to Sarah Annie, Gus Smythe also described the president's visit:

> We had great doings in town yesterday. The President, you know, arrived and they made a great fuss receiving him, with soldiers and bands and nurses and speeches. He is a fine looking man with a very intellectual countenance, but only one eye. He spoke very well, his delivery clear and emphatic. To-day he visited Sullivan's Island and the [sic] Charleston. To-morrow he goes over to James Isl. & there is to be a grand review. I should like very much to see it.

From the portico of City Hall, the beleaguered president addressed the people of Charleston. At one point he said that it would be better to leave the city "a heap of ruins" than "prey for Yankee spoils." The crowd chanted in agreement, "Ruins! Ruins!" The president opined, however, that Charleston would never be taken. He continued:

> Let us trust to our commanding general, to those having the charge and responsibilities of our affairs. . . . It is by united effort, by fraternal feeling, by harmonious co-operation, by casting away all personal considerations . . . that our success is to be

James L. Petigru, the state's preeminent lawyer and one of the few Unionists left in Charleston during the Civil War. Mary Chesnut noted in her diary, "Mr. Petigru alone in South Carolina has not seceded."

JAMES L. PETIGRU

James Louis Petigru was a self-made man who rose to the first ranks of the South Carolina legal profession and became a legend in his own lifetime both at the bar and in politics. He was born in the South Carolina upcountry district of Abbeville to parents of modest means. He was part Huguenot, or French Protestant, and part Irish. His family spelled the name Pettigrew, but James changed the spelling of his name while he was a college student. Mary Chesnut wrote in her famous diary that he had "Huguenotted" the spelling to make his name appear to be French. But, she added, he "could not tie up his Irish."

Petigru supported himself by teaching in Columbia and Beaufort and studied law in the Beaufort area. He practiced at Coosawhatchie, was elected solicitor (district attorney or prosecutor) in 1816, and married the daughter of a local planter. He moved to Charleston in 1819 to join in the practice of law with James Hamilton, Jr. In 1822 he was elected attorney general of South Carolina.

Petigru was a nationalist and Federalist in all respects. He opposed John C. Calhoun and the nullification movement with great vigor in the 1830s and believed Calhoun to be a very dangerous man. According to Lacy Ford, he "often handled controversial and politically sensitive cases. He defended a man accused of being a Negro trying to 'pass' as white, and in the 1850's represented a Northern emigrant to Goose Creek who was accused of preaching abolitionist doctrines. In politically motivated litigation, Petigru challenged the 'test oath' passed by the nullifiers."

Petigru was a devout Episcopalian and served as a vestryman for St. Michael's Church. Two of the classic stories told about him by the great Civil War historians have to do with religion. Allan Nevins relates the first in his monumental *Ordeal of the Union:* "The respected jurist James L. Petigru, just entrusted with the codification of the State laws, protested to the last against the flowing tide. Charlestonians long remembered one dramatic moment of his career. Listening attentively to the reading of Sunday prayers from the pulpit of his beloved St. Michael's, he started when he heard the usual invocation for the President of the United States omitted, and without hesitation walked up the aisle and out the door."

The other story is an observation by Mary Chesnut: "When they pray for our president, [Mr. Petigru] gets up from his knees. He might risk a prayer for Mr. Davis. I doubt if it would seriously do Mr. Davis any good. Mr. Petigru is too clever to think himself one of the righteous whose prayers avail so overly much."

He derided the secessionists and apparently did not believe until very late that secession would actually occur. He opposed all efforts by the Confederate government; one example of this was his representing Northern shipping interests in litigation against the Confederate Sequestration Act. The war, however, hurt him deeply. His home at Broad and Legare was burned in the Great Fire of 1861, prompting Mary Chesnut to write, "So being anti-secessionist does not save. The fire, as the rain, falls on the just and the unjust." His summer house on Sullivan's Island, like the houses of many of his neighbors, was destroyed to make way for military fortifications along the beach.

Robert Barnwell Rhett, Jr., the fanatic editor of the *Mercury,* wrote an editorial early in the war implying that Petigru had described himself to Rhett as a monarchist. Petigru would make no public comment on the absurd editorial. He told his friends, however, "Rhett, Jr. is fool enough to call me a monarchist because I am a Union man. . . . [My] attachment to popular government [however] would outlast that of a whole brigade of Secessionists."

President Lincoln was urged by a group of prominent northerners to appoint Petigru to the United States Supreme Court as a kind of political statement to replace Justice McLean or Justice Campbell. "His unspotted character . . . , his steadiness and truth to the Union in the midst of treachery," the letter to Lincoln read, "are known to the whole nation." But Petigru was too old by then and was not in good health. The president had even considered foregoing the bombardment of Charleston because of Petigru. This story was told in *Harper's Magazine* in July 1877: " 'How many righteous men did the Lord accept?' asked a listener. 'I don't know exactly,' said the narrator. 'I know Abraham beat down the Lord a good deal.' 'So,' said Mr. Lincoln, 'they may beat us down to Mr. Petigru and save Charleston.' "

At his death, the city closed down to mourn Petigru despite his refusal to recognize the Confederacy. He was buried in St. Michael's churchyard. General Winfield Scott wrote Edwin M. Stanton upon learning of Petigru's death: Petigru, he said, was the "greatest moral hero of the age."

In 1888 Caroline Petigru Carson, Petigru's daughter, made a claim against the United States on account of the plundering of her silver by Union troops. She asked her old family friend, William Tecumseh Sherman, to give her an affidavit in support of her claim. The old general had to decline, as officers could not make voluntary statements against the government. "Nevertheless I shall always be glad if any good luck comes to you from that or any other source," he wrote. "I would however, much prefer that your father's loyalty to his country should be specifically rewarded, the value of whose example was worth more to the Union than the money value of both Charleston and Columbia. . . . Wishing you and yours all possible happiness, and with a grateful remembrance of the days long gone in Charleston and on Cooper River, I am sincerely yours, W. T. Sherman."

Petigru is reputed to have told his grandchildren that he would not be remembered, but if he were it would be as a "good lawyer." He became well known to history, however, as "the Union man of South Carolina," the one brave patriot who withstood the popular tide. Lacy Ford wrote that it is "certainly ironic, that no public figure's memory was more cherished by postbellum Charleston, that cradle of the Confederacy, than that of James Louis Petigru, the diehard Unionist and devoted Charlestonian."

James L. Petigru's famous epitaph, written with the help of George Bancroft, Robert Winthrop, and Charles Dana, so moved President Woodrow Wilson that he had the postmaster in Charleston cable it to him at Versailles at the end of World War I:

JAMES LOUIS PETIGRU

Born at
Abbeville May 10th. 1789,
Died at Charleston March 9th. 1863.

JURIST, ORATOR, STATESMAN,
PATRIOT.

Future times will hardly know how great a life
This simple stone commemorates,—
The tradition of his Eloquence, his
Wisdom and Wit may fade;
but he lived for ends more durable than fame.
His eloquence was the protection of the poor
and wronged
His Learning illuminated the principles of
Law—
In the admiration of his Peers,
In the respect of his People
In the affection of his Family,
His was the highest place;
The just meed

Of his kindness and forbearance.
His dignity and simplicity
His brilliant Genius and his unwearied
industry,
Unawed by Opinion,
Unseduced by Flattery
Undismayed by disaster.
He confronted Life with antique Courage
And Death with Christian Hope.

In the great Civil War
He withstood his People for his country,
But his People did homage to the Man
Who held his conscience higher than their
praise;
And his country
Heaped her honours on the grave of the
Patriot,
To whom, living,
His own righteous self-respect sufficed,
Alike for Motive and Reward.

IRISH-AMERICAN CHARLESTONIANS AND THE CIVIL WAR

Irish Charlestonians loyally supported the Confederacy, and several Charleston Irish-American companies joined the Confederate Army. The Charleston Meagher Guard, named for a famous Irish-American soldier, changed its name to the Emerald Light Infantry when Meagher became a general in the Union Army. McGowan's Brigade was the first Confederate colors to enter Gettysburg. The Irish Volunteers fought valiantly in numerous battles. It is said they were the first company to volunteer for the duration of the war. William H. Ryan, a native of Charleston, served as first lieutenant of the Irish Volunteers and then as captain of the Charleston Battalion. He was a hero of the Battle of Secessionville but was killed in the brutal 1863 assault on Battery Wagner.

Irish Charlestonians also served on the submarine *Hunley,* which one historian claims was designed by an Irishman, J. R. McClintock. The crew of the ironclad *Chicora* included a McCarthy, a McGovern, a McQuinn, a Noonan, a Scanlon, a Conrad, a Cleary, and a Kelly. Captain John C. Mitchell of the First Regiment, S.C. Artillery, was an Irish-American whose dying words at Fort Sumter on July 20, 1864, inspired his comrades: "I willingly give my life for South Carolina. Oh, that I could have died for Ireland."

The Charleston Irish community was especially proud of the Irish Volunteers. The students at the Academy of Our Lady of Mercy made a flag, which the bishop, Patrick N. Lynch, presented in the Cathedral. It was described as follows:

> The ground of its face is white, watered silk, in the center of which is the emblem of Old Erin—the Irish Harp wrought most exquisitely in raised gold work adorned with brilliants. Encircling the harp is a wreath of needlework, representing the oak, the olive and the native shamrock of Ireland . . . over the wreath . . . eleven stars—the number [of] states in the Confederacy, and above in gold letters are the words 'Erin go Bragh.' The reverse was a green field with a palmetto and crescent in white.

achieved. He who would now seek to drag down him who is struggling, if not a traitor, is first cousin to one; for he is striking the most deadly blows that can be [struck]. He who would attempt to promote his own personal ends . . . is not worthy of the Confederate liberty for which we are fighting.

Davis prayed "for each and all, and above all for the sacred soil of Charleston." Young Gus Smythe agreed with the President. "I don't think the Yankees will ever get into Charleston," he wrote in November, 1863.

In his remarks and speeches Davis pointedly snubbed General Beauregard, whose brilliant defense of Charleston certainly merited praise. This aspect of Davis's personality was most unfortunate for the Confederacy, and his treatment infuriated Beauregard, who declined to have dinner with the president. Davis, he said to a friend, "has *killed* my enthusiasm for our holy cause!"

Despite the bombardment, Davis enjoyed his week-long stay in Charleston. He had last come to the city in 1850, in the company of other dignitaries, for the funeral of his fellow senator John C. Calhoun. Now he relaxed and dined with members of a frayed and dying but nevertheless charming Charleston aristocracy. He enjoyed his reception at council chambers following his speech. He especially enjoyed former Governor William Aiken's hospitality at his mansion at 48 Elizabeth Street, on Wragg Square. (The William Aiken House still stands; it is owned today by the Charleston Museum.) "Beauregard, Rhetts, Jordan to the contrary notwithstanding," Mary Chesnut wrote, "Mr. Aiken's perfect old Carolina style of living delighted [Davis, as did] those old grey-haired darkies and their automatic, noiseless perfection of training."

It was one of the last moments of the Old South for Jefferson Davis, William Aiken, and the Charleston aristocracy.

THE BISHOP OF CHARLESTON AND THE CONFEDERACY

Patrick N. Lynch was consecrated as the Catholic bishop of Charleston on March 14, 1858, in the Cathedral of St. John and St. Finbar on Broad Street, which burned in the Great Fire of 1861. It was the first consecration of a new bishop in Charleston.

Bishop Lynch's appointment was a popular one. He had been a priest for eighteen years and was a favorite speaker. "Father Lynch preached and his sermon impressed me profoundly," William T. Sherman, then a lieutenant, wrote home from Fort Moultrie in the 1840s.

The Catholic community staunchly supported the Confederacy. "Long years of menace, insult, outrage and unconstitutional aggression have been at last brought to a close by the event—the election of a Black republican President," the diocesan newspaper, the *U.S. Catholic Miscellany,* editorialized on Lincoln's election.

Bishop Lynch was active in support of the Confederacy. He said a mass for the Meagher Guard at Castle Pinckney on December 26, 1860. He presented the Irish Volunteers with their new flag, saying as he did so, "Peace is a blessing. It is a blessing for which we all pray to heaven; while it is a blessing not always granted. When granted we return our thanks for it; when it is withheld, we bow before the will of heaven, and strive to do our duty."

The Great Fire of 1861 burned the Catholic cathedral. The siege of Charleston forced Bishop Lynch and his secretary to move to St. Joseph's, in Ansonborough. St. Mary's Church, on Hasell Street, the mother church of Catholicism in the South, was struck by Federal shells on several occasions. Few parishioners could attend church in downtown Charleston.

When Jefferson Davis visited Charleston in November, 1863, Bishop Lynch accompanied him on his tour of fortifications. The bishop had been particularly active and helpful in the exchange of prisoners between Charleston and the Federal forces on Morris Island. Dr. Craven later recalled the exchange in a book:

Bishop Patrick Lynch, the spiritual leader of South Carolina's Catholics at the time of the Civil War. Born in Ireland, Bishop Lynch immigrated to South Carolina in 1819. In 1840 he was ordained as a priest in Rome. In 1857 he was appointed vicar-general and was consecrated bishop in 1858. He was bishop in Charleston for twenty-four years, and he served as the Confederacy's special envoy to the Vatican.

"The Bishop had been extremely kind, receiving the blessing of our boys, who spoke in warm terms of his Christian humanity. So far as I could judge from the specimen, our wounded had not anything to complain of in their treatment. At least nothing which the necessities of this situation rendered unavoidable."

In 1864 Bishop Lynch was asked to come to Richmond to discuss with the Confederate secretary of state the possibility of obtaining the Vatican's recognition of the Confederacy. The bishop accepted the assignment and left Charleston for Rome with the title Special Commissioner of the Confederate States of America to the States of the Church. He ran the blockade from Wilmington in April, 1864; Conrad Wise Chapman, on furlough to visit his family in Rome, was a fellow passenger. Lynch reached Rome in June, 1864, and met with Pope Pius IX. The pope, however, felt he "could not say anything directly to conform and strengthen slavery" and would not give diplomatic recognition to the Confederate States, so Bishop Lynch's mission failed. Before he could return from Rome, the war was lost.

CHAPTER 7

SHERMAN MARCHES AND CHARLESTON SURRENDERS

In December, 1864, Jacob Schirmer said in his diary, "The circumference of the Confederacy appears to be getting smaller every day—and our enemies are exalting. . . . From all reports starvation is almost before us." Susan Middleton now wrote to her sister Harriott, in Flat Rock, North Carolina, about "consolation parties" in Charleston where everyone sang psalms until midnight, "when the band begins to play and the company dances till daylight." As to the city itself, she noted that "they say not a pane of glass is to be found in Broad Street." In fact, the siege of Charleston had failed in its main goal: the capture of the city. It went on much longer than the generals could have imagined, and as Stephen R. Wise pointed out, the "results were inconclusive. The reason for the failure was that neither the plan nor the leaders had proven flexible. . . . In the Spring of 1863, Fort Sumter was the key to Charleston, but by the Summer, Sullivans Island had become the main harbor defense." Sullivan's Island had become an impregnable fortress, and Fort Sumter, like a mirage in the desert, had evaporated as a significant military target. The siege succeeded, however, in blockading the port, tying up a large number of Confederate troops, and boosting Northern morale.

On December 24, 1864, General Sherman confidently wrote to General Grant that his strategy for South Carolina, the home of secession, was to keep the Confederates in doubt as to his real objective. Sherman reasoned that after he crossed the Savannah River, whether his object was Augusta or Charleston, the Confederates would divide their forces; he would then ignore both Charleston and Augusta and occupy Columbia. "Charleston" he told Grant, "is now a mere desolated wreck, and is hardly worth the time it would take to starve it out."

Writing to his sister in December, Gus Smythe could not believe Sherman might appear in Charleston. In September, 1864, he had felt the Confederacy might still win, especially if McClellan was elected president. Lincoln, he thought, could be elected only by military interference. "So do not give way yet, dear Mother. I believe there are many, very many happy days yet in store for you and Father here in old Charleston." By December, however, he was writing, "The city is full of wild rumors of all kinds & about everything. No one tho', seems to know anything about Sherman, save that he is near Savannah & Hardee not fighting him. The city is under the strictest martial law. No one is allowed to leave it without permission from Hd. Qrs., not even the Provost Martial's [sic] pass being respected. So we are in for a siege anyhow. We shall have stirring times here until Sherman is disposed of, & if they let him get to the coast, we shall have plenty to do.

So we are in no danger of rusting out just now."

The siege of Charleston had gone on and on. Rowena Reed described it in *Fighting For Time* as the longest campaign of the Civil War. It was also a losing campaign for the Union forces. In May, 1864, General Gillmore had given up and asked to be reassigned. Major General John G. Foster succeeded him and tried to take the city, defended by 5,000 Confederates, with his 15,000-man army. Both Fort Sumter and Fort Moultrie were still very much in operation in the summer and fall of 1864. In July, 1864, 2,500 men under Brigadier General Hatch landed on Johns Island in an attempt to draw troops from Fort Johnson. Then 500 Union troops attempted a surprise attack on Fort Johnson, which was, as the Federals hoped, undermanned. The attack failed, however, because of logistical problems of tides and channels. But the Confederacy was in desperate need of men.

Thus by December, 1864, General Sherman and his massive army were close by. Charleston waited in anticipation. The general was quite familiar with the Charleston area, having been stationed at Fort Moultrie for four years in the 1840s. He believed the Confederate general in charge of Charleston's defense, William J. Hardee, would probably evacuate Charleston, but that if it were attacked by way of "the neck back of Charleston" the city would be "impregnable to assault, and we will hardly have time for siege operations."

C hristmas night, Mother, but oh, how different from what it used to be.
From a letter by Augustine Smythe to his mother, December 25, 1864.

The siege of Charleston continued unabated into January, 1864. This view shows the ongoing bombardment of the city from Fort Putnam, the name the Union Army gave the former Confederate Battery Gregg on Cummings Point, Morris Island, in honor of Colonel Haldiman S. Putnam, who was killed in the assault on Wagner. Putnam thought the charge at Wagner was foolish, but he said at the time, "Seymour overruled me. Seymour is a devil of a fellow for dash."

Should you capture Charleston, I hope that by some accident the place may be destroyed, and if a little salt should be sown upon its site it may prevent the growth of future crops of nullification and secession.
—General H. W. Halleck to General Sherman, December 1864.

I will bear in mind your hint as to Charleston, and do not think "salt" will be necessary. When I move, the Fifteenth Corps will be on the right of the right wing, and their position will naturally bring them into Charleston first; and, if you have watched the history of that corps, you will have remarked that they generally do their work pretty well. The truth is, the whole army is burning with an insatiable desire to wreak vengeance upon South Carolina. I almost tremble at her fate, but feel that she deserves all that seems in store for her.

Many and many a person in Georgia asked me why we did not go to South Carolina; and, when I answered that we were en route for that State, the invariable reply was, "Well, if you will make those people feel the utmost severities of war, we will pardon you for your desolation of Georgia."

I look upon Columbia as quite as bad as Charleston, and I doubt if we shall spare the public buildings there as we did at Milledgeville.
—General Sherman to General Halleck, December 24, 1864.

Sherman's Seventeenth Army Corps crossing the South Edisto River on pontoons, February 9, 1865. "We must all turn amphibious," he wrote, "for the country is half under water."

There was apparently some debate in the administration as to whether Sherman should occupy and destroy Charleston or Columbia. The general's correspondence indicates that his superiors were torn between Charleston's lack of military importance and its symbolic value. "I am aware," Sherman wrote, "that, historically and politically, much importance is attached to the place." He said in his memoirs that he was authorized to march his army north and decided to secure a foothold or starting point on the South Carolina side, designating Pocotaligo and Hardeeville as the points of rendezvous for the two wings of his army. He remained in doubt, however, about the wishes of the administration as late as January 2 on whether he should take Charleston or continue to break up the railways of South and North Carolina and unite his forces with those of General Grant before Richmond. On January 29, 1865, Sherman wrote Grant that Admiral Dahlgren wanted to launch another combined army and navy assault on Fort Moultrie, "but I withhold my consent, for the reason that the capture of all Sullivans Island is not conclusive as to Charleston; the capture of James Island would be, but all pronounce that impossible at this time." Beauregard's defense of Charleston still held, even though Beauregard was no longer there.

Charlestonians were convinced that Sherman was going to march on Charleston. "Our affairs are gloomy indeed," Schirmer wrote in his diary on January 27, 1865. "Sherman with his army has succeeded to pass thro' Georgia with no interruption and he is now moving on thro' So. Car. and there is no doubt there is plenty of trouble ahead for us and I know not what our armies are about." Governor Andrew G. Magrath, whose resignation as Federal judge in 1861 so electrified the public, called on Jefferson Davis to abandon Richmond and save Charleston. He wrote the president, "The force on the coast is not sufficient to make effectual resistance to General Sherman. If that is so, Charleston falls; if Charleston falls, Richmond follows. Richmond may fall and Charleston be saved, but Richmond cannot be saved if Charleston falls." Sherman recalled in his memoirs, "The fact was, that General Hardee, in Charleston, took it for granted that we were after

WILLIAM TECUMSEH SHERMAN AND CHARLESTON

General William Tecumseh Sherman was Lieutenant Sherman in the United States Army of the 1840s. He was stationed at "that dream of any lieutenant's heart," Fort Moultrie, on Sullivan's Island in Charleston harbor, from June, 1842, to May, 1846. While he was there the young lieutenant enjoyed all the social amenities of the island and the city and learned to paint with watercolors. It was also in Charleston that Sherman began his study of the law. He eventually left the army and went on to become a lawyer before he reenlisted as a colonel when the Civil War began.

Sherman wrote his brother in 1843:

When they move to Charleston and the country, they send invitations which must be accepted, or give offence. The consequence was that two or more of us had to go constantly as representatives of the whole, —always in rotation, unless duty or pleasure coincided, when a greater number would cross the water. These parties are very various, from the highly aristocratic and fashionable, with sword and epaulettes, or horse-racing, picnicing, boating, fishing, swimming, and God knows what not. A life of this kind does well enough for a while, but soon surfeits with its flippancy, —mingling with people in whom you feel no permanent interest, smirks and smiles when you feel savage, tight boots when your fancy would prefer slippers.

In his letters home, Sherman evinced a great affection for the Southern way of life: "It is impossible to appreciate any blessing or pleasure without being separated from it a while," wrote Sherman. It is "one of the neatest cities in this country, policed to perfection and guarded by soldiers, enlisted by the State, who enforce order with the Bayonet. . . . Never does any riot or disturbance occur in the streets, never are you disturbed by crowds about the doors of inns or brothels, nor roused from sleep by their yells." He did however, complain about the heat: "Florida is a Greenland to this," he wrote to his stepbrother Philemon Ewing. "It is hot as hell."

The future Yankee general who marched to the sea found slavery to be perfectly acceptable: "The Negroes are well-dressed & behaved, never impudent or pushing and so far as I can judge feeling very lightly indeed the chains of bondage that we read of. Servants are treated with remarkable kindness and in no instance would I see a difference in them and ours of the north were it not for the market place where they are exposed for sale. I am no advocate of slavery as a means of wealth or national advancement, yet at the same time I know that the idea of oppression and tyranny that some people consider as the necessary accompaniment of slavery is a delusion of their own brain."

At first Lieutenant Sherman apparently did not understand the local customs when it came to courting. He found himself in an embarrassing situation when he went for a buggy ride with a Charleston lady and then refused to marry her. People thought they were engaged, he wrote Ewing, since "to ride side by side with a lady in a buggy shows an intimacy that could only subsist between persons in that condition."

Sherman was not known for his strong opinions in those days. He was sent on one occasion to make peace among a group of quarreling officers, and he stopped a duel between Braxton Bragg, then a lieutenant but later to become a Confederate general, and a journalist who had insulted Bragg's native North Carolina by calling it "a strip of land lying between two states." Ironically in hindsight, Sherman was friendly with Captain Robert Anderson, his old instructor at West Point. "With this Kentucky-born officer he stood on the battlements and watched cotton ships from the North dump their ballasts of rock at a certain point in the shallows not far from them, across the water. Army engineers were building there a new fort to be named Sumter," wrote Lloyd Lewis in *Sherman The Fighting Prophet.*

There will always be a healthy suspicion that Sherman did not "march to the sea" in South Carolina and burn Charleston because of his affection for people he once knew well and liked a great deal. Consciously or unconsciously, he may have wanted to avoid desecrating Charleston. His public statements, private letters, and memoirs are all consistent, however, in making the point that Charleston was already a wreck. In addition, Lee had not surrendered, and neither Grant nor Sherman knew for sure that Lee could be defeated without Sherman's army.

There is an oral tradition in Charleston that Sherman spared the city because he was in love with a Charleston lady. The same tale, however, is told in Augusta, Georgia, the other city which Sherman appeared to threaten in order to divide the remnant of the Confederate army.

General William Tecumseh Sherman was stationed at Fort Moultrie on Sullivan's Island in the 1840s and remembered fondly his days in the South. He closed a letter to James L. Petigru's daughter in 1888 "with a grateful remembrance of the days long gone in Charleston and on Cooper River." Sentimentality, however, did not prevent Sherman from wreaking havoc in South Carolina.

Alfred R. Waud's drawing of Sherman's troops crossing the Little Salkehatchie River in the South Carolina Lowcountry.

Charleston; the rebel troops in Augusta supposed they were 'our objective'; so they abandoned poor Columbia to the care of Hampton's cavalry, which was confused by the rumors that poured in on it, so that both Beauregard and Wade Hampton, who were in Columbia, seem to have lost their heads."

Obviously, Charlestonians believed, Charleston was more important than Columbia, and obviously Sherman would want to destroy the one city that, more than any other, began the war. Local citizens of all classes and descriptions therefore packed up their valuables and sent them to Columbia for safekeeping. Practically every person, family, group, or organization, including religious congregations from St. Michael's Episcopal Church to the Kahal Kadosh Beth Elohim Jewish Temple, later had a story about how important papers and valuable objects were destroyed because they had been sent to Columbia for safekeeping. James L. Petigru had taken his daughter Caroline's silver to Columbia in 1861 "and safely deposited [it] in the vault of the Commercial Bank." The bank was burned and the silver lost. Sherman himself had a good story. It seems he found himself in Cheraw, South Carolina, and was invited to lunch by General Blair at the occupied home of a blockade runner. In the dining room, the table was spread with an excellent meal. When Sherman requested wine, General Blair served him some and asked, "Do you like it?" Sherman did. He insisted on knowing where the wine came from, but Blair was mysterious. Later Blair sent to Sherman's bivouac a case containing a dozen bottles of the finest Madeira wine Sherman had ever tasted. "I learned," Sherman recalled, "that he had captured, in Cheraw, the wine of some of the old aristocratic families of Charleston, who had sent it up to Cheraw for safety, and heard afterward that Blair had

Plate 13

The U.S.S. Niagara *(in the foreground to the right) was the first warship sent to block the port of Charleston. In early 1861 the* Niagara *was in Japan, sent there by a pro-Southern secretary of the navy under President Buchanan. The vessel swiftly returned to take up the boring but important task of keeping war matériel out of the Confederacy and preventing cotton from leaving the port of Charleston. The* Niagara *was a steam-powered frigate which had helped lay the first transatlantic cable in 1854, an event which this contemporary engraving illustrates. Designed as an oceangoing craft, the* Niagara *found it difficult to come close to shore.*

Plate 14
The Economist, *a blockade runner, shown leaving Charleston in this 1864 painting by William York. To the left is Fort Sumter.*

Plate 15
The Stone Fleet, an idea of Gustavus V. Fox, consisted of sixteen whalers from New England sunk in Charleston harbor in December, 1861, to block shipping, and thirteen more sunk in January, 1862. The tides carried all twenty-nine away. Robert E. Lee, commanding Confederate troops in South Carolina, was appalled at what he termed the "malice & revenge" of the Northerners.

Plate 16

*The ironclad attack on Fort Sumter, April 7,
1863. "The ironclads," Shelby Foote wrote, "might
indeed be invincible; some said so, some said not;
but one thing was fairly certain. The argument was
likely to be settled on the day their owners tested
them in Charleston harbor." The forts won. This
colorful and somewhat exaggerated version of the
great battle was printed by Currier & Ives.*

Plate 17
A view of Charleston harbor, Fort Sumter, and
Sullivan's Island (to the left) by Frank Vizetelly,
looking from Fort Johnson on James Island in
February, 1863.

Plate 18
*The sinking of the Union ironclad Keokuk
in April, 1863, which sealed Admiral
Samuel F. DuPont's decision to end his
attack on Charleston. Later, General
Beauregard ordered the heavy cannons of
the Keokuk salvaged in 18 feet of water.*

Plate 19
The famous charge of the Massachusetts 54th on Battery Wagner. The charge, said the New York Tribune, "made Fort Wagner such a name for the colored race as Bunker Hill has been for ninety years to the white Yankees."

Plate 20
Conrad Wise Chapman's panoramic view of Fort Moultrie in November, 1863. The ironclad fleet battered the fort throughout the fall of that year. There was a constant bombardment of all of the harbor forts until the end of the war.

Plate 21
Chapman's view of Charleston harbor from Fort Johnson on James Island. The Chicora *and* Charleston, *two ironclads, are in the foreground; Castle Pinckney is at the right; the city of Charleston is in the background.*

Plate 22
*White Point Battery, also known as Battery
Ramsay, at White Point Gardens in Charleston.
There were numerous batteries on the peninsula,
constituting an "inner ring" of defenses.*

Plate 23
*Battery Marion on Sullivan's Island was an
intermediate work between Battery Bee and Fort
Moultrie.*

Plate 24
The Confederate flag is lowered at sunset on a defiant Fort Sumter in 1863. Conrad Wise Chapman painted this inspiring view of the fort and the City of Charleston in the background. Another version of this view was painted by John Gadsby Chapman, Conrad's father, from Conrad's sketch.

Plate 25
The Laurens Street battery in the city of Charleston by Conrad Wise Chapman. This battery was located on the peninsula on the Cooper River near present-day Calhoun Street. Fort Sumter is in the background; Sullivan's Island is to the left.

Plate 26
William Aiken Walker's famous view of the
ironclad attack on Fort Sumter in 1864 as seen
from the Battery.

Plate 27

The Confederate submarine H. L. Hunley *was named for its designer, Alabama lawyer Horace L. Hunley. It is shown in this painting by Conrad Wise Chapman on a wharf at Mt. Pleasant, near Charleston harbor. Some called the vessel "Fish" or "Porpoise" for obvious reasons. Twenty-five volunteers, including Hunley, died in test runs. The* Hunley *did, however, prove successful on February 17, 1864, when it sank the U.S.S. Housatonic. This encounter is regarded by historians as the first successful submarine attack in history, though the* Hunley *was only partially submerged at the time. Unfortunately, the* Hunley *sank as well, killing its final crew.*

Plate 28
A bird's-eye view of James Island and Lighthouse Inlet. The Federal ships are shown sailing into the inlet to support the Union invasion. Morris Island is to the right; the City of Charleston is top center.

Plate 29

The 55th Massachusetts Infantry Regiment marches down Broad Street after Charleston's evacuation by Confederate troops in February, 1865. They sang "John Brown's Body" and were greeted joyously by many black Charlestonians. White Charlestonians, however, agreed with diarist Jacob Schirmer that "God has left us to work out our own destruction."

Plate 30
Fort Sumter after the war.
Painting by Seth Eastman.

Plate 31
The Charleston Market in 1872. The city was still occupied by the Union Army. Its recovery astonished Robert E. Lee in 1870. In this 1872 painting one sees a Union officer, a black policeman, and liberated black Charlestonians. Much of the damage from the war seems to have been repaired.

found about eight wagon-loads of this wine, which he distributed to the army generally, in very fair proportions." Incredibly, Sherman also noticed a soldier with a silver pitcher belonging to the Petigru family and had it sent to Petigru's daughter, Caroline, then in New York.

In February, 1865, Charleston was the "mere desolated wreck" Sherman had described. Susan Middleton reported to Harriott that the "houses in the lower part of town are constantly broken open and plundered." The lower half of the city was now totally uninhabited. "To one walking through," one Charlestonian later recalled, "it seemed more like a city of the dead than anything else." As Gus Smythe described it in one of his last letters from Charleston, "No law down in this part of town now. Assaults every night or so. The other night they robbed a man here, just at our door, & another night pulled our Courier off his horse, robbed him, & then put him on again & sent him off. It is horrible; the lawless state of old Charleston, formerly so orderly." Some Charlestonians felt betrayed by those who had led them to this unhappy pass. Smythe said, "My! My! But the people do curse Jeff Davis now! And the Mercury! is it not savaged?" Jacob Schirmer wrote, "We are cut off from all communication. . . . Total ruin is staring us in our faces."

Charleston was abandoned by the Confederate Army in February, 1865, following General Sherman's capture of Atlanta and then Savannah in December, 1864. The March to the Sea was naturally expected—as late as February 11, 1865—to lead to the Cradle of Secession, but ironically, the lowcountry's natural geography protected her from General Sherman just as it has protected her from twentieth-century highways which would have destroyed her coast. Sherman bypassed Charleston for the same reason Interstate 95 bypasses Charleston today: it is out of the way if one is going north to Richmond. Sherman bogged down marching through the lowcountry marshes. "We must all turn amphibious," he wrote, "for the country is half under water." Instead he headed inland toward Columbia. "If I am able to reach certain vital points," he said, "Charleston will fall of itself."

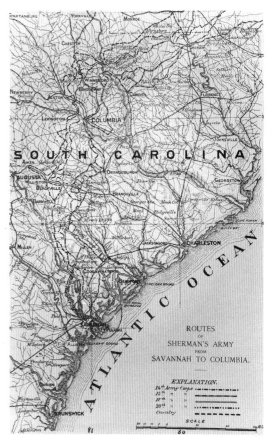

The route of Sherman's army from Savannah, Georgia, to Columbia, South Carolina. Sherman bypassed Charleston for the same reason Interstate 95 does today: he was on his way to Richmond, Virginia. In any case, by this time he considered Charleston "a mere desolated wreck," as he described it to General Grant in December, 1864.

A view from Fort Johnson looking toward Castle Pinckney in Charleston harbor after the war.

On the morning of February 17, 1865, the Confederates at Fort Sumter raised a brand-new flag. That evening it was lowered for the last time. The Confederate defense of Fort Sumter, "a feat of war unsurpassed in ancient or modern times," according to Major John Johnson, was at an end. The city was evacuated. Emma Holmes wrote, "The City's being evacuated! I am afraid Charleston is doomed. . . . Fires rage all over the City, cotton is burned in the parks to prevent it falling into enemy hands. The depot [is] crowded with furniture to its capacity. The trains are more crowded than ever. . . . Poor old Charleston . . . after she has withstood the assault for so long and now we must leave her to these wretches." The soldiers left later, under cover of darkness. General Hardee ordered the evacuation. The next day no flag appeared over Sumter; the fort which had received the first shot of the war was again in Federal hands. "And thus after a siege which will rank among the most famous in history," a Union officer wrote, "Charleston became ours." Rowena Reed concluded, "And so the siege ended. For twenty-two months Charleston's harbor outposts held against an ironclad fleet and a superior army. While geography, aided by Confederate tenacity and skill, favored the defense, the Federals often failed to press their attacks. Too much reliance was placed on the physical and moral impact of bombardment. Union Army leadership changed too often, and troops were not the best. The monitors, designed for brief ship-to-ship engagements, held up badly during extended service against shore batteries, and the admirals were too reluctant to risk ships in an all-out push to the city. Finally, the strategic priorities of the Northern high command lay elsewhere. Yet at one time the Charleston campaign was the only Civil War action seriously studied in Europe. It remains one of the war's most interesting chapters."

This battle on February 9, 1865, in which James Island fell to Union troops, was one of the final ones in and around Charleston.

The American flag is raised over the ruins of Fort Sumter by Captain H. M. Bragg of Gillmore's staff. Note Charleston burning in the background.

The city was occupied by Union troops on February 18. Befitting Charleston's history, a small child lit a fire near a large stockpile of powder left at a railroad station by the Confederate Army. Hardee had ordered the burning of torpedo boats, naval vessels, and cotton warehouses. A Blakely cannon at White Point Gardens, weighing 38 tons, was exploded so that it would not fall into enemy hands. The debris was scattered over the neighborhood, and a 500-pound piece of metal ended up in the roof of the Roper House, 9 East Battery, where it remains today. Soon a great fire began near the Cooper River. On the other side of town, the Ashley River bridge was intentionally burned, and it, too, started a major fire. The fires soon met in the center of the peninsula. Emma Holmes heard from a friend that the flames were so great "one could almost see to read on James Island." As Milby Burton succinctly put it in *The Siege of Charleston*, "The night of February 17–18 was one of horror and chaos, undoubtedly the worst ever experienced in the history of the city . . . with evacuation a certainty [the cotton piled in public squares] was set on fire . . . casting an eerie glow over the entire city." The city was at the mercy of roving mobs and looters and was rocked by explosions from a magazine on Sullivan's Island and from the destruction of the gunboats *Palmetto State* and *Chicora*. Schirmer wrote, "If these records should . . . be preserved, may my descendants never forget the diabolical atrocities committed by those who once were considered friends and brethren."

Benjamin Quarles in *The Negro in the Civil War* describes the surrender this way: "While the proud metropolis—the Confederate Holy of Holies—still smoldered, the Union forces took possession of the harbor defenses—Forts Sumter, Ripley, and Moultrie, and Castle Pinckney—which had so valiantly withstood all previous efforts." At ten in the morning, Lieutenant Colonel A. G. Bennett, of the Twenty-first U.S. Colored Troops, arrived in Charleston and demanded that the mayor formally surrender, which he immediately did. The African-American troops helped put out fires and restore order. The Union lawyer Charles Cowley recalled years later, "Never, while memory holds power to retain anything, shall I forget the thrilling strains of the music of the Union, as sung by our sable soldiers when marching up Meeting Street with their battle stained banners flapping in the breeze."

Gradually more Federal troops arrived. Some looted. Some tried to restore order. The 55th Massachusetts Colored Regiment, among others, paraded down the streets of Charleston. The old Citadel became a Federal fort. The Miles Brewton House, once used by the British occupying army, now became the Union headquarters.

The looting continued for months, despite some half-hearted Federal efforts to reestablish law and order. General Gillmore wrote to General Hatch in Charleston, "I hear on all sides very discouraging accounts of the state of affairs in Charleston; that no restraint is put upon soldiers; that they pilfer and rob houses at pleasure; that large quantities of valuable furniture, pictures, statuary, mirrors, etc., have mysteriously disappeared."

The caption of this drawing from a contemporary newspaper reads, "Enthusiastic crowd of citizens of Charleston, South Carolina, assembled on Vanderhost's Wharf, February 20 [1865], to greet the second visit of General Gillmore and staff." It is apparent, however, that while the Federal soldiers and black Charlestonians are "enthusiastic," some white Charlestonians are not so happy.

Susie King Taylor was a former slave who escaped in 1862 when the Union Army arrived near her home in Savannah, Georgia. She went along with her uncle, who had joined a black regiment on Port Royal Island, and for the remainder of the war served as an army laundress and nurse. She accompanied her unit, the First South Carolina Volunteers, later the 33rd U.S. Colored Troops, to Morris Island, Battery Wagner, and into defeated Charleston at the end of the war. She worked side by side with Clara Barton, the heroic nurse who was one of the founders of the American Red Cross.

This is her firsthand account of the occupation of Charleston on February 28, 1865:

On February 28, 1865 the remainder of the regiment were ordered to Charleston, as there were signs of the rebels evacuating that city. Leaving Cole Island, we arrived in Charleston between nine and ten o'clock in the morning, and found the "rebs" had set fire to the city and fled, leaving women and children behind to suffer and perish in the flames. The fire had been burning fiercely for a day and night. When we landed, under a flag of truce, our regiment went to work assisting the citizens in subduing the flames. It was a terrible scene. For three or four days the men fought the fire, saving the property and effects of the people, yet these white men and women could not tolerate our black Union soldiers, for many of them had formerly been their slaves; and although these brave men risked life and limb to assist them in their distress, men and even women would sneer and molest them when ever they met them.

Susie King Taylor, former slave who escaped slavery and worked in the Union Army as a nurse. In 1902 she published her Reminiscences of My Life in Camp, *one of the few memoirs of its kind.*

SENATOR WILSON AT THE GRAVE OF ROBERT Y. HAYNE

Previous to sailing, I took a walk with Senator Wilson to the churchyard of St. Michael's Church, and showed him, in a thicket, covered with brambles and weeds, the grave of the eloquent Hayne, the antagonist of Webster, Wilson's own predecessor in the Senate, in the great Nullification Debate of 1830. Neither of us spoke for some minutes. Words had lost their power, as we stood by the grave of that apostle of secession, and gazed on the ruin which his doctrines had brought upon the city of his love.

Tears filled Mr. Wilson's eyes, and his features bore the evidence of strong emotion as he stood thoughtful, silent, motionless, as if rivetted to that charmed spot. At length, I broke the silence by saying that, if I only had the power of a painter, I would try my hand on a scene which, in the hands of a good artist, would live for centuries. "What do you mean?" inquired Wilson. "Why, I would take for my subject 'The Successor of Daniel Webster at the Grave of Robert Y. Hayne!'" "It would be good," Wilson rejoined. "I would not have missed this for all there is in Charleston besides!"
—Charles Cowley, Esquire, in his memoirs, *Leaves from a Lawyer's Life Afloat and Ashore* (1879)

Sidney Andrews, a Northern reporter for the *Boston Advertiser* and the *Chicago Tribune,* came to Charleston in September, 1865. This is what he saw:

A city of ruins, of desolation, of vacant houses, of widowed women, of rotting wharves, of deserted warehouses, of weed-wild gardens, of miles of grass-grown streets, of acres of pitiful and voiceful barrenness, —that is Charleston, wherein Rebellion loftily reared its head five years ago, on whose beautiful promenade the fairest of cultured women gathered with passionate hearts to applaud the assault of ten thousand upon the little garrison of Fort Sumter!

Physically, the city *was* in ruins. The damage done by the Great Fire of 1861 had never been repaired. The bombardment of the city below Calhoun Street had left a virtual ghost town. The destruction was unimaginable. Mrs. Ravenel recorded what she saw:

Everything was over-grown with rank, untrimmed vegetation. Not grass merely, but bushes, grew in the streets. The gardens looked as if the Sleeping Beauty might be within. The houses were indescribable: the gable was out of one, the chimneys fallen from the next; here a roof was shattered, there a piazza half gone; not a window remained. The streets looked as if piled with diamonds, the glass lay shivered so thick on the ground.

Another visitor recorded her impressions in April:

The splendid houses are all deserted, the glass in the windows broken, the walls dilapidated, the columns toppled over . . . arches demolished, mantels shattered, while fragments, great and small, of every description strew the floors . . . but where are the owners of these estates—where are they? Fled— . . . they are fugitives and vagabonds, wandering up and down the interior mountains and plantations of South Carolina. . . . upon some houses, we found placards to the following effect: "To be occupied by the owner, who has taken the oath of allegiance to the United States."

Charlestonians, of course, survived, but their way of life was forever altered. For the white aristocratic elite, civilization was almost at an end. "No one in the country in which you live," Williams Middleton wrote his sister in Philadelphia, "has the slightest conception of the real condition of affairs here—of the utter topsy-turveying of all of our institutions." Most of the former slaves had run away or refused to work. Nathaniel Russell Middleton, Jr., recalled,

After . . . the announcement to the negro population that they were free by the virtue of the Emancipation Proclamation, the servants, with few exceptions, left their masters. Considering the excitement of the times and the many reasons why they might have behaved far worse, I think the verdict must be that they did not act badly. Many of them doubtless had some real or supposed grievance, and it is not surprising that exceptions occurred, but on the whole they stood the test well. Our servants were respectful and affectionate to the last, but they all announced that they were going . . . and having said good-bye, took their departure.

Middleton Place, like many other estates, had been burned by Union troops. Governor Aiken had to abandon "his elegant mansion," one diarist noted, "for one a little out of range of Gilmore's guns." Capital was nonexistent. Family fortunes, invested in

Meeting Street near the Battery after the war. It appears the Confederate Army was building a fortification in the middle of Meeting Street.

The celebration of Emancipation Day in Charleston, January 8, 1877, twelve years after the Civil War. Charleston's African-American community continued to celebrate with parades and festivities similar to those of April, 1865. The top frame of this contemporary newspaper shows participants assembling at the old Citadel on Calhoun Street. The middle frames depict people watching the parade, the Boy Drum Corps, thirteen young ladies dressed to represent the thirteen original states, and members of the Union League. The bottom frame depicts the reading of the Emancipation Proclamation on the Battery. Note the presence of black police officers and firemen.

This is an excerpt from "Our Women in the War, the Lives they Lived; the Deaths they Died," published in the *Charleston News & Courier* in 1885. The writer is Mrs. Pauline Dufort, who was one of a number of Charleston women who contributed to this series of reminiscences of the war. She describes the city during the bombardment and at the end of the war.

The city was now deserted from the Battery to Calhoun street. Grass and moss were growing upon the crumbling walls, and all that was required to intensify the horror of the desolation was the cry of the voracious hyena. Save the occasional whiz and crash of a shell, there was nothing to break the monotony of the silence drear and the mute angel kept sentinel over all.

. . . I was requested by the bereaved widow to play the Requiem at [St. Mary's] church, and though anxious to oblige her, I hesitated when I thought of the danger. She pleaded and assured me no harm would come for God, who was ever good, would hear her prayers for our safety. Yielding to her entreaties I started, in company with my husband and my little boy of seven summers, for the church. While waiting for the doors to be opened a shell fell in front of the Charleston Hotel, but did not explode. This was somewhat of a relief, for it was a rare thing to have two shells strike in the same place on the same day. It was apparent that the artillerymen shifted their guns a little every time they fired. The funeral services were concluded without any further annoyance, but just as my husband was closing the organ another whiz was heard, then a flash was seen, followed by a tremendous explosion. A shell had burst in the rear of the graveyard. We were glad to hurry away, and a week later St. Mary's organ was smashed by a shell.

My mother owned the large bakery on East Bay below Broad street, and as that section was in a better condition than other portions of "Shell district" we turned our steps in that direction. On reaching the place we found the bakers at work, and learned that the baking was done in the day time, as the danger was less—the shelling being heavier at night. Sixteen shells had already struck the building but no one had been hurt and the oven was still fit for use. One of the shells, like Truth, lies hidden in the bottom of the well. The master of the establishment made us quite welcome, and as a token of his appreciation presented us with a hot loaf of bread, all he had to offer. On our return we sat down on the steps of the bank, at the corner of East Bay and Broad streets, and ate our dry bread with a gusto more easily imagined than described. How strange! How unlike those *ante-bellum* times, when our care was to guard against a surfeit of foreign and domestic luxuries. I could not refrain from remarking to my companion: "When in after years we tell our children that we sat on these stone steps eating dry bread, for the want of something better, they will hardly believe us."

Union troops guard City Hall in 1865. Note tree-lined Broad Street.

East Battery in 1865. An exploded Blakely gun destroyed by retreating Confederates lies in the street.

The King Street Battery, White Point Garden, as it appeared after the surrender of Charleston in 1865.

Confederate bonds or currency, had disappeared. D. E. Huger Smith recalled, "It must be remembered that money simply did not exist in the South. Our plantations had been seized by the conquering Government; every bank in Charleston had lost its capital; every railroad in the South had been smashed; every industrial enterprise had been destroyed." Townhouses were looted by Union troops and criminals of both races. People took what work they could find. Hall T. McGee, who had served with Captain George Lamb Buist in the Palmetto Guard, wrote later that he had "returned from the Army a beggar and in rags." Lieutenant General Richard H. Anderson worked in the railroad yards. The James Heyward family took in sewing. D. E. Huger Smith worked as a porter in a wholesale establishment "at a dollar a day and all the cheese I could eat." Other Charleston aristocrats rented rooms in once fashionable homes or ran boarding schools. Some drove streetcars; others became tellers in banks. Others tried to get their plantations back in production. Slowly life began to return to some new kind of order. The poverty and even outright hunger in the first year after the surrender were grinding.

There was bitter resentment of the occupying army, worsened, if that were possible, by the fact that the army was largely black. Mrs. Francis J. Porcher wrote a friend,

> Nat Fuller, a Negro caterer, provided munificently for a miscegenat dinner, at which blacks & whites sat on an equality, & gave toasts and sang songs for Lincoln & freedom. Miss Middleln [*sic*] and Miss Alston, young ladies of colour, presented a coloured regiment with a flag on the Citadel green, and nicely dressed black sentinels turn back white citizens, reprimanding them for their passes not being correct.

D. E. Huger Smith recalled in later years, "During the bitter years of misrule, miscalled 'Reconstruction,' many of us who survived believed that those who died in the flush of

Citizens of Charleston taking the oath of allegiance to the United States. The city was under martial law, in the charge of Brigadier General Alexander Schimmelfennig, a Prussian immigrant. He established his headquarters in the Miles Brewton House at 27 King Street, the same building that had been chosen as headquarters by the commander of the occupying British Army in 1780, during the American Revolution.

A view of the Mills House from Queen Street, taken in 1865. The destruction in this picture was caused by the Great Fire of 1861.

Battery Ramsay (or White Point Battery) in 1865.

JUDAH P. BENJAMIN

It is interesting, and a little mysterious, that the two most prominent men in the Confederate government with any connection to Charleston were both outsiders to Charleston society. The secretary of the treasury, Christopher Memminger, was foreign-born and an orphan. Judah P. Benjamin, successively attorney general, secretary of war, and secretary of state, was born in Saint Thomas, British West Indies, and grew up in Charleston. In the words of his biographer, Eli Evans, Benjamin "achieved greater political power than any other Jew in the nineteenth century—perhaps even in all American history." Jefferson Davis called him "a master of law and the most accomplished statesman I have ever known." He was Davis's closest supporter in Richmond and, according to some historians, the Confederate president's alter ego. Historians often refer to Benjamin as the Brains of the Confederacy.

The Benjamin family was of Spanish Jewish ancestry. Judah Benjamin's parents migrated to the West Indies and then the Carolinas. By 1822 they were living in Charleston, where Benjamin grew to young adulthood. Philip Benjamin, Judah's father, became an American citizen in 1825; he probably took the oath of citizenship in the Federal courtroom at the county courthouse on Broad Street. The Benjamin family was poor and struggling; Philip Benjamin ran a dry goods store at 165 King Street. Though he was an active member of the Reformed Society of Israelites at Beth Elohim Synagogue on Hasell Street, the family was not observant; their store was open on Saturday, the Jewish Sabbath. The elder Benjamins had a tumultuous marriage and eventually separated. Philip Benjamin was buried in a Jewish burial ground in Charleston, probably the old Da Costa Cemetery on Hanover Street, which is no longer in existence.

The future Confederate statesman undoubtedly was perceived early in life as brilliant. Tradition has it that he was educated in the private academy of Rufus Southworth on St. Michael's Alley through the generosity of the Hebrew Orphan Society and Moses Lopez, its president. The headquarters of the society still stands at 88 Broad Street, and the Hebrew inscription is still visible on the second story.

In 1825, at the age of fourteen, Judah Benjamin matriculated at Yale. It has been reported that his tuition was paid by some benefactor, either Lopez or "a lady from Massachusetts." Quitting Yale in 1827, Benjamin set off from Charleston with five dollars in his pocket, bound for New Orleans to make his fortune. There he clerked in a commercial house, tutored the children of the well-to-do, and, in 1833, married a Creole aristocrat, Natalie St. Martin. He studied law and wrote a book on the law of Louisiana that greatly enhanced his career. He rose to national prominence as a lawyer for large commercial interests, was elected to the United States Senate in 1852 (the second Jew to be elected to that body), and was reelected in 1858.

As a senator, Benjamin defended slavery. In this he was not unique among Americans of Jewish ancestry. Rabbi Morris J. Raphall of New York had preached a sermon, "The Bible View of Slavery," in which he argued that the Ten Commandments supported slavery. Benjamin Wade, an abolitionist senator from Ohio, lambasted Senator Benjamin: "I have listened with intense interest," said he, "as I always do to the eloquent speech of my friend, the Senator from Louisiana—an Israelite with Egyptian principles." An ardent secessionist, Benjamin ably defended Southern rights. He made one of the most brilliant speeches of any of the departing Southern senators.

Benjamin served only briefly as the Confederacy's first attorney general, becoming secretary of war in September, 1861. He failed miserably in that role, although it should be said of him, as it was of Memminger, that he had been given an almost impossible assignment. Davis next appointed him secretary of state, a job to which Benjamin gave all of his considerable energy and intellect. He set up spy rings in Canada, organized acts of terrorism, wooed the great Jewish bankers of Europe on behalf of the Confederacy, and tried to persuade both Napoleon III and the British prime minister to intervene in the war. It all ended in failure.

In 1865, after Lee's surrender, Secretary of State Benjamin departed Richmond with the presidential party. After a harrowing four-month flight to avoid capture, which included hiding in swamps, traveling in disguise, and taking passage on a ship which sank not long after sailing, Benjamin arrived in London bereft of assets or an occupation. He studied law again, was admitted to practice, wrote another classic law treatise, and began yet another legal career, this time as an English barrister. He became phenomenally successful and beloved at the English bar. Years later he saw Varina and Jefferson Davis again on their visits to London.

Benjamin died in 1884 in Paris, where his estranged wife lived. He is buried there in Père Lachaise cemetery.

Judah P. Benjamin, successively attorney general, secretary of war, and secretary of state of the Confederacy, lived in Charleston in his youth. His father operated a dry goods store on King Street, and young Judah was educated at a private academy on St. Michael's Alley. When he was United States senator from Louisiana, he was described by Senator Wade of Ohio as "an Israelite with Egyptian principles"—a reference to Benjamin's defense of slavery.

MUSTERING OUT THE FIRST SOUTH CAROLINA VOLUNTEERS, THE FIRST AFRICAN-AMERICAN TROOPS IN AMERICAN HISTORY

General Order,
No. 1.

Comrades: The hour is at hand when we must separate forever, and nothing can take from us the pride we feel, when we look upon the history of the "First South Carolina Volunteers," the first black regiment that ever bore arms in defense of freedom on the Continent of America. . . .

Soldiers, you have done your duty and acquitted yourselves like men who, actuated by such ennobling motives, could not fail; and as the result of your fidelity and obedience you have won your freedom, and oh, how great the reward! It seems fitting to me that the last hours of our existence as a regiment should be passed amidst the unmarked graves of your comrades, at Fort Wagner. Near you rest the bones of Colonel Shaw, buried by an enemy's hand in the same grave with his black soldiers who fell at his side; where in the future your children's children will come on pilgrimages to do homage to the ashes of those who fell in this glorious struggle. . . .

Officers and soldiers of the 33d U.S. Colored Troops, once the First So. Carolina Volunteers, I bid you all farewell!

By order of

Colonel C. T. Trowbridge,
Commanding regiment.

In modern-day Charleston, members of the African-American community do indeed make a pilgrimage to Morris Island every year.

hope for their country, and of self-sacrifice for duty, were to be envied by us, who were facing daily for eleven years rancorous ill-treatment, and supercilious and contemptuous oppression."

For black Charlestonians, civilization was not at an end; it was just beginning. They would not have disagreed with Williams Middleton's remark about the "utter topsy-turveying of all our institutions." The difference was that they were happy about it. Slavery was at end. The Day of Jubilee had arrived. Charleston was now the Promised Land. The gloom and doom which pervaded white aristocratic Charleston were unknown in black Charleston. It was a time of celebration.

And celebrations were frequent. On March 3, 1865, a huge crowd of black Charlestonians assembled at Marion Square and watched as thirteen black women, elegantly dressed to symbolize the thirteen original states, presented the Union commander with a flag, a bouquet of flowers, and a fan for Mrs. Lincoln. On March 4 Major Martin R. Delany, editor, explorer, and the highest ranking African-American military officer in the army, arrived in Charleston. On March 29 one of the largest parades ever held in Charleston began at noon. Four thousand blacks participated. There were companies of soldiers, tailors, coopers, 50 butchers, 1,800 schoolchildren and their teachers, 8 companies of firemen, sailors, and many other tradesmen. Most dramatically there followed two carts, one carrying an auction block and an "auctioneer" selling two black women and their children. The other carried a coffin with signs proclaiming the death of slavery and that "Sumter dug his grave on the 13th of April, 1861." Other celebrations took place in Zion church.

The greatest celebration was held on April 14, 1865, when Robert Anderson returned to Charleston to raise the garrison flag he had taken with him on that fateful day in April, 1861. President Lincoln had been invited to attend but could not. He sent a letter which was read later that evening. The president had a great deal on his mind. He had wired the secretary of war, Edwin Stanton,

> I feel quite confident that Sumter fell on the 13th, and not the 14th of April, as you have it. It fell on Saturday, the 13th; the first call for troops on our part was got up on Sunday, the 14th, and given date and issued on Monday, the 15th. Look up the old almanac and other data and see if I am not right.

Stanton changed the date, but as it turned out, Lincoln's memory was inexplicably in error, and the correct date was soon substituted.

The secretary of war had begun planning for this celebration weeks before. On March 27, he had written General Order No. 50:

> ORDERED—
>
> *First.* That at the hour of noon on the 14th day of April, 1865, Brevet Major General Robert ANDERSON will raise and plant upon the ruins of Fort Sumter, in Charleston harbor, the same United States flag which floated over the battlements of that Fort during the rebel assault, and which was lowered and saluted by him and the small force of his command when the works were evacuated on the 14th day of April, 1861.

GEORGE A. TRENHOLM

George A. Trenholm was born in Charleston in 1807. His father died young, and Trenholm left school in order to support himself. He was employed by John Fraser & Company, cotton exporters and shippers. Working his way up the company's ladder, he became the principal owner and senior partner in 1853. On the eve of the Civil War, he was believed to be the wealthiest man in the South. His vast holdings included hotels, plantations, shipping companies, commercial buildings, steamships, warehouses, and cotton presses. His home was Ashley Hall, now a private girls' school of the same name, at 172 Rutledge Avenue. He owned, among other things, the Planter's Hotel, now the Dock Street Theatre.

Trenholm was described as "the absolute master of local banking, and the cotton trade." He was a director of the Bank of Charleston and was regarded as one of the great financial minds of the South. He and Christopher Memminger were friends. He was also actively involved in politics, serving in the South Carolina General Assembly from 1852 to 1856.

When the Civil War began, Trenholm offered his services. He assisted in the production of ironclad boats to defend Charleston and paid personally for the construction of twelve small offensive craft. His companies became the virtual European bank of the Confederate government. Fraser, Trenholm and Company in Liverpool held and disbursed Confederate funds for boatbuilding and arms purchases, assisted in procuring loans for the Confederate government, and generally advanced the Southern cause.

Trenholm was one of the originators of blockade running and accumulated great wealth in that pursuit, according to Stephen Wise, author of *Lifeline of the Confederacy* and the leading modern authority on blockade running. At one time during the war he owned as many as fifty ships. He carried necessities for general consumption as well as more profitable items.

Most Southerners believed Trenholm to be an outstanding patriot despite the great profits he reaped from blockade running. He was appointed secretary of the treasury of the Confederacy to succeed his friend Memminger in June, 1864, when the currency was already collapsing.

When the war ended in April, 1865, Trenholm fled with Jefferson Davis and his party to Greensboro, North Carolina, and then to Fort Mill. He was arrested and taken to Fort Pulaski. Later he was pardoned and resumed his business activities in Charleston. In 1867 his companies were involved in bankruptcy proceedings. After the war, the federal government sought to take his property through litigation—claiming, ironically, that he had failed to pay import and export duties during the war. There were rumors for years about the missing Confederate treasury and that Trenholm, the last secretary of the treasury, took a large suitcase of gold with him when he left Richmond.

Trenholm remained popular with the people of Charleston. He was elected to the General Assembly again in 1874 as a Democrat while the Reconstruction era Republicans controlled the state. He died in 1876.

The Reverend A. Toomer Porter thought Trenholm "the greatest man who ever lived" in Charleston. "He had his ships, and his word in Broad Street and on East Bay was law."

George A. Trenholm, shipping tycoon and businessman. He ran the South's largest blockade-running companies, helped finance the Confederacy, and became secretary of the treasury of the Confederate States of America late in the war. There are those who believe that Margaret Mitchell based her fictional hero, Rhett Butler, on Trenholm.

Second. That the flag, when raised, be saluted by one hundred guns from Fort Sumter, and by a National salute from every fort and rebel battery that fired upon Fort Sumter.

Third. That suitable ceremonies be had upon the occasion, under the direction of Major General WILLIAM T. SHERMAN, whose military operations compelled the rebels to evacuate Charleston, or, in his absence, under the charge of Major General Q. A. GILLMORE, commanding the Department. Among the ceremonies will be the delivery of a public address by the Reverend HENRY WARD BEECHER.

Fourth. That the naval forces at Charleston, and their Commander on that station, be invited to participate in the ceremonies of the occasion.

BY ORDER OF THE PRESIDENT OF THE UNITED STATES:

EDWIN M. STANTON,

Secretary of War.

The Federal fleet, which had taken four years to prevail, ran up their most colorful flags for the occasion.

The city closed down for the festivities. Three thousand African Americans went to Fort Sumter to watch the ceremonies. Robert Smalls was there with the *Planter*. John G. Nicolay, President Lincoln's secretary, was there. Major Delany and his son, a soldier in the Massachusetts 54th, were there. Denmark Vesey's son was there. Leading abolitionists, including Henry Ward Beecher and William Lloyd Garrison, were there. Beecher, Harriet Beecher Stowe's brother, shared the platform with another leading abolitionist, Theodore Tilton. (In later years Beecher created a national scandal by having an affair with Tilton's wife.) Just after noon, Sergeant Hart, the man who had lowered the tattered flag four years earlier, raised it again. "As the banner reached its apex," Benjamin Quarles wrote, "the acclamation became ear-splitting. The bay thundered with the roar of cannon from ship and shore." The harbor was filled with boats, large and small. A steamer had bought down a large contingent of visitors from the North.

General Robert Anderson, tired and broken at age sixty, spoke:

> I am here, my friends, my fellow citizens, and fellow soldiers, to perform an act of duty to my country dear to my heart, and which all of you will appreciate and feel. Had I observed the wishes of my heart, it should have been done in silence; but in accordance with the request of the honorable Secretary of War, I make a few remarks, as by his order, after four long, long years of war, I restore to its proper place this flag which floated here during peace, before the first act of this cruel Rebellion. I thank God that I have lived to see this day, and to be here to perform this, perhaps the last act of my life, of duty to my country.

In his speech, Beecher, who had been burned in effigy in Charleston four years earlier, called for national unity and education for black South Carolinians. He blamed the war on "the polished, cultured, exceedingly capable and wholly unprincipled ruling aristocracy who wanted to keep power." He also congratulated President Lincoln:

> On this solemn and joyful day, we again lift to the breeze our father's flag, now, again, the banner of the United States, with the fervent prayer that God would crown it with honor, protect it from treason, and send it down to our children, with all the blessings of civilization, liberty and religion. Terrible in battle, may it be beneficent in peace. . . . We offer to the President of the United States our solemn congratulations that God has sustained his life and health under the unparalleled burdens and sufferings of four bloody years, and permitted him to behold this auspicious occasion of that national unity for which he has waited with so much patience and fortitude, and for which he has labored with such disinterested wisdom.

Later in the evening there were a ball, a supper, and fireworks. General Anderson made a toast to the president: "I beg you, now that you will join me in drinking the health of . . . the man who, when elected President of the United States, was compelled to reach the seat of government without an escort, but a man who now could travel all over our country with millions of hands and hearts to sustain him. I give you the good, the great, the honest man, Abraham Lincoln."

That same night, in Washington, Abraham Lincoln was assassinated.

In Trinity Church of New York City the Reverend Dr. Francis Vinton . . . construed the latest inscrutable events: "President Lincoln had arrived at the end of his mission. On the very day not only of our Lord's crucifixion, but the day on which the raising of the flag over Sumter typified the resurrection of the nation, God had said to him, 'Well done, thou good and faithful servant, enter thou into the joy of the Lord.' It may be that President Lincoln was unfitted by the natural gentleness and humanity of his disposition, to execute the stern justice of Christ's viceregent. And so let us say, "God's will be done."
—Carl Sandburg, *Abraham Lincoln, The War Years*

The raising of the American flag at Fort Sumter on Good Friday, April 14, 1865, four years to the day after it was lowered by Major Anderson. President Lincoln's secretary, John G. Nicolay, was in Charleston for the event, along with a host of Northern dignitaries. The flag was lowered to half-mast after Lincoln's assassination the following day.

Robert Anderson, whose reluctant devotion to duty had helped begin the Civil War, was there on April 14, 1865, to raise his old flag as a symbolic end to "this cruel rebellion." Anderson died six years later.

The Race Course Prison, also called the Fair Grounds Prison, was, at the time of the Civil War, located on the outskirts of the city, and consisted of about forty acres. The area is now Hampton Park. According to a former prisoner, it was "without shelter, except such as might be constructed from garments and blankets." This illustration from Harper's Weekly shows the cemetery as it appeared in 1867. It gained notoriety when the first Union Memorial Day ever was held in Charleston at this cemetery on May 1, 1865. Lincoln's assassination had prompted James Redpath, a northerner living in occupied Charleston, to organize a march to the thousands of Union graves. The mourners brought arms full of flowers. "News of this observance," Lloyd Lewis wrote, "came North through the army and spread as the soldiers, mustured out, passed to their homes through the summer of '65." After the war, the Union dead were removed to the National Cemetery in Beaufort, South Carolina.

EPILOGUE

On the day following the flag-raising ceremonies at Fort Sumter, an immense throng crowded the African Church to greet and hear William Lloyd Garrison, George Thompson, Senator Henry Wilson of Massachusetts, and others from the North who had crusaded against slavery. Before the war, Garrison had been the most hated man in Charleston except perhaps John Brown himself. Because thousands were unable to gain admittance, another meeting had to be held at Citadel Square. "There was one scene in the church . . . which those who witnessed it will never forget," a Union officer recalled. "It was that of the eloquent natural orator, Samuel Dickerson, and his two daughters, full-blooded blacks, and emancipated slaves, presenting to the brave old Garrison a wreath of the most beautiful flowers of that semi-tropical climate, together with a welcome to Charleston, and the thanks and benedictions of their race. . . . Mr. Garrison's unstudied speech, —'I have been an out-law, with a price set upon my head, for thirty years, for your sakes; but I never expected to look you in the face, or that you would ever hear of anything I might do in your behalf.'" It was the moment antebellum Charleston had always dreaded.

Thirty-two years later, on May 31, 1897, on a grey and misty Decoration Day (now called Memorial Day), a crowd of people both black and white met on the steps of the Massachusetts capitol in Boston to unveil the Robert Gould Shaw monument. It was a bas-relief statue showing Colonel Shaw on horseback leading the first African-American soldiers into battle, on Morris Island near Charleston harbor. The sculptor, Augustus Saint-Gaudens, wrote later (around 1905) of the surviving old soldiers of the Massachusetts 54th who had returned for the dedication:

> The impression of these old soldiers passing the very spot where they left for the war so many years before, thrills me even as I write these words. They seemed as if returning from the war, the troops of bronze marching in the opposite direction—the direction in which they left for the front, the young men in the bas-relief showing these veterans the hope and vigor of youth. . . . It was a consecration.

The renowned psychologist and author William James also spoke. His younger brothers Robertson and Wilkinson had fought at Battery Wagner and had been wounded there. He said,

> And this, fellow citizens, is why, after the great generals have had their monuments, and long after the abstract soldiers'-monuments have been reared on every village-green, we have chosen to take Robert Shaw and his regiment as the subjects of the first soldiers'-monument to be raised to a particular set of comparatively undistinguished men. The very lack of external complication in the history of these soldiers is what makes them represent with such typical purity the profounder meaning of the Union Cause.

*The Robert Gould Shaw Monument by Augustus
Saint-Gaudens on the Boston Common (to the left)
is a monument to both the "Black rank and file"
and the "White officers taking life and honor in their
hands." This 1897 photograph shows the veterans
of the Fifty-Fourth Massachusetts attending the
dedication of the memorial.*

We do not, as the black race, properly appreciate the old veterans, white or black, as we ought to. I know what they went through, especially those black men, for the Confederates had no mercy on them; neither did they show any toward the white Union soldiers. I have seen the terrors of that war. I was the wife of one of those men who did not get a penny for eighteen months for their services, only their rations and clothing.

—Susie King Taylor, *Reminiscences of My Life in Camp with the 33d United States Colored Troops Late 1st S.C. Volunteers* (1902)

The monument at White Point Gardens to the defenders of Fort Sumter was dedicated on October 20, 1932. Eight thousand Charlestonians attended. So did the last Confederate veteran of Fort Sumter still living in Charleston.

Finally, the leading African American in the South, Booker T. Washington, spoke. The *Boston Evening Transcript* reported his talk:

> You could see tears glisten in the eyes of the soldiers and civilians. Then the orator turned to the coloured soldiers on the platform, to the colour-bearer of Fort Wagner [Sgt. William H. Carney], who smilingly bore still the flag he had never lowered even when wounded, and said: "To you, to the scarred and scattered remnants of the Fifty-Fourth, who with empty sleeve and wanting leg, have honoured the occasion with your presence, to you, your commander is not dead. Though Boston erected no monument and history recorded no story, in you and the loyal race which you represent, Robert Gould Shaw would have a monument which time could not wear away."

Thirty-five years after that ceremony in Boston, on October 20, 1932, the people of Charleston dedicated a monument at White Point Gardens, the Battery, to the Confederate defenders of Fort Sumter. Though the speakers were not so eloquent or so famous as those in Boston had been, the feelings of the orators and their audience were as strong. Many present had fathers, uncles, and grandfathers who had fought in what many still called "the Confederate War." The sculptor Herman A. MacNeil said of the monument, "Its motif in brief, is that the stalwart youth, standing in front with sword and shield symbolizes by his attitude the defense not only of the fort, but also of the fair city behind the fort in which are his most prized possessions, wife and family. And she, the wife, glorified into an Athena-like woman, unafraid, stands behind him with arms outstretched toward the fort, thus creating an inseparable union of the city and Fort Sumter."

Just as the Union veterans of Fort Wagner returned to Boston in 1897, so the last Confederate veteran of Fort Sumter still living in Charleston in 1932, Colonel William Robert Greer, attended this ceremony. He described the heroic defense of the fort and praised Andrew B. Murray, the philanthropist who bequeathed $100,000 to the city to help fund the monument. There was never "at any time any lack of courage," Colonel Greer said, "but a determination unalterable that this great Gibraltar of Charleston should never be captured or surrendered. . . . There were many flags shot down in the fort during the siege, but before the force embarked for the city the commander, the gallant and intrepid [Thomas A.] Huguenin, removed the standard and consigned it as a sacred relic to the care of the Sumter Guards, where it is held in perpetue with love and veneration."

The monument was unveiled by four young ladies, all descendants of members of the Confederate garrison of the fort: the granddaughter of Colonel Alfred Rhett, the first commanding officer of Fort Sumter; the granddaughter of Captain Thomas A. Huguenin, the last Confederate commander; the grandniece of Major Stephen Elliott, second in command under Colonel Rhett; and the granddaughter of Major John Johnson, a member of the Confederate Engineers and author of *The Defense of Charleston Harbor*. Two ushers placed on the monument the last Confederate flag which flew over Fort Sumter. "The young ladies," the *News & Courier* reported, "then placed on the base of the monument two wreaths of red and white carnations."

The main speaker was Gerald W. Johnson, a writer and journalist from Baltimore who was in the process of writing a book about the start of the war, *The Secession of the Southern States*. He defended the Confederacy and the protectors of Fort Sumter. "They were told

began my return on the 2d of May. We went into Charleston Harbor, passing the ruins of old Forts Moultrie and Sumter without landing. We reached the city of Charleston, which was held by part of the division of General John P. Hatch, the same that we had left at Pocotaligo. We walked the old familiar streets—Broad, King, Meeting, etc.—but desolation and ruin were everywhere. The heart of the city had been burned during the bombardment, and the rebel garrison at the time of its final evacuation had fired the railroad depots, which fire had spread, and was only subdued by our troops after they had reached the city.

I inquired for many of my old friends, but they were dead or gone, and of them all I only saw a part of the family of Mrs. Pettigru. I doubt whether any city was ever more terribly punished than Charleston, but, as her people had for years been agitating for war and discord, and had finally inaugurated the civil war by an attack on the small and devoted garrison of Major Anderson, sent there by the General Government to defend them, the judgment of the world will be, that Charleston deserved the fate that befell her.

—*Memoirs* of William Tecumseh Sherman (1875)

The Palmetto flag raised on Fort Sumter after the surrender of Major Anderson in 1861. It was the first flag raised on Sumter and is pictured here in the hands of John Styles Bird in 1899. This picture was taken during the reunion of Confederate veterans in Charleston.

They each went up and signed the paper, and the deed was done, which cost millions and millions of money, tens of thousands of lives, destruction of cities and villages, plantations and farms, the emancipation of five millions of African slaves, the entire upheaval of society, the impoverishment of a nation; and let loose a demoralization which has left its impress on the whole land, North and South. It was a deed which made the North rich and the South poor, and has made Southern life one great struggle from that day to this.

—The Reverend A. Toomer Porter writing in his memoirs, *Led on, Step by Step* (1898), on the signing of the Ordinance of Secession in 1861

Augustine Smythe, the young Confederate soldier, as an older man.

that the fight was a fight in defense of their liberties," he exclaimed, "and they believed it. This was their motive, this was their incentive: and for this ideal they laid their good lives down."

One can only imagine the pride, the sadness, and perhaps the bitterness felt by the 8,000 Charlestonians gathered on the Battery that day. The monument itself was, like the Shaw memorial, a monument to lost youth. It was also a monument to a gallant fight for liberty and freedom. As President Lincoln had said in his second inaugural address, "Both read the same Bible, and pray to the same God; and each invokes His aid against the other. . . . The prayers of both could not be answered."

Charleston's role in the war had been remarkable. The Civil War began there when the political fabric of the nation tore irrevocably at the Democratic Party national convention in April, 1860. It began militarily with the first shot at Fort Sumter. Though Charleston was not a main theater of the war, it was center stage for the long, slow-motion opening act of the great drama and the anticlimactic closing act of the flag-raising ceremony of April 14, 1865. Indeed, this ceremony had been intended by President Lincoln and Secretary of War Stanton to capture the nation's attention and bring a symbolic end to the war. But it was upstaged by a much bigger news story, Lincoln's assassination. Charleston was the site of the opening act of the war for African-American troops in 1863 at the Battle of Battery Wagner and a preview of the military genius of General Robert E. Lee.

Many of the main characters of the war were in Charleston at one time or another before, during, and after that event. William Tecumseh Sherman was stationed at Fort Moultrie beforehand and visited afterward; Lee was in command of the area in 1861 and 1862; General Beauregard's finest moments were in his defense of Charleston; Judah Benjamin was raised in Charleston; two secretaries of the treasury of the Confederacy, Memminger and Trenholm, were Charlestonians; Jefferson Davis traveled to Charleston during the siege of the city in 1863; and Ulysses S. Grant visited shortly after the war, in December, 1865, on an inspection tour.

The crushing defeat of the city which was once so proud is now impossible to imagine. Abner Doubleday reflected on that pride in his *Reminiscences of Forts Sumter and Moultrie*. "It was an hour of triumph for the originators of secession in South Carolina," he wrote of the opening of the war, "and no doubt it seemed to them the culmination of all their hopes; but could they have seen into the future with the eye of prophecy, their joy might have been turned into mourning." The abolitionist leader Wendell Phillips asked, "Can you conceive a bitterer drip that God's chemistry could mix for a son of the Palmetto State than that a Massachusetts flag and a colored regiment should take possession of Charleston?" These memories were blotted out of the city's collective mind as the nineteenth century gave way to the twentieth.

Even so pious and decent a man as the Reverend A. Toomer Porter could not bear the thought of the military occupation of Charleston by black troops. He came back to Charleston after the war to find his house at the corner of Rutledge Street and Spring taken over by the Union Army and the Freedman's Bureau, his furniture stolen, and all his worldly possessions gone. Porter, an Episcopal priest, had to enter his own home forcibly. He had no money and no food.

He went downtown the next day to post a notice about a service about his church. On his way through the market, he met George Shrewsbury, a black butcher he had known before the war. He told Shrewsbury of his plight.

Later that evening George Shrewsbury appeared at Porter's house. The butcher had come to offer the priest a hundred dollars in greenbacks with which he had intended to buy cattle. "To think that a gentleman in my position had no money was an idea he could not take in," Porter recalled. He declined the loan, as he had no security to offer. Shrewsbury insisted, saying that refusal would imply that the offer had been a liberty on his part. Porter finally replied, "I will give you my note for it." "I do not wish your note, sir," Shrewsbury responded. "You know you owe it, and I know it; when you can return it I know you will. If you never can do it, it will be all the same; I am paid enough in knowing that I have added to your comfort." Porter later recalled, "I confess my eyes were not dry; first, from the thought that I should be in the condition to need such aid, and next that it should come from one not in my own sphere, nor even of my own race. Money was then worth in Charleston anything the most extortionate chose to ask." Porter could not repay the hundred dollars for eighteen months, but when he returned the last five of it, he offered to pay Shrewsbury interest. "You owe no interest," the butcher told the priest. "I have been abundantly repaid in feeling I was the means of relieving you in a sore time of need, and whenever you wish it again it is at your disposal."

And what of that young Confederate soldier Gus Smythe? He went on to become a successful lawyer and lived to a ripe old age. According to the *News & Courier*, he entertained a party of distinguished Confederate veterans at the reunion of Confederate veterans in Charleston in 1899, and his wife, as president of the United Daughters of the Confederacy, led the effort in that same year to erect a memorial at White Point Gardens to the men lost in the first submarines. The monument stands there today.

Nothing remains of Battery Wagner. Much of Morris Island has washed away. Paul Hamilton Hayne wrote in 1886, "One who visits Morris Island to-day will vainly search for a solitary fragment of the grand old Confederate earth-work. The winds, with unseen, ethereal fingers, have twisted up the former foundations, and with stormy breath have blown the ancient boundaries afar." The sea has carried off the remains of Colonel Shaw and his men. Fort Sumter is now Fort Sumter National Monument, and Fort Moultrie too is a part of the National Park Service.

And Gus Smythe's perch, the steeple of St. Michael's Church? It stands there still, towering over the old forts, still as Henry James described them in 1905, "faintly blue on the twinkling sea . . . like vague marine flowers."

The Confederate memorial at Magnolia Cemetery.

Ode at Magnolia Cemetery
Henry Timrod

Sleep sweetly in your humble graves,
Sleep, martyrs of a fallen cause;
Though yet no marble column craves
The pilgrim here to pause.

In seeds of laurel in the earth
The blossom of your fame is blown,
And somewhere, waiting for its birth,
The shaft is in the stone!

Meanwhile, behalf the tardy years
Which keep in trust your storied tombs,
Behold! your sisters bring their tears,
And these memorial blooms.

Small tributes! but your shades will smile
More proudly on these wreaths to-day,
Than when some cannon-moulded pile
Shall overlook this bay.

Stoop, angels, hither from the skies!
There is no holier spot of ground
Than where defeated valor lies,
By mourning beauty crowned.

On April 26, 1870, an aged and infirm Robert E. Lee, traveling from Florida to Virginia, stopped over in Charleston for a visit. The *Courier* reported the event on April 28, 1870:

Yesterday afternoon, after the engines had dismissed from the parade, the various white companies in the department, assembled in Meeting-street, procured a band, and proceeded to call upon General LEE. Arrived there, loud calls were made for the old veteran; and, in obedience to the cheers, the General stepped out upon the portico. He was introduced to Chief NATHAN and the Board of Fire Masters by Major E. WILLIS. Brief remarks were made by Chief NATHAN, Messrs. W. A. KELLY, A. T. SMYTHE, F. L. O'NEILL, and Hon. C. G. MEMMINGER, the latter responding in behalf of the General. This, however would not satisfy the enthusiastic firemen, who continued to cry for "Just one word," and in obedience to their loud demands, the General thanked them for their kind attention, and pleaded his indisposition as an excuse for his silence. The procession then moved off, and quietly disbanded.

The next day the *Courier* reported:

A grand reception on Wednesday night, at the residence of W. J. BENNETT, Esq., bore testimony, ample and grateful, of the veneration and affectionate esteem in which ROBERT E. LEE, the great chief of the (so-called) "Lost Cause," is held by the *elite* of our people. From 8 P.M. to 12, there was no cessation of the overflow of comers. Old and young, the grey beards and sages of the country, the noble, pure, honorable, poor and wealthy, with hardly an exception, were present, and glad to do him honor. Stately dames of the old school, grand-mothers of seventy, and a long train of grand-daughters, all flocked around the noble old chief, glad of a smile, of a shake of the hand; and happy was the girl of twelve, or fourteen, who carried away on her lips the parting kiss of the grand old soldier. Such has been his welcome in Charleston, but O! how much more fervent it would have been, had his health been sufficient to have permitted him to yield himself freely to the popular anxiety to see him, feel the pressure of his hand, and hear his words, however few, in those subdued and mellow tones which declare the gentleman. . . .

Among the visitors present, we noted two of the Secretaries of President DAVIS' cabinet, the Honorables Messrs. MEMMINGER AND TRENHOLM;—and the Hon. Judge BRYAN, District Judge of the United States, did not conceive it inconsistent with his loyalty, to do reverence to the great man in seclusion! . . .

But the tributes of the ladies were even more profuse than those of the gentlemen. Very beautiful was the collection, and it spelled the eye and charmed the senses of the veteran. He remarked: "It is so grateful to see so much elasticity among your people; and I am astonished to see Charleston so wondrously recuperated after all her disasters."

General Lee died six months later.

Robert E. Lee a week after the surrender of his army, photographed by Mathew Brady. Lee was beloved by all Southerners, including Charlestonians, who flocked to get a glimpse of him in 1870 when he came through their city on his way from Florida to Virginia.

SELECT BIBLIOGRAPHY

The literature on the Civil War is immense. It comprises more than 50,000 books and pamphlets, excluding those devoted to the prewar years. To list each work that discusses Charleston's role in the war or each work relied on in writing this book would require listing hundreds of general works. This bibliography, therefore, lists only the significant works relied upon by the author. Each of them contains important information on and analyses of Charleston during the Civil War era. These works are also listed in the index under both title and author.

The most comprehensive and the best history of the Civil War yet written is the work of Allan Nevins, *Ordeal of the Union*, 8 vols. (New York: Charles Scribner's Sons, 1947–71). Each volume has a different title, and each is cited herein by its individual title, such as *the Emergence of Lincoln* or *The War for the Union*. The best modern one-volume history of the Civil War is James M. McPherson's *Battle Cry of Freedom: The Civil War Era* (New York: Oxford University Press, 1988), a volume of the Oxford History of the United States series. Other excellent general histories of the War are Shelby Foote's three-volume work, *The Civil War: A Narrative* (New York: Random House, 1958, 1963, 1974); Bruce Catton's three-volume work, *The Centennial History of the Civil War* (New York: Doubleday, 1961–65) (*The Coming Fury* [1961], *Terrible Swift Sword* [1963], and *Never Call Retreat* [1965]); Emory M. Thomas, *The Confederate Nation 1861–1865* (New York: Harper & Row, 1979); R. U. Johnson and C. C. Buel (eds.), *Battles and Leaders of the Civil War*, 4 vols. (New York: Century, 1884–87); and William C. Davis (ed.), *The Image of War*, 6 vols. (Garden City, N.Y.: Doubleday, 1981–88). A good old-fashioned Southern volume is E. Merton Coulter's *The Confederate States of America 1861–1865* (Baton Rouge: Louisiana State University Press, 1950), vol. 7 of the series *A History of the South*. A classic work on the literature of the period is Edmund Wilson's *Patriotic Gore: Studies in the Literature of the American Civil War* (New York: Oxford University Press, 1962).

Because this work is illustrated, I am indebted to the many authors of illustrated and photographic histories of the war. Johnson and Buel's *Battles and Leaders* and Davis's *The Image of War* (both noted in the previous paragraph) contain excellent and classic drawings and photographs. Other fine illustrated histories are Geoffrey C. Ward, *The Civil War: An Illustrated History* (New York: Alfred A. Knopf, 1990); Richard M. Ketchum (ed.), *The American Heritage Picture History of the Civil War* (New York: Doubleday, 1960); Gerald Simons (ed.), The Time-Life Civil War Series, especially *Brother against Brother: The War Begins* (Alexandria, Va.: Time-Life Books, 1983); *First Blood: Fort Sumter to Bull Run* (Alexandria, Va.: Time-Life Books, 1983); *The Blockade* (Alexandria, Va.: Time-Life Books, 1983); and *The Coastal War* (Alexandria, Va.: Time-Life Books, 1984); Robert Paul Jordan, *The Civil War* (Washington, D.C.: National Geographic Society, 1969); Stephen W. Sears (ed.), *The American Heritage Century Collection of Civil War Art* (New York: McGraw Hill, 1974); and Philip Van Doren Stern, *The Confederate Navy: A Pictorial History* (Garden City, N.Y.: Doubleday, 1962). P. C. Coker's lavishly illustrated volume *Charleston's Maritime Heritage* (Charleston: CokerCraft Press, 1987) is an excellent study of Charleston as a port.

The best general history of South Carolina during the Civil War (which, of necessity, focuses on Charleston) is Charles E. Cauthen's *South Carolina Goes to War, 1860–1865* (Chapel Hill: University of North Carolina Press, 1950).

While virtually unknown to the general reader, the Democratic Party's national convention in Charleston in 1860 has been the subject of numerous scholarly works. Among them are Emerson D. Fite, *The Presidential Campaign of 1860* (New York, 1911); Robert W. Johannsen, "Douglas at Charleston," in Norman A. Graebner (ed.), *Politics and the Crisis of 1860* (Urbana: University of Illinois Press, 1961); and Ray Franklin Nichols, *The Disruption of American Democracy* (New York: Macmillan, 1948). Both Allan Nevins in *The Emergence of Lincoln*, vol. 2 of his series The Ordeal of the Union, and Bruce Catton in *The Coming Fury*, a volume of his Centennial History, discuss the Charleston convention in detail. The reporter all historians rely on extensively is Murat Halstead, whose accounts are published in William B. Hesseltine (ed.), *Three Against Lincoln: Murat Halstead Reports the Caucuses of 1860* (Baton Rouge: Louisiana State University Press, 1960).

Secession and the road to secession are topics as great as the war itself. The best general work is David M. Potter, *The Impending Crisis, 1848–1861* (New York: Harper & Row, 1976). Potter's other classic is *Lincoln and His Party in the Secession Crisis* (New Haven: Yale University Press, 1942; reissued 1962). The first history of secession was written by a Union officer who served with Major Anderson at Fort Sumter, Samuel Wylie Crawford. It is *The Genesis of the Civil War: The Story of Sumter, 1860–1861* (New York: Charles L. Webster & Company, 1887). Other works which focus on Charleston and South Carolina are William W. Freehling, *Prelude to Civil War: The Nullification Controversy in South Carolina, 1816–1836* (New York: Harper & Row, 1968); Steven A. Channing, *Crisis of Fear: Secession in South Carolina* (New York: Simon & Schuster, 1970); Avery Craven, *The Coming of the Civil War* (New York: Charles Scribner's Sons, 1950); and *Civil War in the Making, 1815–1860* (Baton Rouge: Louisiana State University Press, 1972). The secession crisis is also portrayed in the definitive work on the Confederate judiciary, William M. Robinson, Jr., *Justice in Grey: A History of the Judicial System of the Confederate States of America* (Cambridge: Harvard University Press, 1941); and the history of the ordinance itself is expertly described by Charles H. Lesser in a pamphlet published by the South Carolina Department of Archives and History entitled "Relic of the Lost Cause, The Story of South Carolina's Ordinance of Secession" (1990).

The first shot of the Civil War has been the subject of countless works and is, according to James McPherson, "one of the most thoroughly studied questions in American history." As discussed in the text, the analysis I have relied on most heavily is that of Charles W. Ramsdell in "Lincoln and Fort Sumter," *Journal of Southern History*, 3 (1937): 259–88. Ramsdell is dismissed by both Allan Nevins and James G. Randall, author of *Lincoln The President: Springfield to Gettysburg*, 2 vols. (New York: Dodd, Mead, 1945). The following contain excellent accounts of the first shot: Catton, *The Coming Fury*; W. A. Swanberg, *First Blood: The Story of Fort Sumter* (New York: Charles Scribner's Sons, 1957); Richard N. Current, *Lincoln and the First Shot* (Philadelphia: J. B. Lippincott, 1963); Potter, *The Impending Crisis* and *Lincoln and His Party in the Secession Crisis*; Cauthen, *South Carolina Goes to War*; E. Milby Burton, *The Siege of Charleston, 1861–1865* (Columbia: University of South Carolina Press, 1970); Carl Sandburg, *Abraham Lincoln: The War Years*, vol. 1 (New York: Harcourt, Brace & World, 1936); and Ashley Halsey, Jr., *Who Fired the First Shot?* (New York: Hawthorn Books, 1963).

My account is also based on Stephen A. Hurlbut's report to President Lincoln later published under the title *Between Peace & War: A Report to Lincoln from Charleston, 1861* (Charleston: St. Albans Press, 1953); Ward Hill Lamon, *Recollections of Abraham Lincoln, 1847–1865* (Washington, D.C., 1911); and Abner Doubleday, *Reminiscences of Forts Sumter and Moultrie in 1860–61* (New York: Harper & Brothers, 1870). Excellent articles on the subject are Robert Lebby, "The First Shot on Fort Sumter," *South Carolina Historical and Genealogical Magazine* 12, 3 (July, 1911): 141–45; and Kenneth M. Stampp, "Lincoln and the Strategy of Defense in the Crisis of 1861," *Journal of Southern History* 11 (1945): 297–323.

The blockade and blockade runners have been ably discussed by Stephen R. Wise in *Lifeline of the Confederacy* (Columbia: University of South Carolina Press, 1988); Daniel Ammen, *The Navy in the Civil War: The Atlantic Coast* (New York, 1905); and Hamilton Cochran, *Blockade Runners of the Confederacy* (Indianapolis & New York, 1958). Naval warfare is the subject of numerous works including Van Doren Stern, *The Confederate Navy*; William M. Fowler, Jr., *Under Two Flags: The American Navy in the Civil War* (New York: Avon Books, 1990); and James M. Merrill, *The Rebel Shore: The Story of Union Sea Power in the Civil War* (Boston: Little, Brown, 1957). A good recent work on the submarine *Hunley* is James E. Kloeppel's *Danger Beneath the Waves: A History of the Confederate Submarine, H. L. Hunley* (Orangeburg, S.C.: Sandlapper, 1992).

The siege of Charleston from 1863 to 1865 is the chief subject of Burton's *The Siege of Charleston, 1861–1865*; Samuel Jones's work by the same name (New York: Neale Publishing Company, 1911); and John Johnson's *The Defense of Charleston Harbor* (Charleston, 1890). Major Robert Gilchrist published a booklet entitled *The Confederate Defense of Morris Island, Charleston Harbour* (Charleston: News and Courier Book Presses, 1887). *Fighting for Time*, vol. 4 of the series Image of War, contains an excellent essay on the siege by Rowena Reed as well as many photographs. The Time-Life series volume *The Coastal War* by Peter Chaitin is also excellent on the siege. The works on the Massachusetts 54th are set forth below in a paragraph on ethnic history and African Americans.

Sherman's march is also a subject unto itself. I have relied on John G. Barrett, *Sherman's March Through the Carolinas* (Chapel Hill: University of North Carolina Press, 1956); and Burke Davis, *Sherman's March* (New York: Vintage Books, 1988).

The memoirs, letters, and diaries of Charlestonians and others before, during, and after the war are extensive. The best memoir by a Charlestonian by far is the Reverend A. Toomer Porter's *Led On! Step By Step* (New York & London, 1898; rpt. Charleston: Porter-Gaud School, 1988). Mary Chesnut's diary is well known, having been published in a definitive volume edited by C. Vann Woodward, *Mary Chesnut's Civil War* (New Haven: Yale University Press, 1981). Her contemporary diary (without the later additions) has been published as *The Private Mary Chesnut: The Unpublished Civil War Diaries*, ed. C. Vann Woodward and Elisabeth Muhlenfield (New York: Oxford University Press, 1984). Other important diaries are the Jacob Schirmer diary at the South Carolina Historical Society, Charleston; the diary of Captain Alfred Marple, a Union officer on Morris Island (copy at the South Caroliniana Library, University of South Carolina,

Columbia); *The Diary of Miss Emma Holmes, 1861–1866* (Baton Rouge: Louisiana State University Press, 1979), edited by John F. Marszalek; *A Woman Doctor's Civil War: Esther Hill Hawks' Diary* (Columbia: University of South Carolina Press, 1984), edited by Gerald Schwartz; and William H. Russell, *My Diary North and South* (Boston, 1863).

Other important memoirs are Abner Doubleday's *Reminiscences*; Susie King Taylor, *A Black Woman's Civil War Memoirs* (New York: Markus Wiener, 1988); Alvah F. Hunter, *A Year on a Monitor and The Destruction of Fort Sumter* (Columbia: University of South Carolina Press, 1987); Warren Ripley (ed.), *Siege Train: The Journal of a Confederate Artilleryman in the Defense of Charleston* (Columbia: University of South Carolina Press, 1986); Johnson Hagood, *Memoirs of the War of Secession* (Columbia: State, 1910); Charles Cowley, *Leaves From a Lawyer's Life Afloat and Ashore* (Boston: Lee and Shepard, 1870); William T. Sherman, *Memoirs*, 2 vols. (New York, 1875) (Library of America, New York, reprinted Sherman's *Memoirs* in 1993); Gideon Welles, *The Diary of Gideon Welles*, 3 vols. (New York: Norton, 1960); and Johnson and Buel (eds.), *Battles and Leaders of the Civil War*. I have made extensive use of the letters of the Smythe family in the collection of the South Carolina Historical Society and in particular the letters of Augustine T. Smythe. I have also used the Middleton correspondence published in the *South Carolina Historical Magazine*, 64 (July, 1963): 158–68, and 65 (January, 1964): 33–44, and edited by Isabella M. Leland. Copies of Clara Barton's letters from Morris Island and copies of William Tecumseh Sherman's letters from Fort Moultrie are at Fort Moultrie, where the National Park Service maintains a wonderful little library and an informal archive. The staff is exceedingly cooperative.

Biographical material was derived from a variety of general sources including *Battles and Leaders of the Civil War* (previously cited above); *The Dictionary of American Biography*; Patricia L. Faust (ed.), *Historical Times Illustrated Encyclopedia of the Civil War* (New York: Harper & Row, 1986); and Burton J. Hendrick, *Statesman of the Lost Cause* (New York: Literary Guild of America, 1939). The best work on Robert E. Lee remains Douglas Southall Freeman, *R. E. Lee: A Biography*, 4 vols. (New York: Charles Scribner's Sons, 1934–35); on Beauregard, T. Harry Williams, *P. G. T. Beauregard: Napoleon in Gray* (Baton Rouge: Louisiana State University Press, 1955); Eli N. Evans, *Judah P. Benjamin, The Jewish Confederate* (New York: Macmillan, 1988); on the Grimké Sisters, Gerda Lerner, *The Grimké Sisters From South Carolina* (New York: Schocken, 1971); on Robert Smalls, Okon Edet Uya, *From Slavery to Public Service: Robert Smalls, 1839–1915* (New York: Oxford University Press, 1971); on Sherman, Lloyd Lewis, *Sherman, Fighting Prophet* (New York: Harcourt, Brace, 1932); on Pemberton, Michael B. Ballard, *Pemberton: A Biography* (Jackson: University Press of Mississippi, 1991); on Memminger, Henry D. Capers, *The Life and Times of C. G. Memminger* (Richmond: Everett Waddy, 1893); on James L. Petigru, J. P. Carson (ed.), *Life, Letters and Speeches of James Louis Petigru: The Union Man of South Carolina* (Washington, D.C.: W. H. Loudermilk, 1938); on Clara Barton, Blanche C. Williams, *Clara Barton, Daughter of Destiny* (Philadelphia: J. B. Lippincott, 1941); on Andrew G. Magrath, William M. Robinson, *Justice in Grey*, and U. P. Brooks, *South Carolina Bench and Bar*, vol. 2 (Columbia: State, 1908); on Ambrosio José Gonzales, an article by Lewis P. Jones, "Ambrosio José Gonzales: A Cuban Patriot in South Carolina," *South Carolina Historical Magazine* 56, 2 (April, 1955).

Lincoln is a vast subject all to himself. The chief works on Lincoln relating to

Charleston are Richard N. Current, *The Lincoln Nobody Knows* (New York: Hill and Wang, 1963); Carl Sandburg, *Abraham Lincoln: The War Years*, vol. 1 (New York: Harcourt, Brace & World, 1939) on the firing on Fort Sumter, and vol. 4, on raising the flag over Sumter in 1865; and Randall, *Lincoln the President*; as well as the general works already cited. Lincoln's secretary John G. Nicolay wrote *The Outbreak of the Rebellion* (New York: Charles Scribner's Sons, 1881).

There are a number of good works on Charleston in the Civil War. Two of the most important are long out of print. They are Samuel Jones, *The Siege of Charleston* (New York, 1911); and John Johnson, *The Defense of Charleston Harbor* (Charleston, 1890). The *Post-Courier*, the local Charleston newspaper, published an excellent booklet in 1966 entitled *The Civil War at Charleston*. It contains a collection of newspaper feature articles published during the Centennial celebration of the Civil War. The *Post-Courier* also published a useful pamphlet entitled *The Battery* by Warren Ripley (1977). The National Park Service has published two excellent Official National Park handbooks on Fort Moultrie and Fort Sumter which are readable and informative: *Fort Moultrie: Constant Defender* by Jim Stokeley (Handbook 136)(Washington, D.C., 1985) and *Fort Sumter: Anvil of War* (Handbook 127)(Washington, D.C., 1984).

General works on Charleston's history discuss the war: Isabella G. Leland, *Charleston: Crossroads of History* (Woodland Hills, Calif.: Charleston Trident Chamber of Commerce/Windsor Publications, 1980); Robert Molloy, *Charleston: A Gracious Heritage* (New York: D. Appleton-Century, 1947); (Mrs.) St. Julien Ravenel, *Charleston: The Place and the People* (New York: Macmillan, 1906); Robert Rosen, *A Short History of Charleston* (Charleston: Peninsula Press, rev. ed., 1992); Walter J. Fraser, Jr., *Charleston! Charleston! The History of a Southern City* (Columbia: University of South Carolina Press, 1989); and Coker, *Charleston's Maritime Heritage*.

The ethnic history of Charleston is also a subject in itself. On African Americans I have relied on the general works and on the following: Richard C. Wade, *Slavery in the Cities: The South, 1820–1960* (New York: Oxford University Press, 1964); Joel Williamson, *After Slavery, The Negro in South Carolina During Reconstruction, 1861–1877* (New York: Norton, 1965); Luis F. Emilio, *History of the Fifty-Fourth Regiment of Massachusetts Volunteer Infantry, 1863–1865* (Boston: Boston Book Company, 1894); Benjamin Quarles, *The Negro in the Civil War* (Boston: Little, Brown, 1953); James McPherson, *The Negro's Civil War* (New York: Ballantine Books, 1965); Dudley T. Cornish, *The Sable Arm: Negro Troops in the Union Army, 1861–1854* (New York: Norton, 1966); Russell Duncan (ed.), *Blue-Eyed Child of Fortune: The Civil War Letters of Colonel Robert Gould Shaw* (Athens: University of Georgia Press, 1992); William S. McFeely, *Frederick Douglass* (New York: Simon & Schuster, 1991); Virginia M. Adams, *On the Altar of Freedom: A Black Soldier's Civil War Letter from the Front* (the letters of James Henry Gooding) (Amherst: University of Massachusetts Press, 1991); Richard Benson and Lincoln Kirstein, *Lay This Laurel* (on the Shaw Memorial in Boston) (New York: Eakins Press, 1973); Michael P. Johnson and James L. Roger (eds.), *No Chariot Let Down: Charleston's Free People of Color on the Eve of the Civil War* (Chapel Hill: University of North Carolina Press, 1984); *Black Masters: A Free Family of Color in the Old South* (New York, 1984); and Peter Burchard, *One Gallant Rush: Robert Gould Shaw and his Brave Black Regiment* (New York: St. Martin's Press, 1965).

On Jewish Charlestonians I have relied on Barnett A. Elzas, *The Jews of South Carolina from the Earliest Times to the Present Day* (Philadelphia: J. B. Lippincott, 1905); and Harry Simonhoff, *Jewish Participants in the Civil War* (New York: Arco, 1963). On Catholics and the Irish I have relied on William B. Regan, *The Irish of Charleston: An Oral History* (Charleston: Peninsula Press, 1990); Richard C. Madden, *Catholics in South Carolina: A Record* (Lanham, Md. University Press of America, 1985); Sister M. Anne Francis Campbell, O.L.M., "Bishop England's Sisterhood, 1829–1929" (unpublished Ph.D. dissertation, St. Louis University, St. Louis, Mo., 1968); and general local blarney.

A number of volumes available to the general reader publish contemporary documents such as editorials, letters, and speeches. Among those relied on in this text are Henry Steele Commager, *The Blue and the Grey: The Story of the Civil War As Told by the Participants*, 2 vols. (Indianapolis: Bobbs-Merrill, 1950); Kenneth M. Stampp (ed.), *The Causes of the Civil War* (New York: Simon & Schuster, 1959); and Richard B. Harwell (ed.), *The Civil War Reader* (New York: Mallard Press, 1991).

ILLUSTRATION CREDITS

COLOR ILLUSTRATIONS

Plate 1: Museum of the Confederacy, Richmond, VA. Photograph by Katherine Wetzel.

Plate 2: S. Bernard, *View Along the East Battery, Charleston,* Yale University Art Gallery, Mabel Brady Garvan Collection.

Plate 3: Author's Collection (*Harper's Weekly*).

Plate 4: Architect of the Capitol, United States Capitol Art Collection.

Plate 5: M. A. Villafana Family Collection. Photograph courtesy of Kennedy Galleries, Inc., New York.

Plate 6: Courtesy of the Library of Congress.

Plate 7: Author's Collection (*Harper's Weekly*).

Plate 8: U.S. Naval Academy Museum.

Plate 9: U.S. Naval Academy Museum.

Plate 10: Author's Collection (*Harper's Weekly*).

Plate 11: L/NPG.9.77, National Portrait Gallery, Smithsonian Institution. Oil on canvas adhered to masonite, 121.9 x 76.2 cm. (48 x 30 in.); on loan from Serena Williams Miles Van Rensselaer.

Plate 12: Collection of City Hall, Charleston, S.C.

Plate 13: Courtesy of Dr. Charles V. Peery.

Plate 14: Historic Charleston Collection. Photograph by Priestly Coker.

Plate 15: *Harper's Weekly.* Courtesy of NationsBank, Broad Street Branch, Charleston.

Plate 16: U.S. Naval Academy Museum.

Plate 17: Author's Collection (*Illustrated London News*).

Plate 18: Courtesy of Dr. Charles V. Peery.

Plate 19: Boston Athenaeum.

Plate 20: Gibbes Museum of Art, Carolina Art Commission.

Plate 21: Museum of the Confederacy, Richmond, VA. Photograph by Katherine Wetzel.

Plate 22: Museum of the Confederacy, Richmond, VA. Photograph by Katherine Wetzel.

Plate 23: Museum of the Confederacy, Richmond, VA. Photograph by Katherine Wetzel.

Plate 24: Courtesy of Dr. Charles V. Peery.

Plate 25: Museum of the Confederacy, Richmond, VA. Photograph by Katherine Wetzel.

Plate 26: Historic Charleston Foundation Collection.

Plate 27: Museum of the Confederacy, Richmond, VA. Photograph by Katherine Wetzel.

Plate 28: Author's Collection (*Harper's Weekly*).

Plate 29: M. and M. Karolik Collection, courtesy Museum of Fine Arts, Boston.

Plate 30: Architect of the Capitol, United States Capitol Art Collection.

Plate 31: Abby Aldrich Rockefeller Folk Art Collection, Williamsburg, VA.

BLACK-AND-WHITE ILLUSTRATIONS

Prologue
p. 13: South Caroliniana Library, University of South Carolina.

p. 14: South Caroliniana Library, University of South Carolina.

p. 15: South Caroliniana Library, University of South Carolina.

Chapter 1: The Long Road to Secession
p. 17: Valentine Museum, Richmond, VA.

p. 18: South Carolina Historical Society, Charleston.

p. 19: Courtesy of the Library of Congress.

p. 21: South Caroliniana Library, University of South Carolina.

p. 22: Courtesy of the Library of Congress.

p. 25: Massachusetts Commandery, Military Order of the Loyal Legion and the U.S. Army Military History Institute.

p. 27: *William H. Seward* by Francis D'Avignon, NPG.72.68, National Portrait Gallery, Smithsonian Institution.

Chapter 2: Charleston hosts the Democratic Party National Convention of 1860
p. 29: South Carolina Historical Society, Charleston.

p. 32: *Battles and Leaders of the Civil War* (1884–87).

p. 33: Author's Collection (*Harper's Weekly*).

p. 35: Author's Collection (*Harper's Weekly*).

p. 36: Author's Collection (*Harper's Weekly*).

p. 37: *Battles and Leaders of the Civil War* (1884–87).

Chapter 3: The Cradle of Secession
p. 38: *Battles and Leaders of the Civil War* (1884–87).

p. 39 (top): South Carolina Historical Society, Charleston.

p. 39 (bottom): Author's Collection (*Frank Leslie's The American Soldier in the Civil War,* 1895).

p. 41: *Battles and Leaders of the Civil War* (1884–87).

p. 43: Author's Collection (*Illustrated London News*).

p. 136: *American Heritage* Picture Collection.

p. 137 (top): National Park Service (Fort Sumter National Monument).

p. 137(bottom): *Battles and Leaders of the Civil War* (1884–87).

p. 138: Author's Collection (*Frank Leslie's The American Soldier in the Civil War*, 1895).

p. 139: Author's Collection (*Frank Leslie's The American Soldier in the Civil War*, 1895).

p. 140: Author's Collection (*Frank Leslie's Illustrated Newspaper*).

p. 141: Photographs and Prints Division, Schomburg Center for Research in Black Culture, The New York Public Library, Astor, Lenox and Tilden Foundations.

p. 143: National Archives photo no. 165-C-802.

p. 144: South Carolina Historical Society, Charleston.

p. 145: Courtesy of the Library of Congress.

p. 146 (top): National Archives photo no. 165-C-791.

p. 146 (bottom): National Archives photo no. 165-C-808.

p. 147: Author's Collection (*Frank Leslie's The Civil War in the United States*, 1896).

p. 148 (top): Courtesy of the Library of Congress.

p. 148 (bottom): National Archives photo no. 165-C-799.

p. 149: National Archives photo no. 111-BA-1223.

p. 151: Confederate Museum, Charleston.

p. 152: National Park Service (Fort Sumter National Monument).

p. 153: National Park Service (Fort Sumter National Monument).

p. 154: National Park Service (Fort Sumter National Monument).

p. 155: Author's Collection (*Harper's Weekly*).

Epilogue

p. 157: Massachusetts Historical Society.

p. 158: Author's Collection (Photograph by Jack Alterman).

p. 159: National Park Service (Fort Sumter National Monument).

p. 160: South Caroliniana Library, University of South Carolina.

p. 161: Author's Collection (Photograph by Jack Alterman).

p. 163: Courtesy of the Library of Congress, Mathew Brady Collection.

Endpapers: Chicago Historical Society

INDEX

Page numbers in bold type denote illustrations; the designation "pl." precedes references to color plates.